TESTING PROGRAM

WORD BY WORD

Second Edition

Steven J. Molinsky • Bill Bliss

Contributing Author
Jennifer Bixby

Illustrated by
Richard E. Hill

PEARSON
Longman

Dedicated to Janet Johnston in honor of her wonderful contribution
to the development of our textbooks over three decades.

Steven J. Molinsky
Bill Bliss

Word by Word Testing Program, second edition

Pearson Education, 10 Bank Street, White Plains, NY 10606

Editorial director: Pam Fishman
Vice president, director of design and production: Rhea Banker
Director of electronic production: Aliza Greenblatt
Director of manufacturing: Patrice Fraccio
Senior manufacturing manager: Edith Pullman
Directors of marketing: Oliva Fernandez, Carol Brown
Production editor: Diane Cipollone
Associate paging manager: Paula Williams
Text design: Wendy Wolf
Cover design: Warren Fischbach
Illustrations: Richard E. Hill

ISBN 978-0-13-191615-9; 0-13-191615-7
Pearson Longman on the Web
PearsonLongman.com offers online resources for teachers and students. Access our
Companion Websites, our online catalog, and our local offices around the world.

Visit us at pearsonlongman.com.

Printed in the United States of America
1 2 3 4 5 6 7 8 9 10—V012—18 17 16 15 14 13 12 11 10 09

Name _____

Date _____

(A) WHAT IS IT?

1. apartment number

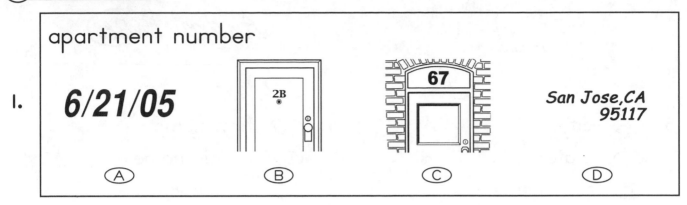

6/21/05 (A)   2B (B)   67 (C)   *San Jose, CA 95117* (D)

2. e-mail address

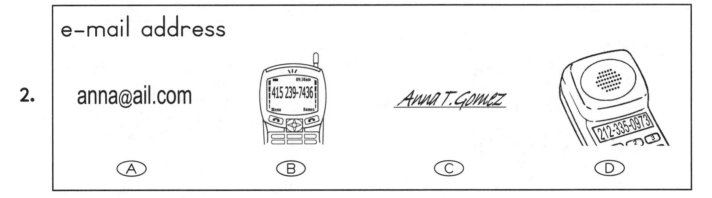

anna@ail.com (A)   415 239-7436 (B)   *Anna T. Gomez* (C)   212-335-0973 (D)

3. social security card

43 Center Street (A)   Los Angeles, CA (B)   (C)   SOCIAL SECURITY 227-94-0001 ANNA T. GOMEZ (D)

4. children

(A)   (B)   (C)   (D)

B WHAT'S THE WORD?

FLORIDA

5.
- (A) city
- (B) state
- (C) first name
- (D) street

6.
- (A) first name
- (B) middle name
- (C) middle initial
- (D) last name

Andrew P.(Lee)

09:30am
305-853-2296
Menu   Names

47 River Road
Dallas,TX (75201)

7.
- (A) cell phone number
- (B) date of birth
- (C) social security number
- (D) street number

8.
- (A) area code
- (B) city
- (C) zip code
- (D) street number

9.
- (A) name
- (B) sex
- (C) area code
- (D) place of birth

10.
- (A) son
- (B) nephew
- (C) niece
- (D) uncle

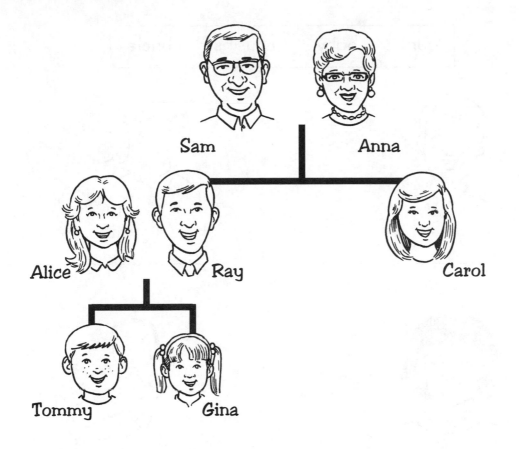

| aunt | father | grandmother | son |
| daughter | grandfather | mother | |

11. Sam is the _ _ _ _ _ _ _ _ _ _ _ .

12. Anna is the _ _ _ _ _ _ _ _ _ _ _ .

13. Ray is the _ _ _ _ _ _ _ .

14. Alice is the _ _ _ _ _ _ _ .

15. Carol is the _ _ _ _ .

16. Tommy is the _ _ _ .

17. Gina is the _ _ _ _ _ _ _ _ .

aunt	baby	cousins	uncle

18. _____

19. _____

20. _____

21. _____

E PERSONAL INFORMATION

NAME: (22.) _____

First Name   Middle Initial   Last Name

ADDRESS: (23.) _____

Number   Street

(24.) _____

City   State   Zip Code

TELEPHONE NUMBER: (25.) _____

Name _____

Date _____

A WHAT IS IT?

1. pencil

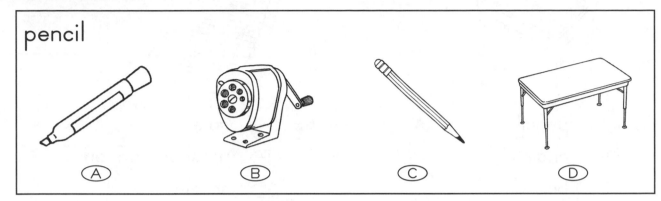

   A   B   C   D

2. notebook

   A   B   C   D

3. bookcase

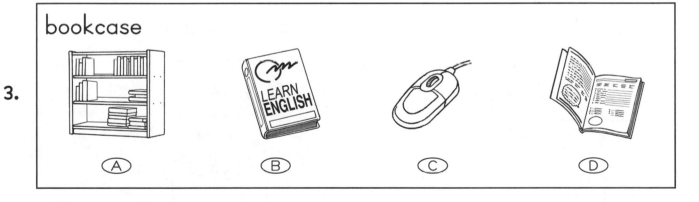

   A   B   C   D

4. computer

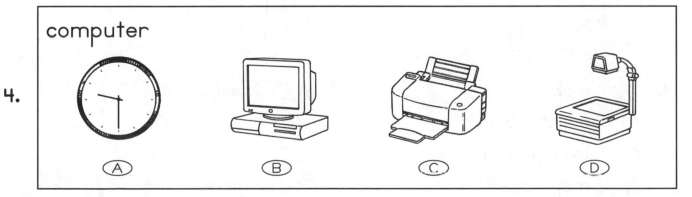

   A   B   C   D

B WHAT'S THE WORD?

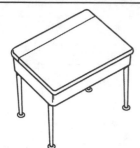

5. (A) pencil
   (B) chair
   (C) board
   (D) desk

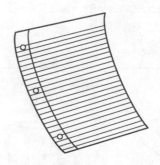

6. (A) ruler
   (B) notebook paper
   (C) screen
   (D) graph paper

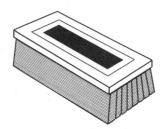

7. (A) eraser
   (B) chalk
   (C) pen
   (D) thumbtack

8. (A) spiral notebook
   (B) dictionary
   (C) monitor
   (D) binder

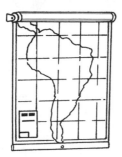

9. (A) globe
   (B) bulletin board
   (C) loudspeaker
   (D) map

10. (A) keyboard
    (B) whiteboard
    (C) wastebasket
    (D) table

C WHAT'S THE WORD?

| Go | Raise | Read | Stand | Write |

11. _____ your hand.

12. _____ page six.

13. _____ on a separate piece of paper.

14. _____ to the board.

15. _____ up.

D WHERE IS IT?

| behind |
| in |
| in front of |
| on |
| under |

16. The wastebasket is _____ the table.

17. The teacher is _____ the table.

18. The textbook is _____ the table.

19. The dictionary is _____ bookcase.

20. The chair is _____ the table.

E WHAT'S THE ACTION?

Circle the correct answer.   Turn off the lights.

Put away your book.   Work with a partner.

Spell your name.

21. _____

22. _____

23. _____

24. _____

I'm from Chicago 1985 phone number

25. _____

Name _____

Date _____

A **WHAT THE ACTION?**

get up

1.
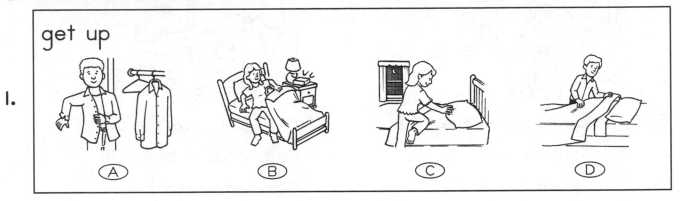

take a shower

2.
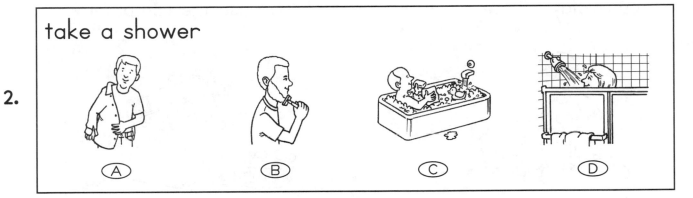

make breakfast

3.

brush my teeth

4.

B WHAT'S THE ACTION?

5.
- Ⓐ go to the store
- Ⓑ leave work
- Ⓒ go to school
- Ⓓ play

6.
- Ⓐ practice the piano
- Ⓑ read a book
- Ⓒ go to work
- Ⓓ use the computer

7.
- Ⓐ walk the dog
- Ⓑ feed the cat
- Ⓒ exercise
- Ⓓ get home

8.
- Ⓐ clean the house
- Ⓑ write a letter
- Ⓒ do the laundry
- Ⓓ get dressed

9.
- Ⓐ make lunch
- Ⓑ have dinner
- Ⓒ iron
- Ⓓ relax

10.
- Ⓐ play basketball
- Ⓑ listen to music
- Ⓒ swim
- Ⓓ plant flowers

C) WHAT DO YOU SAY?

Excuse me.	I don't understand.
Good morning.	See you later.

11. _____

12. _____

13. _____

14. _____

D) EVERYDAY CONVERSATION

Fine, thanks.	Yes. Hold on a moment.
Nice to meet you, too.	You're welcome.
Not much.	

15. What's new with you? _____

16. How are you? _____

17. Thank you. _____

18. Nice to meet you. _____

19. May I please speak to Alice? _____

| cloudy | raining | sunny |
| lightning | snowing | windy |

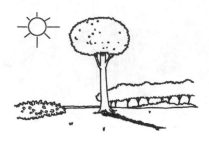

20. _____

21. _____

22. _____

23. _____

24. _____

25. _____

Name _____

Date _____

A **WHAT IS IT?**

dime

1.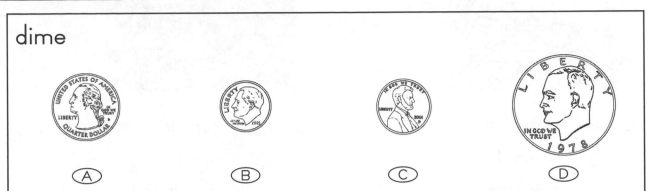

   Ⓐ   Ⓑ   Ⓒ   Ⓓ

quarter

2.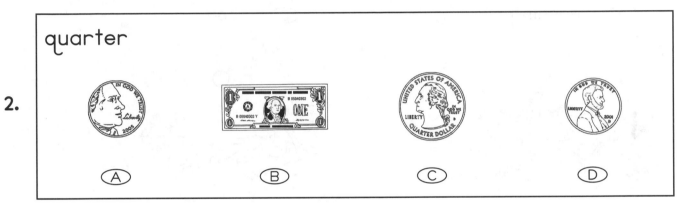

   Ⓐ   Ⓑ   Ⓒ   Ⓓ

First Street

3.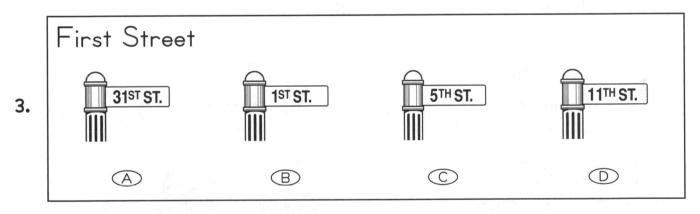

     31ST ST.   1ST ST.   5TH ST.   11TH ST.

   Ⓐ   Ⓑ   Ⓒ   Ⓓ

8:00 P.M.

4.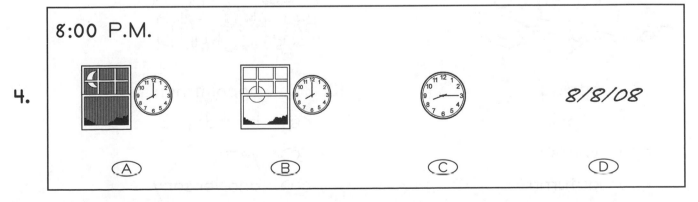

                                                            8/8/08

   Ⓐ   Ⓑ   Ⓒ   Ⓓ

5.
- Ⓐ date
- Ⓑ tonight
- Ⓒ evening
- Ⓓ morning

6.
- Ⓐ season
- Ⓑ night
- Ⓒ afternoon
- Ⓓ noon

7.
- Ⓐ afternoon
- Ⓑ evening
- Ⓒ last night
- Ⓓ midnight

8.
- Ⓐ month
- Ⓑ October
- Ⓒ fall
- Ⓓ summer

9.
- Ⓐ spring
- Ⓑ April
- Ⓒ winter
- Ⓓ autumn

10.
- Ⓐ appointment
- Ⓑ birthday
- Ⓒ year
- Ⓓ anniversary

C WHAT TIME IS IT?

| 5:10 | 8:45 | 9:15 | 10:05 |

11. _____   12. _____   13. _____   14. _____

D HOW MUCH IS IT?

| $.18 | $.65 | $6.50 | $10.25 |

15. _____   16. _____

17. _____   18. _____

| December | March | May | September |

19. January, February, _____

20. April, _____ , June

21. July, August, _____

22. October, November, _____

| Sunday |
| Thursday |
| Tuesday |

23. Monday, _____ , Wednesday

24. _____ , Friday

25. Saturday, _____

Name _____

Date _____

A WHAT IS IT?

dresser

1.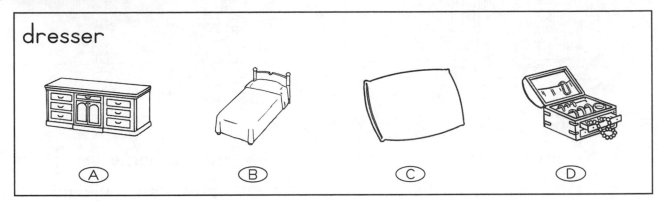

(A)   (B)   (C)   (D)

blanket

2.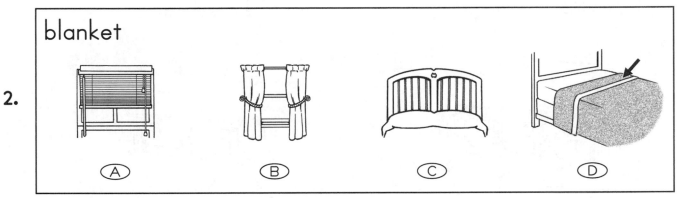

(A)   (B)   (C)   (D)

napkin

3.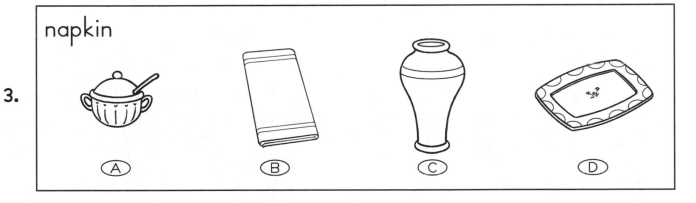

(A)   (B)   (C)   (D)

bowl

4.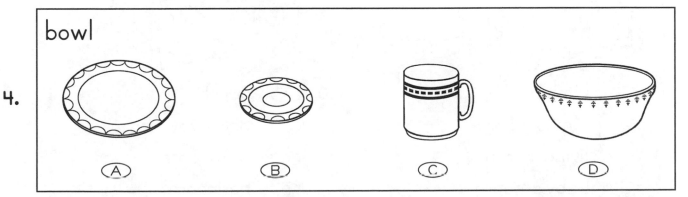

(A)   (B)   (C)   (D)

5. Ⓐ farm
   Ⓑ city
   Ⓒ suburb
   Ⓓ town

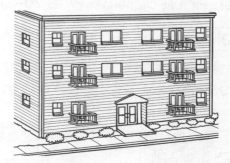

6. Ⓐ duplex
   Ⓑ mobile home
   Ⓒ apartment building
   Ⓓ houseboat

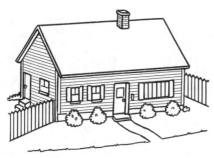

7. Ⓐ house
   Ⓑ ranch
   Ⓒ dorm
   Ⓓ condo

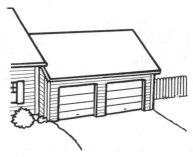

8. Ⓐ mailbox
   Ⓑ patio
   Ⓒ garage
   Ⓓ tool shed

9. Ⓐ kitchen
   Ⓑ dining room
   Ⓒ living room
   Ⓓ baby's room

10. Ⓐ porch
    Ⓑ driveway
    Ⓒ bathroom
    Ⓓ bedroom

C WHAT IS IT?

coffee table	fireplace	mirror	wall
couch	lamp	rug	window

11. _____

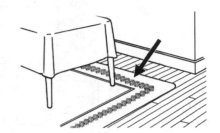

12. _____

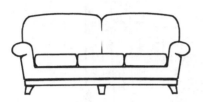

13. _____

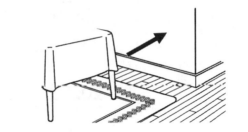

14. _____

15. _____

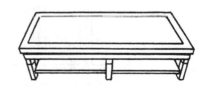

16. _____

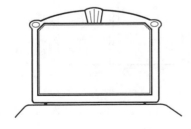

17. _____

18. _____

medicine cabinet   microwave   oven   shower   stove   toaster   tub

19. _____

20. _____

21. _____

22. _____   24. _____

23. _____   25. _____

Name _____

Date _____

A **WHAT IS IT?**

broom

1.

   Ⓐ   Ⓑ   Ⓒ   Ⓓ

sponge

2.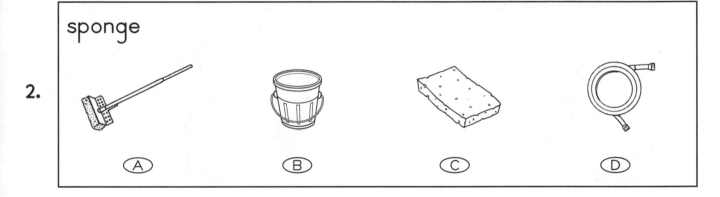

   Ⓐ   Ⓑ   Ⓒ   Ⓓ

hammer

3.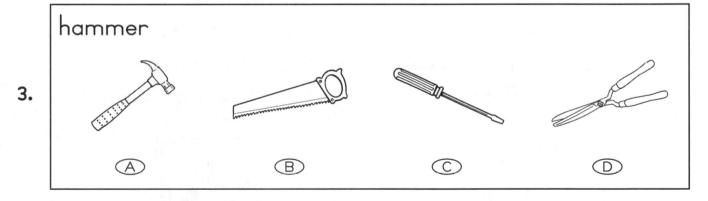

   Ⓐ   Ⓑ   Ⓒ   Ⓓ

paintbrush

4.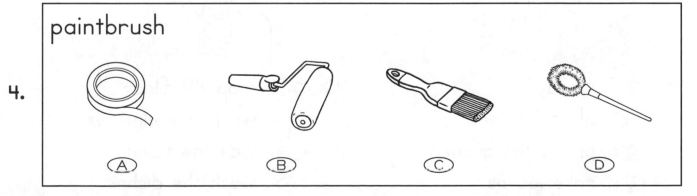

   Ⓐ   Ⓑ   Ⓒ   Ⓓ

B WHAT'S THE WORD?

5.
- Ⓐ trim the hedge
- Ⓑ mow the lawn
- Ⓒ prune the bushes
- Ⓓ plant vegetables

6.
- Ⓐ clean the bathroom
- Ⓑ sweep the floor
- Ⓒ polish the furniture
- Ⓓ dust

7.
- Ⓐ vacuum
- Ⓑ mop the floor
- Ⓒ take out the garbage
- Ⓓ wax the floor

8.
- Ⓐ plant vegetables
- Ⓑ wax the floor
- Ⓒ water the flowers
- Ⓓ polish the furniture

9.
- Ⓐ weed
- Ⓑ plant flowers
- Ⓒ prune the bushes
- Ⓓ rake leaves

10.
- Ⓐ mop the floor
- Ⓑ wash the windows
- Ⓒ wax the floor
- Ⓓ wash the dishes

C WHAT IS IT?

| flashlight | glue | oil | window cleaner |

11. _____

12. _____

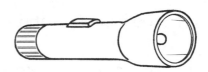

13. _____

14. _____

D WHO IS IT?

| appliance repairperson | exterminator | plumber |
| electrician | locksmith | |

15. There are ants in the kitchen. Call the _____.

16. The bathtub is leaking. Call the _____.

17. The refrigerator isn't working. Call the _____.

18. The lock is broken. Call the _____.

19. The power is out. Call the _____.

basement	lobby	security deposit
floor	lock	smoke detector

20. My apartment is on the fifth _____ .

21. There's a dead-bolt _____ on my door.

22. Give the _____ to the landlord.

23. My mailbox is in the _____ .

24. There's a laundry room in the _____ .

25. There's a _____ in the stairway.

A **WHAT IS IT?**

subway

1.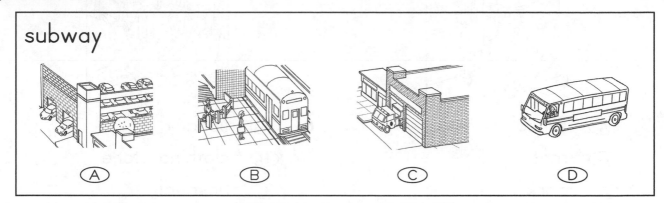

Ⓐ   Ⓑ   Ⓒ   Ⓓ

motorcycle

2.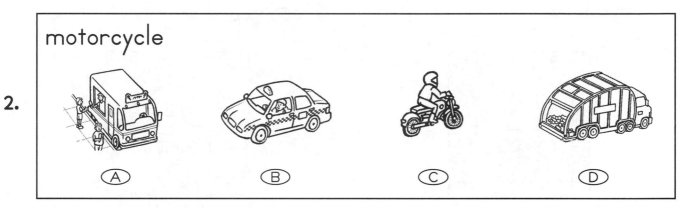

Ⓐ   Ⓑ   Ⓒ   Ⓓ

street sign

3.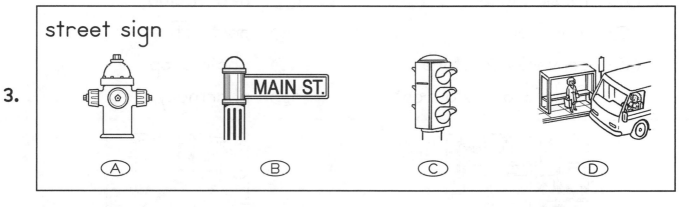

Ⓐ   Ⓑ   Ⓒ   Ⓓ

pedestrian

4.

Ⓐ   Ⓑ   Ⓒ   Ⓓ

5. Ⓐ school
   Ⓑ motel
   Ⓒ park
   Ⓓ bank

6. Ⓐ library
   Ⓑ clothing store
   Ⓒ hospital
   Ⓓ card shop

7. Ⓐ music store
   Ⓑ laundromat
   Ⓒ convenience store
   Ⓓ fast-food restaurant

8. Ⓐ health club
   Ⓑ post office
   Ⓒ photo shop
   Ⓓ pharmacy

9. Ⓐ shoe store
   Ⓑ electronics store
   Ⓒ toy store
   Ⓓ video store

10. Ⓐ gas station
    Ⓑ parking lot
    Ⓒ bus station
    Ⓓ train station

cleaners	movie theater	supermarket
clinic	restaurant	
department store	shopping mall	

11. _____

12. _____

13. _____

14. _____

15. _____

16. _____

17. _____

bakery	deli	donut shop	pizza shop

18. _____

19. _____

20. _____

21. _____

fire alarm box	mailbox	parking meter	sidewalk

22. _____

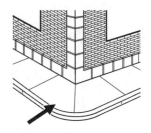

23. _____

24. _____

25. _____

Name _____

Date _____

A WHAT IS IT?

1. infant

2. senior citizen

3. heavy

4. curly

5. (A) mustache
   (B) beard
   (C) bald
   (D) long

6. (A) elderly
   (B) pregnant
   (C) slim
   (D) man

7. (A) young
   (B) middle-aged
   (C) toddler
   (D) woman

8. (A) hot
   (B) hungry
   (C) tired
   (D) thirsty

9. (A) comfortable
   (B) afraid
   (C) worried
   (D) sick

10. (A) mad
    (B) excited
    (C) sad
    (D) bored

C WHAT'S THE WORD?

| confused | nervous | scared | surprised |

11. _____

12. _____

13. _____

14. _____

D WHAT'S THE ANSWER?

| dirty | full | old | open | soft |

15. Is your car new?   No. It's _____.

16. Is the bed hard?   No. It's _____.

17. Is the cup clean?   No. It's _____.

18. Is the store closed?   No. It's _____.

19. Is the glass empty?   No. It's _____.

dry	short	tight
loose	tall	wet

20. _____

21. _____

22. _____

23. _____

24. _____

25. _____

Name _____

Date _____

A WHAT IS IT?

1. pear

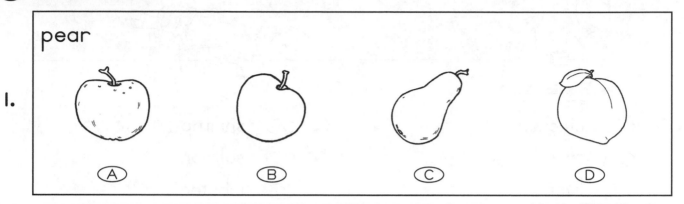

Ⓐ   Ⓑ   Ⓒ   Ⓓ

2. grapes

Ⓐ   Ⓑ   Ⓒ   Ⓓ

3. broccoli

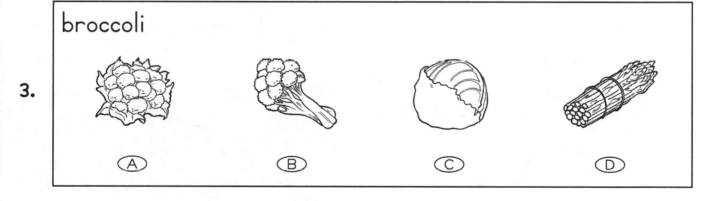

Ⓐ   Ⓑ   Ⓒ   Ⓓ

4. carrot

Ⓐ   Ⓑ   Ⓒ   Ⓓ

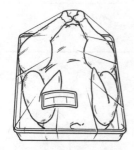

5.
- Ⓐ chicken
- Ⓑ trout
- Ⓒ liver
- Ⓓ roast beef

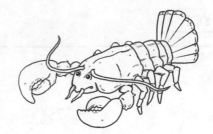

6.
- Ⓐ shrimp
- Ⓑ salmon
- Ⓒ lobster
- Ⓓ duck

7.
- Ⓐ pork
- Ⓑ steak
- Ⓒ pastrami
- Ⓓ halibut

8.
- Ⓐ corned beef
- Ⓑ Swiss cheese
- Ⓒ ham
- Ⓓ salami

9.
- Ⓐ drumsticks
- Ⓑ ribs
- Ⓒ lamb chops
- Ⓓ sausages

10.
- Ⓐ chicken breasts
- Ⓑ crabs
- Ⓒ oysters
- Ⓓ pork chops

liquid soap	paper towels	shopping basket	straws
paper bag	plastic wrap	shopping cart	tissues

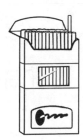

11. _____

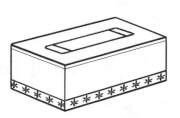

12. _____

13. _____

14. _____

15. _____

16. _____

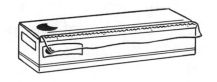

17. _____

18. _____

bottle	dozen	jar	pound
box	head	loaf	

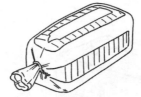

19. I have a _____ of bread.

20. We need a _____ of ground beef.

21. Where is the _____ of cereal?

22. Please open the _____ of soda.

23. We have a _____ of lettuce.

24. We need a _____ of peanut butter.

25. I have a _____ eggs.

A WHAT IS IT?

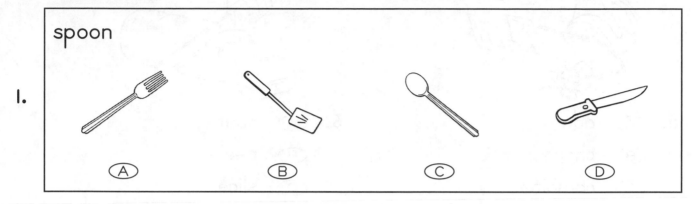

spoon

1. A   B   C   D

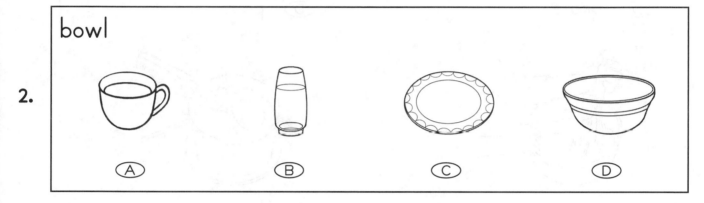

bowl

2. A   B   C   D

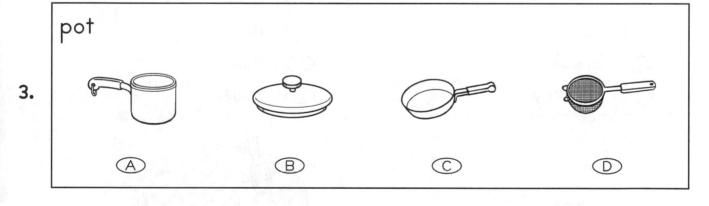

pot

3. A   B   C   D

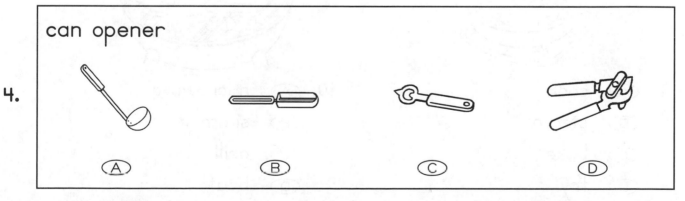

can opener

4. A   B   C   D

B WHAT'S THE WORD?

5.
(A) add
(B) chop
(C) combine
(D) grate

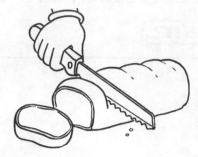

6.
(A) saute
(B) peel
(C) slice
(D) pour

7.
(A) stir
(B) cut
(C) break
(D) stir-fry

8.
(A) broil
(B) boil
(C) mix
(D) roast

9.
(A) cook
(B) steam
(C) bake
(D) fry

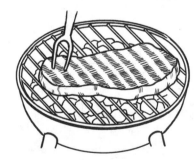

10.
(A) microwave
(B) simmer
(C) grill
(D) beat

C WHAT IS IT?

| gallon   ounce   quart   tablespoon |

11. _____

12. _____

13. _____

14. _____

D WHO IS IT?

| busperson   customer   hostess   server |

15. _____

16. _____

17. _____

18. _____

apple pie	cheeseburger	pancakes	sandwich
baked potato	milkshake	salad	

19. _____

20. _____

21. _____

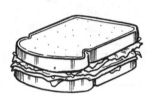

22. _____

23. _____

24. _____

25. _____

Name _____

Date _____

A) WHAT IS IT?

ring

1.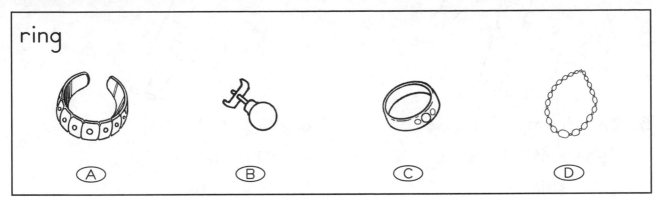

    Ⓐ   Ⓑ   Ⓒ   Ⓓ

belt

2.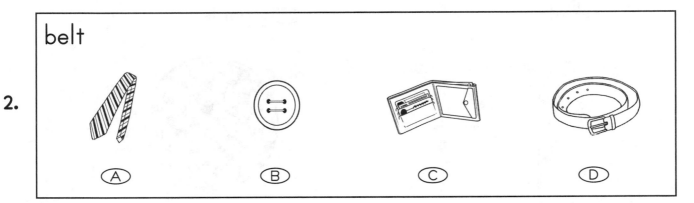

    Ⓐ   Ⓑ   Ⓒ   Ⓓ

sneakers

3.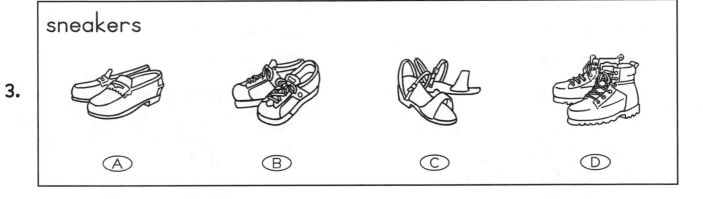

    Ⓐ   Ⓑ   Ⓒ   Ⓓ

high heels

4.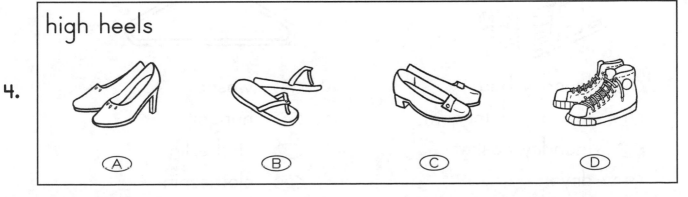

    Ⓐ   Ⓑ   Ⓒ   Ⓓ

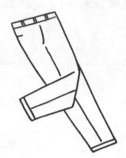

5. (A) coat
    (B) suit
    (C) shirt
    (D) skirt

6. (A) hat
    (B) tie
    (C) robe
    (D) pants

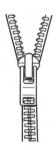

7. (A) collar
    (B) zipper
    (C) button
    (D) sleeve

8. (A) checked
    (B) striped
    (C) plaid
    (D) polka-dotted

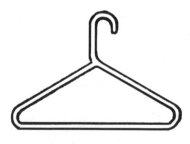

9. (A) laundry bag
    (B) laundry detergent
    (C) laundry basket
    (D) dryer

10. (A) washer
    (B) hanger
    (C) clothesline
    (D) clothespin

blouse	jacket	raincoat	sunglasses
dress	pajamas	socks	umbrella

11. _____

12. _____

13. _____

14. _____

15. _____

16. _____

17. _____

18. _____

| gloves | parka | scarf | shorts | sweater | swimsuit | T-shirt |

Cold Weather Clothing   19–22.

_____

_____

_____

_____

Hot Weather Clothing   23–25.

_____

_____

_____

Name _____

Date _____

A WHAT IS IT?

cell phone

1.

Ⓐ   Ⓑ   Ⓒ   Ⓓ

notebook computer

2.

Ⓐ   Ⓑ   Ⓒ   Ⓓ

clock radio

3.

Ⓐ   Ⓑ   Ⓒ   Ⓓ

tricycle

4.

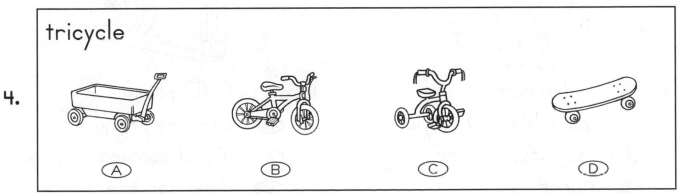

Ⓐ   Ⓑ   Ⓒ   Ⓓ

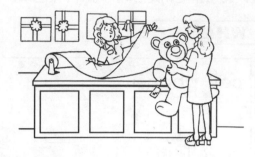

5.
- Ⓐ Furniture Department
- Ⓑ Housewares Department
- Ⓒ Electronics Department
- Ⓓ Household Appliances Department

6.
- Ⓐ Perfume Counter
- Ⓑ Jewelry Counter
- Ⓒ Gift Wrap Counter
- Ⓓ Women's Clothing Department

7.
- Ⓐ customer pickup area
- Ⓑ water fountain
- Ⓒ Customer Service Counter
- Ⓓ snack bar

8.
- Ⓐ escalator
- Ⓑ men's room
- Ⓒ elevator
- Ⓓ stairs

9.
- Ⓐ video game
- Ⓑ portable CD player
- Ⓒ battery charger
- Ⓓ tuner

10.
- Ⓐ DVD player
- Ⓑ cordless phone
- Ⓒ digital camera
- Ⓓ video camera

cable	headphones	mouse	remote control
cassette	monitor	printer	

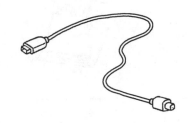

11.    12.

13. _____   14. _____

15. _____   16.

17. _____

D. WHAT IS IT?

label	price tag	receipt	sale sign

18. _____

19. _____

20. _____

21. _____

E. WHAT'S THE WORD?

exchange	pay for	return	try on

22. _____

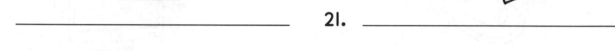

23. _____

24. _____

25. _____

Name _____

Date _____

A **WHAT IS IT?**

1. check

     Ⓐ   Ⓑ   Ⓒ   Ⓓ

2. deposit slip

     Ⓐ   Ⓑ   Ⓒ   Ⓓ

3. ATM card

     Ⓐ   Ⓑ   Ⓒ   Ⓓ

4. safe deposit box

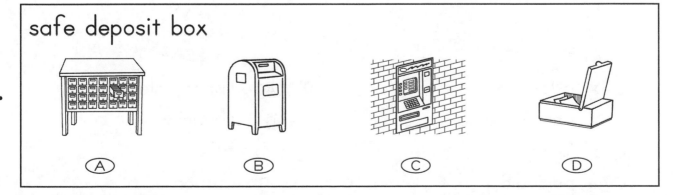

     Ⓐ   Ⓑ   Ⓒ   Ⓓ

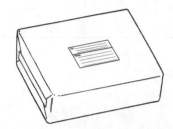

5. Ⓐ mailbox
   Ⓑ package
   Ⓒ money order
   Ⓓ express mail

6. Ⓐ postcard
   Ⓑ postmark
   Ⓒ letter
   Ⓓ priority mail

7. Ⓐ stamp
   Ⓑ address
   Ⓒ envelope
   Ⓓ stamp machine

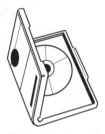

8. Ⓐ videotape
   Ⓑ DVD
   Ⓒ microfilm
   Ⓓ magazine

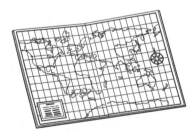

9. Ⓐ atlas
   Ⓑ encyclopedia
   Ⓒ journal
   Ⓓ periodical

10. Ⓐ library clerk
    Ⓑ librarian
    Ⓒ title
    Ⓓ author

C WHAT IS IT?

bank robbery	car accident	fire	gas leak
burglary	chemical spill	gang violence	vandalism

11. ______________________

12. ______________________

13. ______________________

14. ______________________

15. ______________________

16. ______________________

17. ______________________

18. ______________________

D WHAT'S THE WORD?

ambulance	city hall	nursery	senior center
bank	dump	police station	

19. The teller works in the

_____.

20. The police officer works at the

_____.

21. The activity director works in the

_____.

22. The paramedic works in the

_____.

23. The child-care worker works in the

_____.

24. The mayor works at

_____.

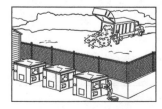

25. The sanitation worker works at the

_____.

Name _____

Date _____

A WHAT IS IT?

1. earache
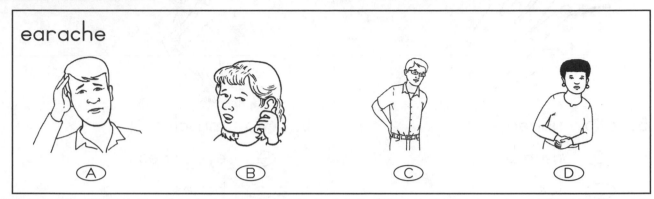

2. fever
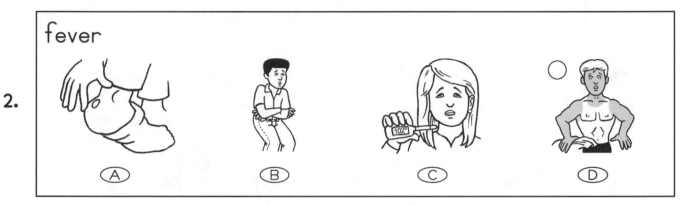

3. cold

4. exhausted

B WHAT'S THE WORD?

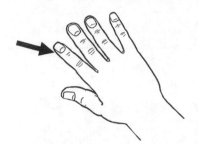

5.
- Ⓐ finger
- Ⓑ thumb
- Ⓒ toe
- Ⓓ face

6.
- Ⓐ muscles
- Ⓑ eyelashes
- Ⓒ bones
- Ⓓ teeth

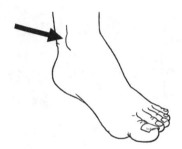

7.
- Ⓐ arm
- Ⓑ ankle
- Ⓒ leg
- Ⓓ elbow

8.
- Ⓐ thigh
- Ⓑ heel
- Ⓒ knee
- Ⓓ chin

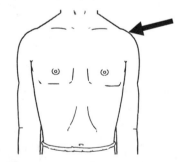

9.
- Ⓐ spinal cord
- Ⓑ shin
- Ⓒ hip
- Ⓓ shoulder

10.
- Ⓐ heart
- Ⓑ lung
- Ⓒ brain
- Ⓓ stomach

| allergic reaction | cough | rescue breathing | splint |
| bandage | insect bite | runny nose | stiff neck |

11. _____

12. _____

13. _____

14. _____

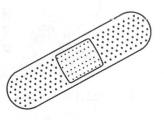

15. _____

16. _____

17. _____

18. _____

D WHAT IS IT?

asthma	heart attack	Heimlich maneuver	influenza
diabetes	heatstroke	high blood pressure	

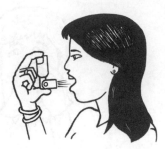

19. _____

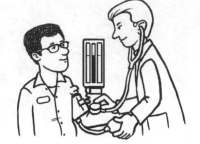

20. _____

21. _____

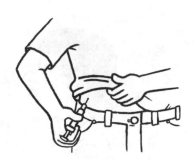

22. _____

23. _____

24. _____

25. _____

A WHAT IS IT?

aspirin

1.

teaspoon

2.

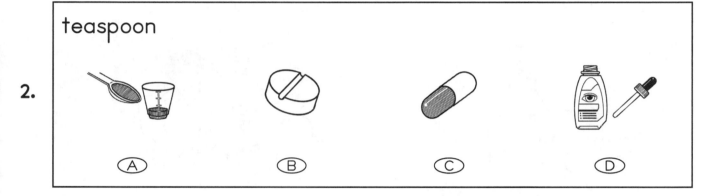

crutches

3.

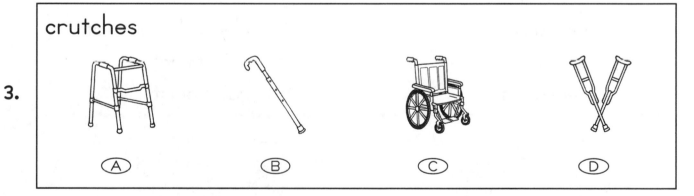

toothpaste

4.

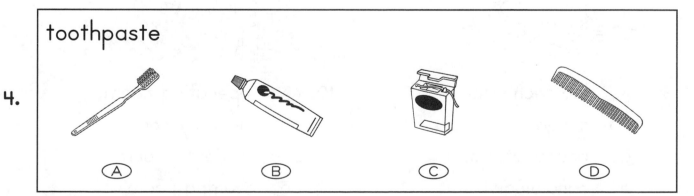

5. Ⓐ patient

Ⓑ volunteer

Ⓒ nurse

Ⓓ orderly

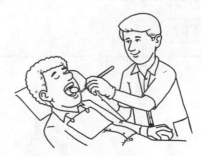

6. Ⓐ psychiatrist

Ⓑ orthopedist

Ⓒ dietician

Ⓓ dentist

7. Ⓐ gynecologist

Ⓑ allergist

Ⓒ pediatrician

Ⓓ receptionist

8. Ⓐ counselor

Ⓑ physical therapist

Ⓒ chiropractor

Ⓓ radiologist

9. Ⓐ lab technician

Ⓑ surgeon

Ⓒ acupuncturist

Ⓓ cardiologist

10. Ⓐ operating room

Ⓑ delivery room

Ⓒ patient's room

Ⓓ waiting room

change the diaper	examine your eyes
check your blood pressure	listen to your heart
drink fluids	take your temperature

11. _____

12. _____

13. _____

14. _____

15. _____

16. _____

D WHAT IS IT?

| cast | prescription | sling | stitches |

17. _____

18. _____

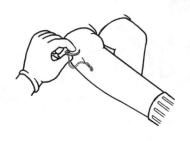

19. _____

20. _____

E WHAT'S THE WORD?

| blow dryer | bottle | deodorant | razor | shampoo |

21. I shave with a _____.

22. I wash my hair with _____.

23. I dry my hair with a _____.

24. I feed the baby with a _____.

25. I put on _____.

A WHAT IS IT?

1. math

A   B   C   D

2. biology

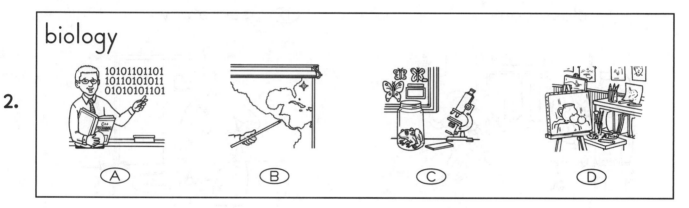

A   B   C   D

3. government

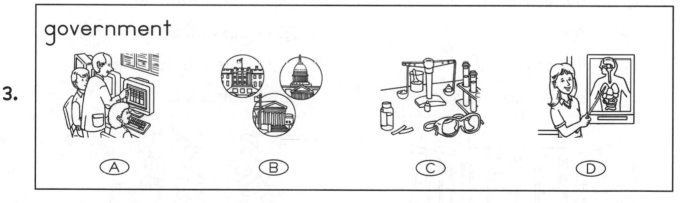

A   B   C   D

4. physical education

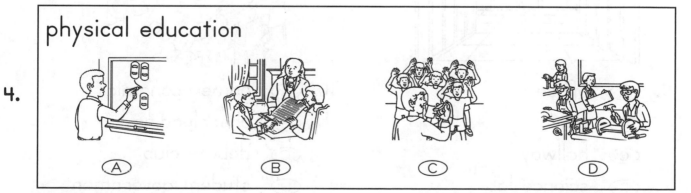

A   B   C   D

B WHAT'S THE WORD?

5.
- Ⓐ locker room
- Ⓑ nurse's office
- Ⓒ preschool
- Ⓓ classroom

6.
- Ⓐ security officer
- Ⓑ principal
- Ⓒ nurse
- Ⓓ secretary

7.
- Ⓐ gymnasium
- Ⓑ track
- Ⓒ library
- Ⓓ cafeteria

8.
- Ⓐ P.E. teacher
- Ⓑ custodian
- Ⓒ science teacher
- Ⓓ librarian

9.
- Ⓐ office
- Ⓑ field
- Ⓒ hallway
- Ⓓ science lab

10.
- Ⓐ home economics
- Ⓑ cheerleading
- Ⓒ debate club
- Ⓓ student government

adult school	band	elementary school	university
auditorium	coach	guidance office	vocational school

11. _____

12. _____

13. _____

14. _____

15. _____

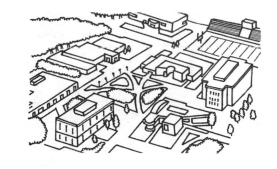

16. _____

17. _____

18. _____

D WHAT IS IT?

chorus	drama	international club	yearbook
community service	football	orchestra	

19. _____

20. _____

21. _____

22. _____

23. _____

24. _____

25. _____

Name _____

Date _____

A **WHAT IS IT?**

1. square

     Ⓐ   Ⓑ   Ⓒ   Ⓓ

2. e-mail

Ⓐ   Ⓑ   Ⓒ   Ⓓ

3. scale

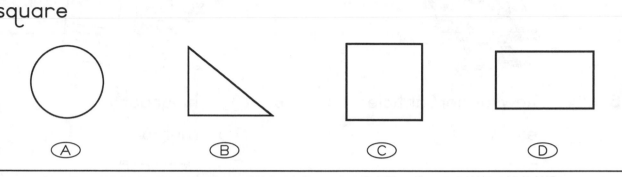

Ⓐ   Ⓑ   Ⓒ   Ⓓ

4. planet

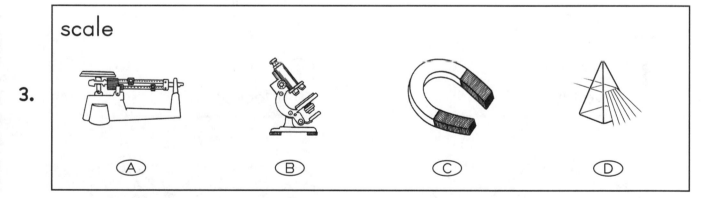

Ⓐ   Ⓑ   Ⓒ   Ⓓ

B WHAT'S THE WORD?

5. Ⓐ newspaper article

    Ⓑ essay

    Ⓒ poem

    Ⓓ novel

6. Ⓐ biography

    Ⓑ memo

    Ⓒ postcard

    Ⓓ thank-you note

7. Ⓐ jungle

    Ⓑ forest

    Ⓒ desert

    Ⓓ valley

8. Ⓐ island

    Ⓑ bay

    Ⓒ pond

    Ⓓ ocean

9. Ⓐ mountains

    Ⓑ hills

    Ⓒ plains

    Ⓓ meadows

10. Ⓐ lake

    Ⓑ river

    Ⓒ waterfall

    Ⓓ stream

| comma | exclamation point | period | question mark |

It's one mile.

Hello, Jim.

11. _____

12. _____

What?

Stop!

13. _____

14. _____

| noun | preposition | pronoun | verb |

It's (on) the table.

It's my (car).

15. _____

16. _____

I (study) English.

(She) is here.

17. _____

18. _____

D WHAT'S THE WORD?

| divided by | minus | plus | times |

19. One _____ two equals three.

20. Two _____ three equals six.

21. Eight _____ three equals five.

22. Ten _____ two equals five.

E WHAT IS IT?

| fifty percent | three quarters | one third |

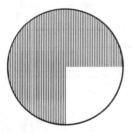

23. _____   24. _____

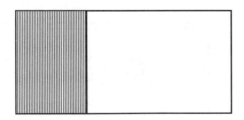

25. _____

(A) WHAT IS IT?

cashier

1.

    Ⓐ   Ⓑ   Ⓒ   Ⓓ

baker

2.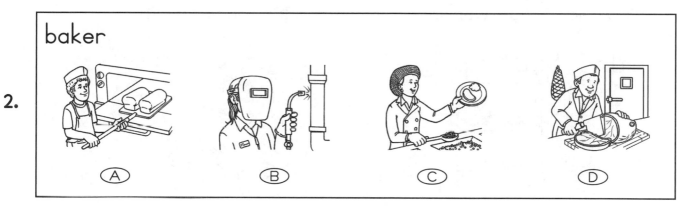

    Ⓐ   Ⓑ   Ⓒ   Ⓓ

assembler

3.

    Ⓐ   Ⓑ   Ⓒ   Ⓓ

security guard

4.

    Ⓐ   Ⓑ   Ⓒ   Ⓓ

5. Ⓐ serviceman
   Ⓑ repairperson
   Ⓒ mover
   Ⓓ sanitation worker

6. Ⓐ manicurist
   Ⓑ manager
   Ⓒ veterinarian
   Ⓓ pharmacist

7. Ⓐ foreman
   Ⓑ homemaker
   Ⓒ farmer
   Ⓓ custodian

8. Ⓐ assemble components
   Ⓑ assist patients
   Ⓒ clean
   Ⓓ use a cash register

9. Ⓐ take inventory
   Ⓑ sew
   Ⓒ repair things
   Ⓓ operate equipment

10. Ⓐ build things
    Ⓑ take care of people
    Ⓒ supervise people
    Ⓓ guard buildings

artist	barber	carpenter	firefighter
babysitter	businessman	delivery person	hairdresser

11. _____

12. _____

13. _____

14. _____

15. _____

16. _____

17. _____

18. _____

D WHAT'S THE WORD?

builds houses	prepares food	speaks Spanish and English
flies airplanes	serves food	teaches students
mows lawns		

19. The landscaper

_____.

20. The waitress

_____.

21. The pilot

_____.

22. The translator

_____.

23. The instructor

Read pages 101-105

_____.

24. The cook

_____.

25. The construction worker

_____.

Name _____

Date _____

(A) WHAT IS IT?

1. envelope

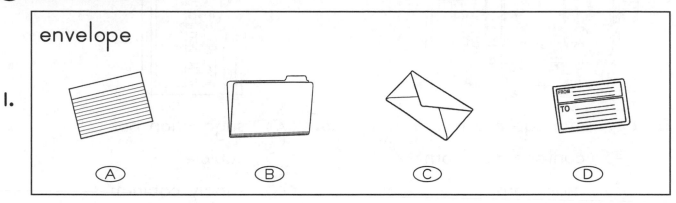

    (A)   (B)   (C)   (D)

2. stapler

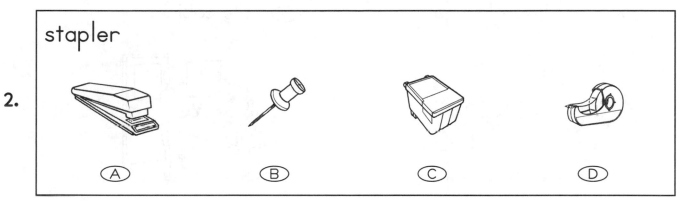

    (A)   (B)   (C)   (D)

3. paper clip

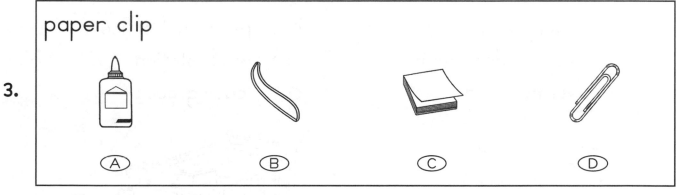

    (A)   (B)   (C)   (D)

4. appointment book

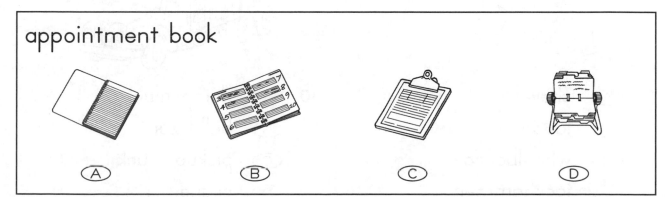

    (A)   (B)   (C)   (D)

5.
- Ⓐ storage room
- Ⓑ conference room
- Ⓒ mailroom
- Ⓓ employee lounge

6.
- Ⓐ suggestion box
- Ⓑ cubicle
- Ⓒ supply cabinet
- Ⓓ file cabinet

7.
- Ⓐ warehouse
- Ⓑ locker room
- Ⓒ shipping department
- Ⓓ assembly line

8.
- Ⓐ payroll office
- Ⓑ personnel office
- Ⓒ work station
- Ⓓ loading dock

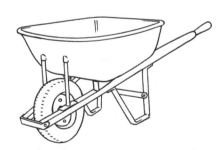

9.
- Ⓐ shovel
- Ⓑ ladder
- Ⓒ wheelbarrow
- Ⓓ jackhammer

10.
- Ⓐ dump truck
- Ⓑ bulldozer
- Ⓒ pickup truck
- Ⓓ crane

| evenings | excellent | experience | full-time | hour | part-time |

11. FT _____

12. PT _____

13. hr. _____

14. eves. _____

15. excel. _____

16. exper. _____

D **WHAT IS IT?**

| fill out an application | make copies |
| go to an interview | take a message |

17. _____   18. _____

19. _____   20. _____

fire extinguisher	goggles	safety vest
first-aid kit	hard hat	

21. _____

22. _____

23. _____

24. _____

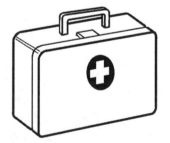

25. _____

Name _____

Date _____

(A) **WHAT IS IT?**

1. bus driver

2. taxicab

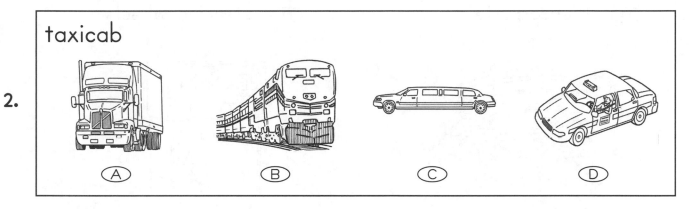

3. sedan

4. pickup truck

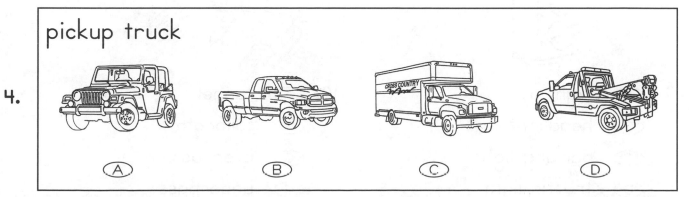

5.
Ⓐ brake
Ⓑ tire
Ⓒ battery
Ⓓ license plate

6.
Ⓐ seat belt
Ⓑ door lock
Ⓒ turn signal
Ⓓ steering wheel

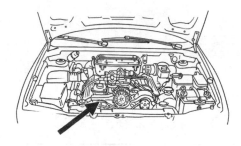

7.
Ⓐ engine
Ⓑ horn
Ⓒ trunk
Ⓓ windshield

8.
Ⓐ bumper
Ⓑ gas tank
Ⓒ gas pump
Ⓓ air pump

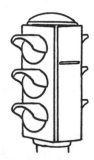

9.
Ⓐ highway
Ⓑ headlight
Ⓒ parking light
Ⓓ traffic light

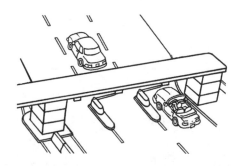

10.
Ⓐ tunnel
Ⓑ tollbooth
Ⓒ overpass
Ⓓ underpass

| no left turn | no right turn | pedestrian crossing | school crossing |

11. _____

12. _____

13. _____

14. _____

| baggage | customs officer | security officer |
| boarding pass | passport | ticket counter |

15. _____

16. _____

17. _____

18. _____

19. _____

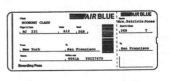

20. _____

behind	in	in front of	into	under

21. The doorman is _____ the hotel.

22. The guest is _____ the lobby.

23. The housekeeper is going _____ the room.

24. The desk clerk is _____ the front desk.

25. The suitcase is _____ the table.

Name _____

Date _____

A **WHAT IS IT?**

draw

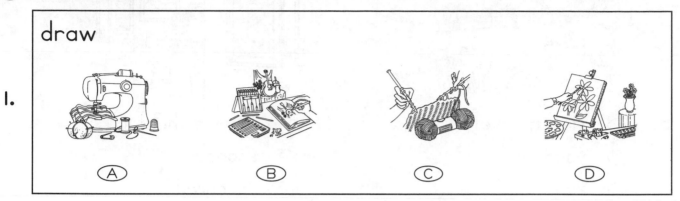

1.

    (A)   (B)   (C)   (D)

cards

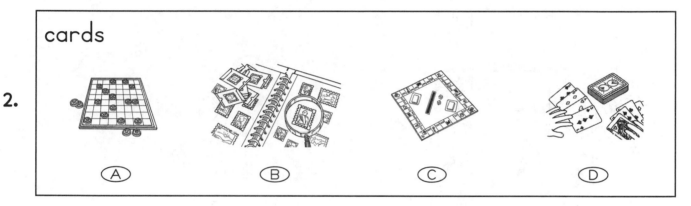

2.

    (A)   (B)   (C)   (D)

bike helmet

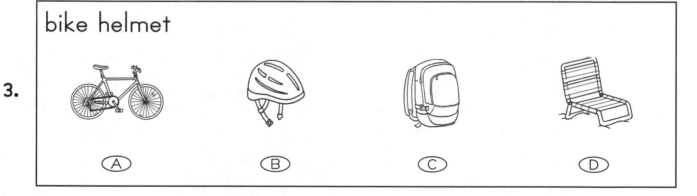

3.

    (A)   (B)   (C)   (D)

pail

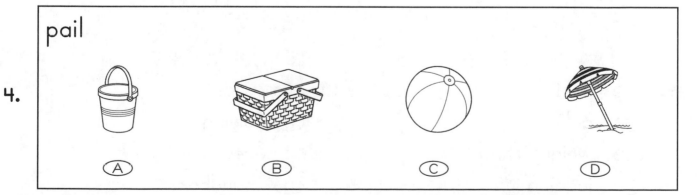

4.

    (A)   (B)   (C)   (D)

5.
- (A) flea market
- (B) yard sale
- (C) zoo
- (D) amusement park

6.
- (A) movie theater
- (B) concert
- (C) carnival
- (D) museum

7.
- (A) playground
- (B) art gallery
- (C) aquarium
- (D) craft fair

8.
- (A) bowling
- (B) ping pong
- (C) badminton
- (D) tennis

9.
- (A) pool
- (B) golf
- (C) weightlifting
- (D) jogging

10.
- (A) slide
- (B) swing
- (C) seesaw
- (D) sandbox

boxing	historic site	national park	surfer
gymnastics	jogging	skateboarding	swimmer

11. _____

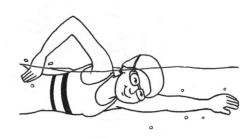

12. _____

13. _____

14. _____

15. _____

16. _____

17. _____

18. _____

| backpack | cooler | grill | kite | picnic table | sun hat | tent |

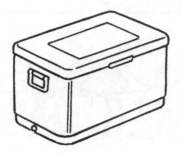

19. _____

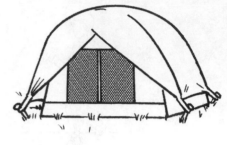

20. _____

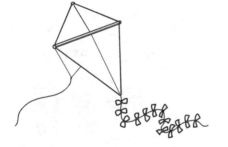

21. _____

22. _____

23. _____

24. _____

25. _____

Name _____

Date _____

A **WHAT IS IT?**

basketball

1.

    Ⓐ   Ⓑ   Ⓒ   Ⓓ

soccer

2.

    Ⓐ   Ⓑ   Ⓒ   Ⓓ

bat

3.

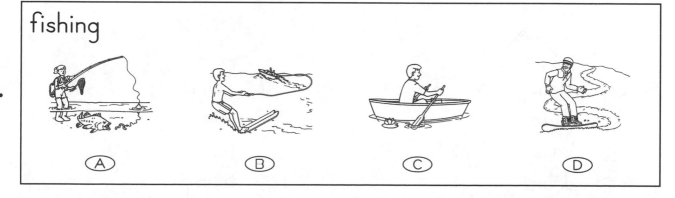

    Ⓐ   Ⓑ   Ⓒ   Ⓓ

fishing

4.

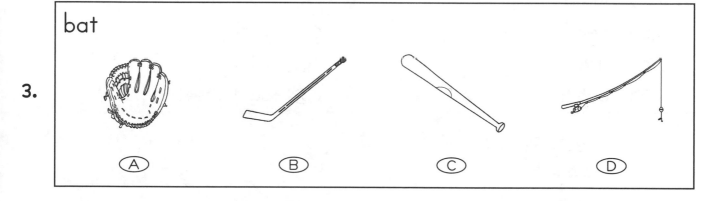

    Ⓐ   Ⓑ   Ⓒ   Ⓓ

5. Ⓐ pass
   Ⓑ kick
   Ⓒ hit
   Ⓓ serve

6. Ⓐ run
   Ⓑ throw
   Ⓒ swing
   Ⓓ lift

7. Ⓐ jump
   Ⓑ bend
   Ⓒ dive
   Ⓓ catch

8. Ⓐ handstand
   Ⓑ push-up
   Ⓒ sit-up
   Ⓓ cartwheel

9. Ⓐ piano
   Ⓑ flute
   Ⓒ bass
   Ⓓ drum

10. Ⓐ violin
    Ⓑ guitar
    Ⓒ tuba
    Ⓓ trumpet

cartoon	comedy	musical	talk show
classical music	game show	rock music	western

11. _____

12. _____

13. _____

14. _____

15. _____

16. _____

17. _____

18. _____

canoeing ice skating sailing skiing sledding snorkeling swimming

Summer Sports 19–22.

_____   _____

_____   _____

Winter Sports 23–25.

_____

_____

_____

A · WHAT IS IT?

1.
barn

Ⓐ   Ⓑ   Ⓒ   Ⓓ

2.
cow

Ⓐ   Ⓑ   Ⓒ   Ⓓ

3.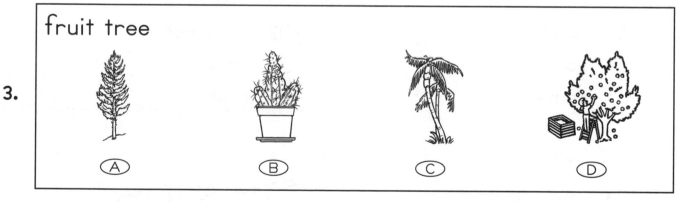
fruit tree

Ⓐ   Ⓑ   Ⓒ   Ⓓ

4.
flowers

Ⓐ   Ⓑ   Ⓒ   Ⓓ

B WHAT'S THE WORD?

5.
- (A) fox
- (B) giraffe
- (C) zebra
- (D) deer

6.
- (A) squirrel
- (B) monkey
- (C) raccoon
- (D) rabbit

7.
- (A) cat
- (B) panda
- (C) lion
- (D) camel

8.
- (A) eagle
- (B) parakeet
- (C) seagull
- (D) robin

9.
- (A) octopus
- (B) whale
- (C) shark
- (D) dolphin

10.
- (A) armadillo
- (B) alligator
- (C) snake
- (D) turtle

| air pollution | flood | hurricane | solar energy |
| earthquake | global warming | recycle | tornado |

11. _____

12. _____

13. _____

14. _____

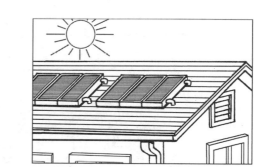

15. _____

16. _____

17. _____

18. _____

D WHICH GROUP?

| bear | chicken | elephant | horse | ostrich | tiger | turkey |

Farm Animals 19–21.

_____

_____

_____

Zoo Animals 22–25.

_____   _____

_____   _____

A **WHAT IS IT?**

1. driver's license

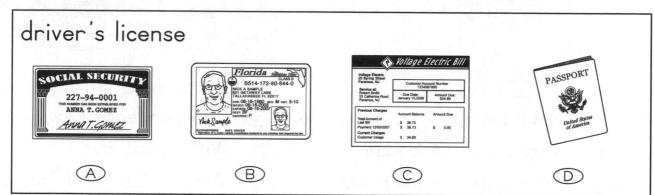

    Ⓐ   Ⓑ   Ⓒ   Ⓓ

2. White House

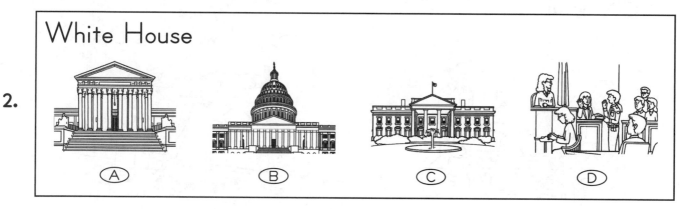

    Ⓐ   Ⓑ   Ⓒ   Ⓓ

3. judge

    Ⓐ   Ⓑ   Ⓒ   Ⓓ

4. jury

    Ⓐ   Ⓑ   Ⓒ   Ⓓ

5. Ⓐ work permit

   Ⓑ employee I.D. badge

   Ⓒ permanent resident card

   Ⓓ visa

6. Ⓐ Independence Day

   Ⓑ Veterans Day

   Ⓒ Martin Luther King, Jr. Day

   Ⓓ New Year's Day

7. Ⓐ Thanksgiving

   Ⓑ Halloween

   Ⓒ Memorial Day

   Ⓓ Valentine's Day

8. Ⓐ appear in court

   Ⓑ be released

   Ⓒ be arrested

   Ⓓ hire a lawyer

9. Ⓐ suspects

   Ⓑ Miranda rights

   Ⓒ handcuffs

   Ⓓ fingerprints

10. Ⓐ obey laws

   Ⓑ stand trial

   Ⓒ make the laws

   Ⓓ be part of community life

C WHAT IS IT?

freedom of the press	freedom of speech	the right to vote
freedom of religion	the Constitution	

11. _____

12. _____

13. _____

14. _____

15. _____

Civil War	Revolutionary War	Vietnam War	World War II

1861–1865   16. _____

1964–1973   17. _____

1939–1945   18. _____

1775–1783   19. _____

apply for citizenship   serve on a jury
follow the news   take a citizenship test
pay taxes   vote

20. _____

21. _____

22. _____

23. _____

24. _____

25. _____

Name _____

Date _____

A WHAT IS IT?

1.
family trip

   Ⓐ   Ⓑ   Ⓒ   Ⓓ

2.
ski trip

   Ⓐ   Ⓑ   Ⓒ   Ⓓ

3.
baggage claim area
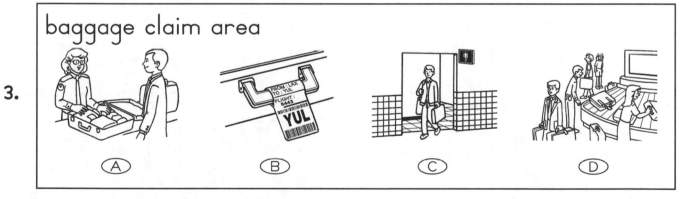
   Ⓐ   Ⓑ   Ⓒ   Ⓓ

4.
immigration
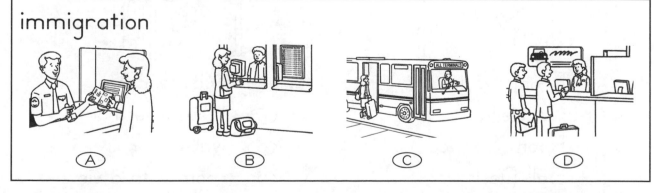
   Ⓐ   Ⓑ   Ⓒ   Ⓓ

5.
Ⓐ expedition
Ⓑ study tour
Ⓒ travel agency
Ⓓ eco-tour

6.
Ⓐ buy tickets
Ⓑ pay with a credit card
Ⓒ make reservations
Ⓓ cash a traveler's check

7.
Ⓐ rent a car
Ⓑ buy souvenirs
Ⓒ mail postcards
Ⓓ visit an historic site

8.
Ⓐ go shopping
Ⓑ go to a club
Ⓒ go to a park
Ⓓ go sightseeing

9.
Ⓐ Front Desk
Ⓑ Concierge
Ⓒ Room Service
Ⓓ Bell Desk

10.
Ⓐ Maintenance
Ⓑ Housekeeping
Ⓒ wake-up call
Ⓓ room with a view

C WHAT IS IT?

| Internet cafe | non-smoking room | shuttle bus | taxi stand |

11. _____

12. _____

13. _____

14. _____

D WHAT'S THE WORD?

| city | days | dinner | tickets | towels |

15. I'd like to get _____ for a show.

16. We need three _____ for our room.

17. I'd like to order _____.

18. I'm here for five _____.

19. How do you like our _____?

Fire!	Please go away!
Help!	Please write that down.
Look out!	What did you say?

20. _____

21. _____

22. _____

23. _____

24. _____

25. _____

A **PERSONAL INFORMATION**

apartment number	last name	street
city	middle initial	street number
first name	state	zip code

1	**2**	**3**
Thomas	S.	Wang

4	**5**	**6**
578	Alden Avenue	7C

7	**8**	**9**
Dallas	TX	75225

1. _____   4. _____   7. _____

2. _____   5. _____   8. _____

3. _____   6. _____   9. _____

B **WHAT'S THE WORD?**

address	date of birth	social security number
area code	e-mail address	telephone number

10. My _____ is 127 Central Avenue.

11. My _____ is 408.

12. My _____ is 555-917-5360.

13. My _____ is lisa87@ail.com.

14. My _____ is 227-12-3456.

15. My _____ is 10/25/90.

C WHO ARE THEY?

| aunt | brother-in-law | cousin | mother | parents |

16. My mother and father are my _____.

17. My father's sister is my _____.

18. My grandmother is my father's _____.

19. My aunt's son is my _____.

20. My wife's brother is my _____.

D WHAT'S THE ANSWER?

21. What's your last name? _____

22. What's your city and state? _____

23. What's your zip code? _____

24. What's your date of birth? _____

25. What's your area code? _____

E WHAT'S THE WORD?

26. My _____ number is 323-1253.
   Ⓐ apartment
   Ⓑ street
   Ⓒ phone
   Ⓓ social security

27. What's your _____ name?
   Ⓐ family
   Ⓑ initial
   Ⓒ zip code
   Ⓓ area code

28. My middle initial is _____.
   Ⓐ Cheng
   Ⓑ T
   Ⓒ T-H-O-M-A-S
   Ⓓ 32904

29. My family name is _____.
   Ⓐ Gonzalez
   Ⓑ TX
   Ⓒ Dallas
   Ⓓ V

30. My grandmother has ten _____.
   Ⓐ husbands
   Ⓑ grandfathers
   Ⓒ grandmothers
   Ⓓ grandchildren

31. I have one brother and two sisters. They're my _____.
   Ⓐ parents
   Ⓑ siblings
   Ⓒ cousins
   Ⓓ children

Lucy   Paul

Allen   Sue   David   Ellen

William   Carol   Stacey

32. Allen is Sue's _____.
   Ⓐ wife
   Ⓑ husband
   Ⓒ brother
   Ⓓ sister

33. William is Paul's _____.
   Ⓐ nephew
   Ⓑ son
   Ⓒ grandson
   Ⓓ granddaughter

34. Carol is David's _____.
   Ⓐ daughter
   Ⓑ son
   Ⓒ nephew
   Ⓓ niece

35. Sue is David's _____.
   Ⓐ sister
   Ⓑ wife
   Ⓒ cousin
   Ⓓ niece

36. Ellen is Lucy's _____.
   Ⓐ daughter-in-law
   Ⓑ daughter
   Ⓒ mother-in-law
   Ⓓ mother

37. Lucy and Paul are Carol's _____.
   Ⓐ parents
   Ⓑ children
   Ⓒ grandchildren
   Ⓓ grandparents

38. Stacey and Carol are _____.
   Ⓐ sisters
   Ⓑ cousins
   Ⓒ siblings
   Ⓓ parents

39. Sue is Ellen's _____.
   Ⓐ uncle
   Ⓑ aunt
   Ⓒ sister
   Ⓓ sister-in-law

40. Allen and Sue have two _____.
   Ⓐ siblings
   Ⓑ sisters
   Ⓒ children
   Ⓓ sons

41. Allen is David's _____.
   Ⓐ brother
   Ⓑ brother-in-law
   Ⓒ father-in-law
   Ⓓ nephew

G WHO ARE THEY?

42. My father's father is my _____.
- Ⓐ uncle
- Ⓑ father-in-law
- Ⓒ grandfather
- Ⓓ father

43. My aunt is my mother's _____.
- Ⓐ mother
- Ⓑ sister
- Ⓒ wife
- Ⓓ sister-in-law

44. My sister's daughter is my _____.
- Ⓐ niece
- Ⓑ nephew
- Ⓒ sibling
- Ⓓ cousin

45. My brother's son is my _____.
- Ⓐ uncle
- Ⓑ sibling
- Ⓒ brother-in-law
- Ⓓ nephew

46. My sister's husband is my _____.
- Ⓐ uncle
- Ⓑ brother-in-law
- Ⓒ cousin
- Ⓓ brother

47. My son's wife is my _____.
- Ⓐ daughter
- Ⓑ niece
- Ⓒ daughter-in-law
- Ⓓ sister-in-law

48. My aunt and uncle's children are my _____.
- Ⓐ nephews
- Ⓑ cousins
- Ⓒ siblings
- Ⓓ sisters

49. My mother-in-law is my _____.
- Ⓐ brother's wife
- Ⓑ cousin's mother
- Ⓒ husband's sister
- Ⓓ husband's mother

50. My brother is my niece's _____.
- Ⓐ nephew
- Ⓑ uncle
- Ⓒ father
- Ⓓ father–in-law

H WRITING SAMPLE

Choose one of these topics and write a paragraph. Use a separate sheet of paper.

- Who are the people in your family? Write about them. What are their names? How old are they?

- Write about your mother's family or your father's family.

Word by Word **Beginning Level**
Unit 2A Test: PICTURE DICTIONARY PAGES 4–8

Name _____

Date _____

A) WHAT'S THE WORD?

| binder | eraser | graph paper | thumbtack |
| calculator | globe | pencil sharpener | wastebasket |

1. _____ 2. _____ 3. _____ 4. _____

5. _____ 6. _____ 7. _____ 8. _____

B) WHICH GROUP?

| bulletin board | chalkboard | keyboard | marker | mouse | pencil |
| chalk | clock | loudspeaker | monitor | pen | printer |

9–12. Items on a Wall   **13–16. Computer Items**   **17–20. Items to Write with**

_____ _____ _____

_____ _____ _____

_____ _____ _____

_____ _____ _____

C) WHAT'S THE WORD?

| book | hand | listen | mistakes | put |

21. Raise your _____.   **24.** Close your _____.

22. Correct your _____.   **25.** _____ the words in order.

23. Please _____ to the answer.

D CLASSROOM ACTIONS

26. _____ the sentences.
    - Ⓐ Copy
    - Ⓑ Close
    - Ⓒ Go
    - Ⓓ Bring

27. _____ away your book.
    - Ⓐ Close
    - Ⓑ Do
    - Ⓒ Look
    - Ⓓ Put

28. Fill in the _____.
    - Ⓐ screen
    - Ⓑ blank
    - Ⓒ group
    - Ⓓ seat

29. Please _____ a book.
    - Ⓐ turn
    - Ⓑ break up
    - Ⓒ share
    - Ⓓ hand

30. _____ up the word in the dictionary.
    - Ⓐ Look
    - Ⓑ Pronounce
    - Ⓒ Work
    - Ⓓ Bring

31. _____ off the lights.
    - Ⓐ Write
    - Ⓑ Read
    - Ⓒ Correct
    - Ⓓ Turn

32. Please _____ up and go the board.
    - Ⓐ sit
    - Ⓑ stand
    - Ⓒ study
    - Ⓓ copy

33. Break up into small _____.
    - Ⓐ groups
    - Ⓑ lights
    - Ⓒ seats
    - Ⓓ notes

E CLOZE READING

At the beginning of class, our teacher asks | notes Ⓐ questions Ⓑ papers Ⓒ |³⁴ about our

weekend. Students | raise Ⓐ open Ⓑ turn Ⓒ |³⁵ their hands to answer. Next she asks us to

| read Ⓐ say Ⓑ take Ⓒ |³⁶ out our homework. We go | over Ⓐ off Ⓑ in Ⓒ |³⁷ the correct answers.

Then we | match Ⓐ look Ⓑ hand Ⓒ |³⁸ in our homework to the teacher. After that, she

| lowers Ⓐ passes Ⓑ crosses Ⓒ |³⁹ out a short test. We write | answers Ⓐ boards Ⓑ blanks Ⓒ |⁴⁰

on a separate sheet of paper. After the test, we | lower Ⓐ unscramble Ⓑ open Ⓒ |⁴¹ our textbooks.

We usually | take Ⓐ work Ⓑ fill Ⓒ |⁴² with a partner.

43. The teacher is _____ the bookcase.
- Ⓐ in
- Ⓑ in front of
- Ⓒ next to
- Ⓓ behind

44. The dictionaries are _____ the bookcase.
- Ⓐ under
- Ⓑ between
- Ⓒ below
- Ⓓ in

45. The screen is _____ the teacher.
- Ⓐ under
- Ⓑ in front of
- Ⓒ to the right of
- Ⓓ to the left of

46. The wastebasket is _____ the teacher's desk.
- Ⓐ between
- Ⓑ under
- Ⓒ on
- Ⓓ in

47. The clock is _____ the bookcase.
- Ⓐ behind
- Ⓑ below
- Ⓒ under
- Ⓓ above

48. The textbook is _____ the teacher's desk.
- Ⓐ in
- Ⓑ on
- Ⓒ under
- Ⓓ next to

49. The overhead projector is _____ the desk.
- Ⓐ in front of
- Ⓑ below
- Ⓒ to the left of
- Ⓓ behind

50. The chalkboard is _____ the screen.
- Ⓐ behind
- Ⓑ above
- Ⓒ in front of
- Ⓓ between

G **WRITING SAMPLE**

Choose one of these topics and write a paragraph. Use a separate sheet of paper.

- What do you see in your classroom? Describe where things are.

- What's happening in a classroom? What are students doing? Write about their classroom actions.

Name _____

Date _____

A WHAT ARE YOU DOING?

cleaning	doing	exercising	going	relaxing	taking
combing	driving	feeding	ironing	studying	walking

1. I'm _____.

2. I'm _____ the dog.

3. I'm _____ the laundry.

4. I'm _____ the house.

5. I'm _____ a shower.

6. I'm _____ to work.

7. I'm _____ my hair.

8. I'm _____ the baby.

9. I'm _____ to the store.

10. I'm _____.

11. I'm _____.

12. I'm _____ my shirt.

B WHAT DO THEY DO?

brushes	gets	puts	uses	washes

13. She _____ the computer every night.

14. He _____ his teeth every morning.

15. She _____ on makeup before a party.

16. He _____ his face before breakfast.

17. She _____ home at 6:30 P.M.

| cloudy | drizzling | foggy | hailing | humid | lightning | snowing | windy |

18. _____

19. _____

20. _____

21. _____

22. _____

23. _____

24. _____

25. _____

D **WHAT'S THE ANSWER?**

26. I _____ breakfast at seven o'clock.
Ⓐ wash
Ⓑ take
Ⓒ have

27. He _____ flowers in the garden.
Ⓐ plants
Ⓑ makes
Ⓒ practices

28. It's a very _____ day. Let's go swimming.
Ⓐ cold
Ⓑ warm
Ⓒ windy

29. The air isn't clear today. It's _____.
Ⓐ sunny
Ⓑ cool
Ⓒ smoggy

30. I watch the weather _____ on the TV.
Ⓐ forecast
Ⓑ temperature
Ⓒ thermometer

31. Where's my umbrella? It's _____ today.
Ⓐ hazy
Ⓑ raining
Ⓒ clear

32. It was very hot last week, and it's hot again this week. We're having a _____.
Ⓐ heat wave
Ⓑ snowstorm
Ⓒ thunderstorm

E   CLOZE READING

Janet [leaves(A)   takes(B)   gets(C)] ³³ up every day at 7:00. She [does(A)   gets(B)   goes(C)] ³⁴

dressed and [makes(A)   irons(B)   cleans(C)] ³⁵ the bed. Then she [reads(A)   eats(B)   feeds(C)] ³⁶

breakfast and [drives(A)   goes(B)   takes(C)] ³⁷ a bus to work. She [makes(A)   leaves(B)   gets(C)] ³⁸

work at 5:00. She [does(A)   comes(B)   uses(C)] ³⁹ home and [makes(A)   takes(B)   feeds(C)] ⁴⁰ dinner. After

dinner, she [reads(A)   writes(B)   listens(C)] ⁴¹ the newspaper and [listens(A)   practices(B)   watches(C)] ⁴² TV.

Then she [makes(A)   takes(B)   washes(C)] ⁴³ a bath and [goes(A)   sleeps(B)   fill(C)] ⁴⁴ to bed.

F   WHAT'S THE ANSWER?

45. What's new?
    - (A) Thanks.
    - (B) And you?
    - (C) Not much.
    - (D) Okay.

46. See you later.
    - (A) Good-bye.
    - (B) Tonight.
    - (C) Hello.
    - (D) I'm busy.

47. How's the weather?
    - (A) I'm fine.
    - (B) It's freezing.
    - (C) No, thanks.
    - (D) Hold on.

48. May I please speak to Mario?
    - (A) Nice to meet you.
    - (B) Hello.
    - (C) I'm not Mario.
    - (D) Yes. Hold on a minute.

49. Thank you.
    - (A) You're welcome.
    - (B) Excuse me.
    - (C) I'm sorry.
    - (D) Fine, thanks.

50. How are you doing?
    - (A) See you later.
    - (B) Not too much.
    - (C) Yes.
    - (D) Fine.

G   WRITING SAMPLE

Choose one of these topics and write a paragraph. Use a separate sheet of paper.

- What do you do every day? What time do you get up? What do you usually have for breakfast? What do you do in the morning? In the afternoon? In the evening?

- What do you do on the weekend? Do you relax? Do you do your laundry? Do you play a sport? What leisure activities do you do?

Name _____

Date _____

A) WHAT'S THE NEXT WORD?

| eleven | fifteenth | ninety | sixth | third |

1. ten, _____, twelve

2. fifth, _____, seventh

3. first, second, _____

4. fourteenth, _____, sixteenth

5. seventy, eighty, _____

B) HOW MUCH IS IT?

6. _____   **7.** _____   **8.** _____

C) WHAT TIME IS IT?

| a quarter after seven | a quarter to seven | half past seven |
| noon | ten to three | three ten |

9. _____   **10.** _____   **11.** _____

12. _____   **13.** _____   **14.** _____

D) IT'S TUESDAY

April	SUN	MON	TUE	WED	THU	FRI	SAT
	1	2	③	4	5	6	7

4/3	4/4	April	Monday	the fifth	Wednesday

15. Yesterday was _____.

16. The month is _____.

17. Thursday is _____.

18. The fourth is on _____.

19. Today's date is _____.

20. Tomorrow's date is _____.

E) WHAT'S THE ANSWER?

21. What day is today? _____

22. What month is it? _____

23. What year is it? _____

24. What's today's date? _____

25. What's your date of birth? _____

F) WHAT'S THE WORD?

26. My favorite day of the week
    is ____.
    Ⓐ Friday
    Ⓑ February
    Ⓒ tomorrow
    Ⓓ fall

27. My favorite season is ____.
    Ⓐ Sunday
    Ⓑ evening
    Ⓒ August
    Ⓓ summer

28. I'm going to study ____.
    Ⓐ yesterday morning
    Ⓑ last night
    Ⓒ this afternoon
    Ⓓ evening

29. I usually go to bed at midnight
    and get up at 7:00 ____.
    Ⓐ morning
    Ⓑ A.M.
    Ⓒ P.M.
    Ⓓ thirty

30. He goes to class ____ a week—on Monday
    and Wednesday.
    Ⓐ one
    Ⓑ two
    Ⓒ once
    Ⓓ twice

31. Today's date is ____.
    Ⓐ 2013
    Ⓑ Wednesday
    Ⓒ April 10, 2013
    Ⓓ April

32. There are _____ days in a week.
   Ⓐ four
   Ⓑ five
   Ⓒ seven
   Ⓓ eight

33. There are _____ months in a year.
   Ⓐ six
   Ⓑ nine
   Ⓒ ten
   Ⓓ twelve

34. There are _____ seasons in a year.
   Ⓐ two
   Ⓑ four
   Ⓒ six
   Ⓓ nine

35. There are _____ hours in a day.
   Ⓐ six
   Ⓑ seven
   Ⓒ twenty-four
   Ⓓ forty-two

36. There are _____ cents in a dime.
   Ⓐ ten
   Ⓑ twenty
   Ⓒ twenty-five
   Ⓓ fifty

37. There are _____ cents in a dollar.
   Ⓐ ten
   Ⓑ twenty-five
   Ⓒ fifty
   Ⓓ one hundred

H **WHAT'S THE ANSWER?**

38. How much is a quarter worth?
   Ⓐ Five cents.
   Ⓑ Forty cents.
   Ⓒ Twenty-five cents.
   Ⓓ Two dimes.

39. How much is a half-dollar worth?
   Ⓐ Fifty cents.
   Ⓑ Two dollars.
   Ⓒ Seventy-five cents.
   Ⓓ Five cents.

40. Can you change a dollar?
   Ⓐ Yes. I have 50 cents.
   Ⓑ Yes. I have three dollars.
   Ⓒ Sure. Here are four quarters.
   Ⓓ Yes. Here are eight dimes.

41. Do you have any cash?
   Ⓐ It's five.
   Ⓑ It's worth ten dollars.
   Ⓒ It's a coin.
   Ⓓ I have a ten-dollar bill.

42. Can you change a twenty?
   Ⓐ Yes. I have two fives.
   Ⓑ Yes. I have a ten and ten ones.
   Ⓒ Yes. I have a twenty-dollar bill.
   Ⓓ Yes. I have a ten and five ones.

43. Do you have enough change for a soda?
   Ⓐ Yes. I have a ten-dollar bill.
   Ⓑ Yes. I have two fives.
   Ⓒ Yes. I have two nickels.
   Ⓓ Yes. I have four quarters.

CLOZE READING

My English class starts at 9:00 A.M. I always like to arrive on time. I usually leave my house

at eight | hours   P.M.   o'clock |⁴⁴. My bus comes at | a quarter   o'clock   half past |⁴⁵ after
     Ⓐ   Ⓑ   Ⓒ   Ⓐ   Ⓑ   Ⓒ

eight. The bus | leaves   costs   has |⁴⁶ seventy-five | quarters   dollars   cents |⁴⁷. I always have
          Ⓐ   Ⓑ   Ⓒ   Ⓐ   Ⓑ   Ⓒ

the correct | change   dollars   cents |⁴⁸. My school is the | four   eight   fourth |⁴⁹ stop. I usually
          Ⓐ   Ⓑ   Ⓒ   Ⓐ   Ⓑ   Ⓒ

arrive at | eight forty-five   eight fifteen   eight o'clock |⁵⁰.
           Ⓐ   Ⓑ   Ⓒ

J **WRITING SAMPLE**

Choose one of these topics and write a paragraph. Use a separate sheet of paper.

- What are the important dates for you during the year? When is your birthday? What other birthdays or anniversaries do you celebrate? List as many important dates as you can.

- Write about your daily schedule. What time do you get up? When do you go to work or to school? How many days a week do you work or go to school? What time do you usually eat breakfast, lunch, and dinner? What time do you do other activities?

- How much money do you usually spend during a day? What do you buy? How much do these things cost? Do you usually pay with cash?

A) **WHERE DO THEY LIVE?**

apartment building	condominium	house	suburbs
city	duplex	nursing home	town

1. _____

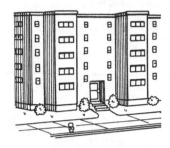

2. _____

3. _____

4. _____

5. _____

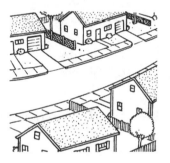

6. _____

7. _____

8. _____

B) **WHAT'S THE WORD?**

armchair	bed	cabinet	dishwasher	plant	rack	vase

9. Please put the flowers in the _____ on the dining room table.

10. I like to sit in my favorite _____ and watch TV.

11. The toothpaste is in the medicine _____.

12. We're going to buy a new mattress for our _____.

13. Please put the wet towel on the towel _____.

14. I water the _____ in the living room twice a week.

15. Our _____ is very loud, but it cleans everything very well.

C WHAT'S THE NEXT WORD?

blanket	box	frame	lamp	player	radio	table	screen	sheet	system

16. coffee _____

17. clock _____

18. DVD _____

19. fitted _____

20. electric _____

21. floor _____

22. jewelry _____

23. bed _____

24. stereo _____

25. fireplace _____

D AROUND THE HOUSE

26. Every evening I sit on the _____ and read.
- Ⓐ headboard
- Ⓑ couch
- Ⓒ playpen
- Ⓓ bed frame

27. It's cold. We need two _____ on the bed.
- Ⓐ blankets
- Ⓑ dust ruffles
- Ⓒ fitted sheets
- Ⓓ tablecloths

28. I have a new _____ on my bedroom floor.
- Ⓐ napkin
- Ⓑ curtain
- Ⓒ mirror
- Ⓓ rug

29. There's a small lamp on the _____.
- Ⓐ blinds
- Ⓑ mattress
- Ⓒ nightstand
- Ⓓ quilt

30. At dinner, we use a _____, a fork, and a spoon.
- Ⓐ knife
- Ⓑ tray
- Ⓒ platter
- Ⓓ cutting board

31. There isn't any sugar in the sugar _____.
- Ⓐ plate
- Ⓑ china
- Ⓒ shaker
- Ⓓ bowl

32. For dinner, we put food in _____.
- Ⓐ drapes
- Ⓑ trays
- Ⓒ serving dishes
- Ⓓ mugs

33. I look in the _____ when I brush my hair.
- Ⓐ mirror
- Ⓑ window
- Ⓒ blinds
- Ⓓ closet

34. I need some new pictures on the _____.
- Ⓐ ceilings
- Ⓑ floors
- Ⓒ walls
- Ⓓ curtains

35. We have a _____ on the wall in our kitchen.
- Ⓐ dish rack
- Ⓑ spice rack
- Ⓒ burner
- Ⓓ blender

36. I keep dishes and glasses in the _____.
- Ⓐ china cabinet
- Ⓑ coffee table
- Ⓒ jewelry box
- Ⓓ chest of drawers

37. The _____ is on the vanity.
- Ⓐ bathroom
- Ⓑ scale
- Ⓒ soap dish
- Ⓓ shower

(continued)

38. I hear the ____. Who's there?
- Ⓐ plunger
- Ⓑ oven
- Ⓒ window
- Ⓓ doorbell

39. We keep the lawnmower in the ____.
- Ⓐ tool shed
- Ⓑ gutter
- Ⓒ grill
- Ⓓ chimney

40. The satellite dish is on the ____.
- Ⓐ buffet
- Ⓑ dining room table
- Ⓒ roof
- Ⓓ ceiling

41. Michael is cooking soup on the ____.
- Ⓐ stove
- Ⓑ placemat
- Ⓒ sink
- Ⓓ cookbook

42. I like to relax in my ____.
- Ⓐ barbecue
- Ⓑ lawn chair
- Ⓒ drainpipe
- Ⓓ shutter

43. The car is in the ____.
- Ⓐ screen
- Ⓑ gutter
- Ⓒ garage door
- Ⓓ driveway

Ⓔ CLOZE READING

My husband and I are going to have a baby soon. We're preparing the baby's

doll	room	fan
Ⓐ	Ⓑ	Ⓒ

⁴⁴. The baby is going to sleep in this

crib	mobile	high chair
Ⓐ	Ⓑ	Ⓒ

⁴⁵.

We're going to keep the baby's clothes in this

potty	mattress	chest
Ⓐ	Ⓑ	Ⓒ

⁴⁶. We're going to use

this

stroller	toy chest	booster seat
Ⓐ	Ⓑ	Ⓒ

⁴⁷ when we take the baby for a walk outside, and we'll

use this

walker	car seat	bumper pad
Ⓐ	Ⓑ	Ⓒ

⁴⁸ when the baby is in the car. Our baby can play

with this stuffed animal and

backpack	playpen	rattle
Ⓐ	Ⓑ	Ⓒ

⁴⁹. And we can listen to the baby at

night with this

swing	baby monitor	cradle
Ⓐ	Ⓑ	Ⓒ

⁵⁰.

Ⓕ WRITING SAMPLE

Choose one of these topics and write a paragraph. Use a separate sheet of paper.

- What kinds of communities do your friends and families live in?
  Describe the communities and the housing. Include as many details as possible.

- Describe your bedroom or your living room.

- Describe the outside of your home. What kind of building is it? What's in the front,
  on the side, and in the back? Give as many details as you can.

A) **WHAT IS IT?**

broom	hammer	ladder	saw	shovel	vacuum cleaner
dustpan	hose	rake	screwdriver	sponge mop	wheelbarrow

1. _____

2. _____

3. _____

4. _____

5. _____

6. _____

7. _____

8. _____

9. _____

10. _____

11. _____

12. _____

B) **WHO IS IT?**

appliance	carpenter	electrician	exterminator	locksmith	plumber

13. We need to call the _____. The sink is clogged.

14. The _____ is coming. There are cockroaches and ants in the kitchen.

15. You should call the _____ repairperson to fix your refrigerator.

16. The _____ will fix the front door lock.

17. We should call a _____ to fix our front steps.

18. The power is out in the kitchen. Let's call the _____.

C   WHAT'S THE WORD?

mow	polish	rake	trim	vacuum	wash	wax

19. I need to _____ the hedges.

20. I have to _____ the lawn.

21. I'm going to _____ the leaves today.

22. We need to _____ the dining room table.

23. We have to _____ the windows in the kitchen.

24. When are you going to _____ the rugs?

25. Let's _____ the floor in the living room.

D   AROUND THE HOUSE

26. My apartment building has _____ in the lobby.
- Ⓐ a parking garage
- Ⓑ a landlord
- Ⓒ an intercom
- Ⓓ a neighbor

27. We have a _____ on our front door.
- Ⓐ key
- Ⓑ fire escape
- Ⓒ lease
- Ⓓ dead-bolt lock

28. When it rains, my roof _____.
- Ⓐ breaks
- Ⓑ leaks
- Ⓒ peels
- Ⓓ opens

29. The front window is broken. Call the _____.
- Ⓐ handyman
- Ⓑ cable TV company
- Ⓒ painter
- Ⓓ plumber

30. I take out the _____ every Tuesday.
- Ⓐ sponge
- Ⓑ wax
- Ⓒ garbage
- Ⓓ dust cloth

31. I use _____ when I wash the windows.
- Ⓐ a hand vacuum
- Ⓑ paper towels
- Ⓒ a mop
- Ⓓ a feather duster

32. Look at all the ants! Where's the _____?
- Ⓐ duct tape
- Ⓑ bucket
- Ⓒ insect spray
- Ⓓ oil

33. I use a brush and a _____ when I paint.
- Ⓐ plunger
- Ⓑ hoe
- Ⓒ weeder
- Ⓓ roller

34. I'm looking in the _____ for an apartment.
- Ⓐ vacancy sign
- Ⓑ classified ads
- Ⓒ moving van
- Ⓓ doorway

35. An appliance repairperson can fix the _____.
- Ⓐ stove
- Ⓑ wall
- Ⓒ lock
- Ⓓ tiles

36. This flashlight needs new _____.
- Ⓐ nails
- Ⓑ batteries
- Ⓒ fuses
- Ⓓ bolts

(continued)

37. It's important to use ____ on your lawn.
   Ⓐ wax
   Ⓑ ammonia
   Ⓒ fertilizer
   Ⓓ cleanser

38. Be very careful when you use a ____!
   Ⓐ power saw
   Ⓑ sprinkler
   Ⓒ level
   Ⓓ plane

39. I cut wood with ____.
   Ⓐ a scraper
   Ⓑ a trowel
   Ⓒ a nozzle
   Ⓓ an ax

40. ____ are very useful tools.
   Ⓐ Duct tape and a hand drill
   Ⓑ A wrench and pliers
   Ⓒ A toolbox and a gas can
   Ⓓ A mallet and sandpaper

41. I need a hammer and ____ to fix the bookcase.
   Ⓐ hose
   Ⓑ locks
   Ⓒ nails
   Ⓓ pails

42. When my toilet is clogged, I use a ____.
   Ⓐ step ladder
   Ⓑ hand drill
   Ⓒ vise
   Ⓓ plunger

E CLOZE READING

Kathy is going to move to a new apartment soon. This afternoon she's going to sign the

| key | lease | listing | 43. Then she's going to write a check for the
| Ⓐ | Ⓑ | Ⓒ |

| security deposit | lock | ad | 44 and give it to the | tenant | landlord | neighbor | 45. Her
| Ⓐ | Ⓑ | Ⓒ | | Ⓐ | Ⓑ | Ⓒ |

new apartment is on the seventh | stairway | roof | floor | 46. It's small, but there's a nice
| Ⓐ | Ⓑ | Ⓒ |

| balcony | peephole | buzzer | 47 for chairs and some plants. Every apartment in the building
| Ⓐ | Ⓑ | Ⓒ |

has a sprinkler system and a smoke | extinguisher | detector | hose | 48. There's also a storage
| Ⓐ | Ⓑ | Ⓒ |

| car | patio | locker | 49 and a | laundry | cleaning | soap | 50 room in the basement.
| Ⓐ | Ⓑ | Ⓒ | | Ⓐ | Ⓑ | Ⓒ |

F WRITING SAMPLE

Choose one of these topics and write a paragraph. Use a separate sheet of paper.

• Do you live in an apartment building? Describe the building, the lobby, the basement, and the outside areas. Include as many details as possible.

• Describe what is broken in your home. What needs repair? Who should you call?

• What do you usually do to clean your home? Do you mop, vacuum, and dust? What else do you do? What do you do every week, and what do you do once a month? What do you use to clean your home?

• What things do you sometimes fix or repair in your home? What tools do you use? What supplies do you use? How long does a repair take? Do you like to make repairs?

A) IN THE CITY

bus stop	fire hydrant	manhole	pedestrian
crosswalk	intersection	parking garage	street vendor
curb	mailbox	parking meter	traffic light

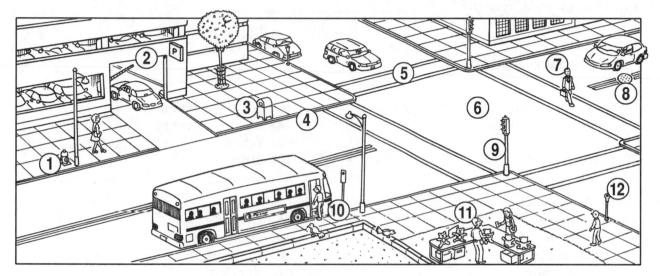

1. _____
2. _____
3. _____
4. _____

5. _____
6. _____
7. _____
8. _____

9. _____
10. _____
11. _____
12. _____

B) WHERE ARE THEY?

furniture store	jewelry store	park	supermarket
hardware store	library	restaurant	

13. They're buying food at the _____.

14. He's riding his bicycle in the _____.

15. She's buying tools at the _____.

16. They're eating dinner in a _____.

17. She's buying a necklace at a _____.

18. They're buying a table and chairs at a _____.

19. I'm looking for books at the _____.

(continued)

barber shop	drug store	pet shop
cleaners	electronics store	video store

20. She's taking some clothes to the _____.

21. He's getting a haircut at the _____.

22. They're looking for movies at the _____.

23. I'm going to buy a new DVD player at the _____.

24. She's buying medicine at the _____.

25. I want to buy a dog at the _____.

C WHAT'S THE WORD?

26. I'm a doctor at the ____ on Main Street.
    Ⓐ deli
    Ⓑ clinic
    Ⓒ pharmacy
    Ⓓ copy center

27. I often have lunch at the ____.
    Ⓐ photo shop
    Ⓑ pet shop
    Ⓒ pizza shop
    Ⓓ barber shop

28. There are three large department stores in the ____.
    Ⓐ mall
    Ⓑ school
    Ⓒ park
    Ⓓ courthouse

29. Henry bakes bread in a ____.
    Ⓐ hair salon
    Ⓑ nail salon
    Ⓒ bank
    Ⓓ bakery

30. I exercise at a ____ three times a week.
    Ⓐ bus station
    Ⓑ music store
    Ⓒ health club
    Ⓓ courthouse

31. Are you a student in this ____?
    Ⓐ child-care center
    Ⓑ school
    Ⓒ store
    Ⓓ shop

32. I like the food at this ____.
    Ⓐ deli
    Ⓑ copy store
    Ⓒ toy store
    Ⓓ dry cleaners

33. Carla sells rings and watches at the ____ on Central Street.
    Ⓐ cleaners
    Ⓑ fire station
    Ⓒ jewelry store
    Ⓓ day-care center

34. I wash my clothes at the ____.
    Ⓐ department store
    Ⓑ laundromat
    Ⓒ school
    Ⓓ grocery store

35. Katherine sells dresses at a ____.
    Ⓐ candy store
    Ⓑ dry cleaners
    Ⓒ convenience store
    Ⓓ clothing store

(continued)

36. We're buying tickets at the _____.
  Ⓐ train station
  Ⓑ shoe store
  Ⓒ ice cream shop
  Ⓓ hotel

37. Aunt Martha is sick. I'm going to visit her in the _____.
  Ⓐ drug store
  Ⓑ hospital
  Ⓒ day-care center
  Ⓓ office building

38. Diane is shopping at a _____. She's going to have a baby.
  Ⓐ hospital
  Ⓑ clinic
  Ⓒ car dealership
  Ⓓ maternity shop

39. I'm looking for a monitor at the _____.
  Ⓐ candy store
  Ⓑ music store
  Ⓒ computer store
  Ⓓ donut shop

40. When we travel, we usually stay in a _____.
  Ⓐ motel
  Ⓑ travel agency
  Ⓒ bus station
  Ⓓ train station

41. Angela takes care of young children at _____.
  Ⓐ a police station
  Ⓑ a parking garage
  Ⓒ an eye-care center
  Ⓓ a day-care center

Ⓓ CLOZE READING

Jack is going into the city this morning. First, he's going to go to the | park Ⓐ bank Ⓑ jail Ⓒ |⁴² to take out some money. He'll sit in his car and use the | drive-through Ⓐ public Ⓑ street Ⓒ |⁴³ window. Then he's going to stop at a | train station Ⓐ taxi stand Ⓑ service station Ⓒ |⁴⁴ to get some gas. He's going to leave his car in a | parking lot Ⓐ crosswalk Ⓑ street sign Ⓒ |⁴⁵ and walk to the | mailbox Ⓐ post office Ⓑ courthouse Ⓒ |⁴⁶ to buy some stamps. He's going to buy a magazine at a | card store Ⓐ library Ⓑ newsstand Ⓒ |⁴⁷. He's going to buy some plants and flowers at the | jewelry store Ⓐ florist Ⓑ park Ⓒ |⁴⁸ and some CDs at the | music store Ⓐ hotel Ⓑ cleaners Ⓒ |⁴⁹

After that, he's going to have lunch at his favorite | day-care Ⓐ fast-food Ⓑ grocery Ⓒ |⁵⁰ restaurant.

Ⓔ WRITING SAMPLE

Choose one of these topics and write a paragraph. Use a separate sheet of paper.

• Describe an area in your city or town. Tell about the stores and services that are located there.

• Tell about a shopping mall in your area. What department stores are in the mall? What other stores and restaurants are there?

A) HOW DO YOU FEEL?

bored	frustrated	happy	hungry	sad	thirsty
cold	furious	hot	nervous	sick	tired

1. _____   2. _____   3. _____   4. _____

5. _____   6. _____   7. _____   8. _____

9. _____   10. _____   11. _____   12. _____

B) WHAT'S THE OPPOSITE?

expensive	loose	narrow	plain	slow
hard	messy	old	poor	smooth

13. new _____

14. fast _____

15. neat _____

16. soft _____

17. wide _____

18. cheap _____

19. rough _____

20. wealthy _____

21. tight _____

22. fancy _____

(continued)

C WHAT DO YOU LOOK LIKE?

23. What color are your eyes? _____

24. Describe your hair. _____

25. Are you tall, average height, or short? _____

D WHAT'S THE WORD?

26. I'm going to bed early tonight. I'm _____.
Ⓐ surprised
Ⓑ sleepy
Ⓒ honest
Ⓓ afraid

27. My sister is going to have a baby. She's _____.
Ⓐ quiet
Ⓑ short
Ⓒ pregnant
Ⓓ loud

28. My neighbor has a new car. I'm _____.
Ⓐ jealous
Ⓑ scared
Ⓒ exhausted
Ⓓ young

29. My cat is in the tree. I'm _____.
Ⓐ homesick
Ⓑ full
Ⓒ tight
Ⓓ worried

30. He doesn't have many friends. He's _____.
Ⓐ lonely
Ⓑ happy
Ⓒ excited
Ⓓ wealthy

31. This knife is dull. Please give me a _____ one.
Ⓐ full
Ⓑ clean
Ⓒ sharp
Ⓓ fancy

32. My son is a good student. I'm very _____.
Ⓐ disappointed
Ⓑ proud
Ⓒ heavy
Ⓓ miserable

33. I'm sorry. I don't understand. I'm _____.
Ⓐ angry
Ⓑ disgusted
Ⓒ confused
Ⓓ annoyed

34. My telephone bill is very expensive this month. I'm _____.
Ⓐ pretty
Ⓑ dishonest
Ⓒ uncomfortable
Ⓓ shocked

35. After dinner, he washes the _____ dishes.
Ⓐ clean
Ⓑ dirty
Ⓒ hot
Ⓓ shiny

36. I can't answer the question. It's _____.
Ⓐ difficult
Ⓑ cheap
Ⓒ ill
Ⓓ ugly

37. It's raining. The streets are _____.
Ⓐ long
Ⓑ open
Ⓒ difficult
Ⓓ wet

(continued)

38. He can't see well. He's _____.
   Ⓐ married
   Ⓑ hearing impaired
   Ⓒ vision impaired
   Ⓓ average weight

39. Sarah doesn't like her new haircut.
   She's _____.
   Ⓐ happy
   Ⓑ clean
   Ⓒ bored
   Ⓓ embarrassed

40. I can't find my keys. I'm _____.
   Ⓐ empty
   Ⓑ upset
   Ⓒ closed
   Ⓓ crooked

41. He's wet, cold, and hungry. He's _____.
   Ⓐ miserable
   Ⓑ dry
   Ⓒ neat
   Ⓓ handsome

Ⓔ CLOZE READING

My neighbor's name is Mr. Wilson. He's a [young Ⓐ   senior Ⓑ   man Ⓒ] ⁴² citizen. He's

[tall Ⓐ   wavy Ⓑ   long Ⓒ] ⁴³ and [short Ⓐ   average weight Ⓑ   shoulder length Ⓒ] ⁴⁴. He's

[bald Ⓐ   pregnant Ⓑ   curly Ⓒ] ⁴⁵, with a short white [hair Ⓐ   age Ⓑ   beard Ⓒ] ⁴⁶ and a

[mustache Ⓐ   height Ⓑ   weight Ⓒ] ⁴⁷. He has two dogs. One dog is [tight Ⓐ   small Ⓑ   narrow Ⓒ] ⁴⁸,

and the other dog is [large Ⓐ   wavy Ⓑ   straight Ⓒ] ⁴⁹. Every morning, Mr. Wilson and his

dogs take a walk. The dogs are always [homesick Ⓐ   open Ⓑ   excited Ⓒ] ⁵⁰ when they leave the

house. I see them when I walk to the bus stop.

Ⓕ WRITING SAMPLE

Choose one of these topics and write a paragraph. Use a separate sheet of paper.

- Describe the people in your family.

- Describe a room in your home. Is it large or small? Is the furniture comfortable? Is it a quiet
  room? Give as many details as you can.

Word by Word **Beginning Level**
Unit 7A Test: PICTURE DICTIONARY PAGES 48–56

Name _____

Date _____

A · WHAT IS IT?

apple	chicken	grapes	lettuce	pear
banana	corn	green bean	milk	steak
cantaloupe	eggs	green pepper	nuts	strawberries
cherries	fish	ham	onion	tomato

1. _____

2. _____

3. _____

4. _____

5. _____

6. _____

7. _____

8. _____

9. _____

10. _____

11. _____

12. _____

13. _____

14. _____

15. _____

16. _____

17. _____

18. _____

19. _____

20. _____

B · WHAT'S THE WORD?

carton	head	jar	loaf	six-pack

21. a _____ of bread

22. a _____ of milk

23. a _____ of mayonnaise

24. a _____ of cabbage

25. a _____ of soda

C WHAT'S THE WORD?

26. My favorite fruit is _____.
- Ⓐ broccoli
- Ⓑ watermelon
- Ⓒ cauliflower
- Ⓓ margarine

27. My favorite meat is _____.
- Ⓐ salmon
- Ⓑ spinach
- Ⓒ roast beef
- Ⓓ mozzarella

28. I'm thirsty. Can I have some _____?
- Ⓐ fish
- Ⓑ eggs
- Ⓒ crackers
- Ⓓ juice

29. We need vegetables. Please buy _____.
- Ⓐ lettuce and tomatoes
- Ⓑ peaches and plums
- Ⓒ mushrooms and limes
- Ⓓ beets and macaroni

30. You can find _____ in the Meat Section.
- Ⓐ lobster and halibut
- Ⓑ figs and avocados
- Ⓒ ground beef and ham
- Ⓓ turkey and soda

31. My favorite shellfish are _____.
- Ⓐ ribs and pork
- Ⓑ scallops and clams
- Ⓒ catfish and crabs
- Ⓓ liver and trout

32. You can find salami and bologna in the _____ Section.
- Ⓐ Deli
- Ⓑ Produce
- Ⓒ Frozen Foods
- Ⓓ Snack Foods

33. These _____ are delicious.
- Ⓐ straws
- Ⓑ blueberries
- Ⓒ coupons
- Ⓓ sandwich bags

34. Please get a _____ of flour when you go to the supermarket.
- Ⓐ bag
- Ⓑ bottle
- Ⓒ can
- Ⓓ bunch

35. There's a _____ of cereal in the cabinet.
- Ⓐ gallon
- Ⓑ loaf
- Ⓒ box
- Ⓓ liter

36. We need two _____ of paper towels.
- Ⓐ pounds
- Ⓑ pints
- Ⓒ liters
- Ⓓ rolls

37. _____ are very popular condiments.
- Ⓐ Cookies and crackers
- Ⓑ Ketchup and mustard
- Ⓒ Rolls and English muffins
- Ⓓ Jam and jelly

38. My favorite snack foods are _____.
- Ⓐ popcorn and pretzels
- Ⓑ flour and sugar
- Ⓒ salt and soap
- Ⓓ spices and cake mix

39. We need some paper products. Please buy _____ when you go to the supermarket.
- Ⓐ soup and salsa
- Ⓑ gum and candy
- Ⓒ tofu and eggs
- Ⓓ napkins and tissues

40. We need _____ for the baby.
- Ⓐ cooking oil
- Ⓑ coffee
- Ⓒ wipes
- Ⓓ chewing gum

41. This store uses paper and _____ bags.
- Ⓐ liquid
- Ⓑ plastic
- Ⓒ aluminum
- Ⓓ waxed

D) CLOZE READING

My favorite supermarket is Super Save-Rite on Pine Street. There are delicious fruits and vegetables in the | Dairy (A) Meat (B) Produce (C) |⁴² Section, and there are wonderful breads and rolls in the | Canned (A) Baked Goods (B) Household (C) |⁴³ Section. There are excellent products in every | aisle (A) line (B) scanner (C) |⁴⁴. There are ten | machines (A) checkout lines (B) magazines (C) |⁴⁵ in the front of the store. | Shoppers (A) Baggers (B) Managers (C) |⁴⁶ take the products from their | coupons (A) bags (B) shopping carts (C) |⁴⁷ and put them on | baskets (A) conveyor belts (B) scales (C) |⁴⁸. Customers pay the | cashiers (A) baggers (B) checkout counters (C) |⁴⁹ for the products, and | scanners (A) packers (B) registers (C) |⁵⁰ put the products in paper or plastic bags.

E) WRITING SAMPLE

Choose one of these topics and write a paragraph. Use a separate sheet of paper.

- What do you have in your refrigerator? What do you need to buy at the supermarket?
- What are your favorite foods? Write about your favorite fruit, vegetable, dairy product, snack food, baked good, and type of meat or fish
- What do you usually have for breakfast? for lunch? for dinner? for a snack? Tell about the foods you eat on a typical day.

Name _____

Date _____

A **WHAT IS IT?**

apple pie	burrito	hot dog	pita bread	shrimp cocktail
bacon	french fries	ice cream sundae	pizza	spaghetti
bagel	fruit cup	mixed vegetables	sandwich	tossed salad
baked potato	hamburger	muffin	sausages	waffles

1. _____ 2. _____ 3. _____ 4. _____

5. _____ 6. _____ 7. _____ 8. _____

9. _____ 10. _____ 11. _____ 12. _____

13. _____ 14. _____ 15. _____ 16. _____

17. _____ 18. _____ 19. _____ 20. _____

B WHAT'S THE WORD?

Bake	Boil	Grate	Peel	Pour

21. _____ the egg.

22. _____ the orange.

23. _____ the cookies.

24. _____ the lemonade.

25. _____ the cheese.

C WHAT'S THE WORD?

26. Please ____ some vegetables for the salad.
    - Ⓐ beat
    - Ⓑ cut up
    - Ⓒ break
    - Ⓓ broil

27. I usually ____ chicken with oil.
    - Ⓐ slice
    - Ⓑ add
    - Ⓒ fry
    - Ⓓ steam

28. ____ the eggs and sugar in this bowl.
    - Ⓐ Mix
    - Ⓑ Cook
    - Ⓒ Roast
    - Ⓓ Steam

29. This soup is cold. We should ____ it.
    - Ⓐ chop
    - Ⓑ barbecue
    - Ⓒ stir-fry
    - Ⓓ microwave

30. Please cover the pot with a ____.
    - Ⓐ beater
    - Ⓑ whisk
    - Ⓒ lid
    - Ⓓ ladle

31. I need a ____. I want to slice the bread.
    - Ⓐ spatula
    - Ⓑ knife
    - Ⓒ colander
    - Ⓓ strainer

32. I make pancakes in a ____.
    - Ⓐ skillet
    - Ⓑ steamer
    - Ⓒ roasting pan
    - Ⓓ saucepan

33. I use a ____ when I stir-fry.
    - Ⓐ casserole dish
    - Ⓑ wok
    - Ⓒ rolling pin
    - Ⓓ double boiler

34. We need a ____ of meat for the recipe.
    - Ⓐ gallon
    - Ⓑ quarter
    - Ⓒ quart
    - Ⓓ pound

35. There are three ____ in a tablespoon.
    - Ⓐ spoons
    - Ⓑ teaspoons
    - Ⓒ ounces
    - Ⓓ cups

36. A quart has 32 ____.
    - Ⓐ ounces
    - Ⓑ fluids
    - Ⓒ pints
    - Ⓓ cups

37. I'd like half a pound of ____, please.
    - Ⓐ milk
    - Ⓑ eggs
    - Ⓒ cheese
    - Ⓓ mustard

(continued)

38. I'll have _____ for dessert.
- Ⓐ noodles
- Ⓑ baked chicken
- Ⓒ pudding
- Ⓓ meatloaf

39. People use _____ at a fast food restaurant.
- Ⓐ wooden spoons
- Ⓑ plastic utensils
- Ⓒ paper forks
- Ⓓ butter knives

40. I like to drink soda with a _____.
- Ⓐ tray
- Ⓑ napkin
- Ⓒ saucer
- Ⓓ straw

41. Here's a _____ for your baby.
- Ⓐ high chair
- Ⓑ table
- Ⓒ booth
- Ⓓ menu

Ⓓ CLOZE READING

It's 6:00 at Mario's Restaurant and all the employees are busy. The

patron	hostess	diner
Ⓐ	Ⓑ	Ⓒ

⁴² is seating a family at a table. The parents need a booster

bar	booth	seat
Ⓐ	Ⓑ	Ⓒ

⁴³ for their three-year-old daughter. At a different table, a waitress

is
taking	making	pouring
Ⓐ	Ⓑ	Ⓒ

⁴⁴ an order. The customers are asking her questions about

the
trays	entrees	checks
Ⓐ	Ⓑ	Ⓒ

⁴⁵ on the menu. At several other tables, people are enjoying

their food. A waiter is showing the dessert
basket	plate	cart
Ⓐ	Ⓑ	Ⓒ

⁴⁶ to several diners. They're

going to order cake. One customer is
serving	giving	paying
Ⓐ	Ⓑ	Ⓒ

⁴⁷ the check and leaving a

tip	top	cup
Ⓐ	Ⓑ	Ⓒ

⁴⁸. In the back of the dining room, a busperson is
taking	setting	leaving
Ⓐ	Ⓑ	Ⓒ

⁴⁹

a table. He's putting silverware and napkins around the table. In the kitchen, the

host	server	chef
Ⓐ	Ⓑ	Ⓒ

⁵⁰ is stirring a big pot of hot soup.

Ⓔ WRITING SAMPLE

Choose one of these topics and write a paragraph. Use a separate sheet of paper.

- What can you cook? Write the recipe. Make a list of ingredients. Then write the instructions.
- Describe your favorite restaurant. Does the restaurant have booths? A salad bar? A dessert cart? What do you usually order there?

A **WHAT ARE THEY WEARING?**

belt	cardigan sweater	jeans	necklace	turtleneck
blouse	high heels	loafers	skirt	vest

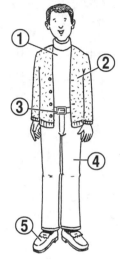

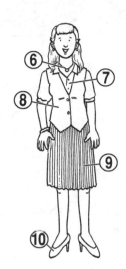

1. _____
2. _____
3. _____
4. _____
5. _____

6. _____
7. _____
8. _____
9. _____
10. _____

B **WHICH GROUP?**

boots	parka	scarf	sweater	T-shirt
down jacket	running shorts	sleeveless shirt	swimsuit	tank top

11–15. Clothing for Hot Weather

_____
_____
_____
_____

16–20. Clothing for Cold Weather

_____
_____
_____
_____

WHAT ARE THEY DOING?

hanging	loading	putting	sorting	unloading

21 **22** **23** **24** **25**

21. He's _____ his laundry.

22. He's _____ the washing machine.

23. She's _____ clothes on the clothesline.

24. She's _____ the dryer.

25. She's _____ things away.

D **WHAT'S THE WORD?**

26. It's going to rain. I think I'll wear ____.
  Ⓐ a jumper
  Ⓑ a raincoat
  Ⓒ a ski jacket
  Ⓓ sunglasses

27. Anne is wearing a ____ because she's going to have a baby.
  Ⓐ nightgown
  Ⓑ hat
  Ⓒ maternity dress
  Ⓓ three-piece suit

28. Tom always wears his ____ to his soccer game.
  Ⓐ blazer
  Ⓑ overalls
  Ⓒ sport jacket
  Ⓓ uniform

29. I usually wear ____ at the beach.
  Ⓐ flip-flops
  Ⓑ pumps
  Ⓒ socks
  Ⓓ stockings

30. Jack is going to a party tonight. He's going to wear a ____.
  Ⓐ poncho
  Ⓑ jogging suit
  Ⓒ jacket and a tie
  Ⓓ muffler and cuff links

31. My children are wearing ____. They're going to bed soon.
  Ⓐ ear muffs
  Ⓑ pajamas
  Ⓒ jumpers
  Ⓓ cover-ups

32. It's cold today. I'm going to wear ____.
  Ⓐ long underwear
  Ⓑ slippers
  Ⓒ suspenders
  Ⓓ polyester pants

33. Marie usually wears ____ when she exercises at the health club.
  Ⓐ denim pants
  Ⓑ a T-shirt and a skirt
  Ⓒ sandals
  Ⓓ sweatpants and a T-shirt

34. My husband gave me a beautiful ____ for my birthday.
  Ⓐ sock
  Ⓑ ring
  Ⓒ cap
  Ⓓ bow tie

35. I'm busy. I'm folding the ____.
  Ⓐ laundry bag
  Ⓑ laundry basket
  Ⓒ laundry
  Ⓓ wet clothing

(continued)

36. I like this dress but it's too _____.
- Ⓐ striped
- Ⓑ low
- Ⓒ broken
- Ⓓ short

37. These shoes are too _____. I need a larger pair.
- Ⓐ small
- Ⓑ wide
- Ⓒ heavy
- Ⓓ fancy

38. I can't wear this shirt. It's _____.
- Ⓐ high
- Ⓑ missing
- Ⓒ stained
- Ⓓ ironed

39. My ski jacket has a broken _____.
- Ⓐ sleeve
- Ⓑ zipper
- Ⓒ sweatband
- Ⓓ collar

Ⓔ CLOZE READING

The Chan family is going to a party tonight. Mrs. Chan is wearing a beautiful black silk

| overcoat Ⓐ | skirt Ⓑ | bowtie Ⓒ | **40.** She's also wearing | earrings Ⓐ | ear muffs Ⓑ | cuff links Ⓒ | **41.** |

and | thongs Ⓐ | high-tops Ⓑ | high heels Ⓒ | **42.** Mr. Chan is wearing his favorite sports

| sweater Ⓐ | jacket Ⓑ | blouse Ⓒ | **43.**, a nice | tie Ⓐ | brooch Ⓑ | down vest Ⓒ | **44.**, and gray wool

| beads Ⓐ | slacks Ⓑ | stockings Ⓒ | **45.** Their son Richard wants to wear a T- | vest Ⓐ | skirt Ⓑ | shirt Ⓒ | **46.**

and | baggy Ⓐ | broken Ⓑ | missing Ⓒ | **47.** jeans. But Mr. and Mrs. Chan are telling him

he has to wear his new | clip-on Ⓐ | V-neck Ⓑ | straw Ⓒ | **48.** sweater and black corduroy

| pants Ⓐ | boots Ⓑ | suspenders Ⓒ | **49.** Their daughter Kathy is wearing her new dress and a

| bracelet Ⓐ | barrette Ⓑ | locket Ⓒ | **50.** with a photo of her best friend.

Ⓕ WRITING SAMPLE

Choose one of these topics and write a paragraph. Use a separate sheet of paper.

- What are you wearing right now? Describe the colors, materials, and patterns. Do any of your clothes have problems? If they do, what are the problems? Are you wearing any jewelry or accessories? What are they?

- You're going to a very special party. What do you think you'll wear? Describe the colors, materials, and patterns. Will you wear jewelry to the party? Describe the jewelry you're going to wear.

Name _____

Date _____

A **WHAT IS IT?**

battery charger	digital camera	portable CD player	remote control
camera case	DVD player	price tag	speakers
cell phone	keyboard	printer	surge protector
clock radio	mouse	receipt	video camera
cordless phone	notebook computer		

1. _____

2. _____

3. _____

4. _____

5. _____

6. _____

7. _____

8. _____

9. _____

10. _____

11. _____

12. _____

13. _____

14. _____

15. _____

16. _____

17. _____

18. _____

| Appliances | Children's | Customer | Electronics | Home | Housewares | Men's |

19. I'm going to buy a new tie in the _____ Clothing Department.

20. We're looking for a sofa in the _____ Furnishings Department.

21. There are a lot of baby clothes in the _____ Clothing Department.

22. There are many different refrigerators in the Household _____ Department.

23. You can find pots and pans in the _____ Department.

24. You can exchange something at the _____ Service Counter.

25. Tuners are on sale in the _____ Department.

C WHAT'S THE WORD?

26. The ____ is on the label.
    (A) receipt
    (B) sales tax
    (C) size
    (D) total price

27. This price is 30% off the ____ price.
    (A) regular
    (B) discount
    (C) tax
    (D) label

28. Read the ____ for your new sweater.
    (A) pager
    (B) sale sign
    (C) software
    (D) care instructions

29. I always ____ shoes before I buy them.
    (A) return
    (B) try on
    (C) pay for
    (D) help

30. Dan is relaxing. He's listening to the ____.
    (A) microphone
    (B) lens
    (C) radio
    (D) camera

31. We watch the news on our new ____.
    (A) PDA
    (B) LCD TV
    (C) film
    (D) portable digital audio player

32. I listen to music on my ____.
    (A) stereo system
    (B) pager
    (C) calculator
    (D) scanner

33. There's a message for you on the ____.
    (A) adding machine
    (B) modem
    (C) adapter
    (D) answering machine

34. I'm looking for a battery pack for my ____.
    (A) record
    (B) camcorder
    (C) tripod
    (D) paint set

35. I need a new ____ for my camera.
    (A) flash attachment
    (B) mouse
    (C) CPU
    (D) tuner

36. I can listen to English tapes on my ____.
    (A) adapter
    (B) scanner
    (C) fax machine
    (D) tape recorder

37. What word-processing ____ do you use?
    (A) program
    (B) game
    (C) protector
    (D) unit

(continued)

38. You need a _____ to connect your hard drive to your monitor.
- Ⓐ screen
- Ⓑ memory disk
- Ⓒ cable
- Ⓓ turntable

39. I often carry my _____ in my briefcase.
- Ⓐ CPU
- Ⓑ notebook computer
- Ⓒ desktop computer
- Ⓓ monitor

40. My son likes to draw pictures with _____.
- Ⓐ clay
- Ⓑ stickers
- Ⓒ blocks
- Ⓓ crayons

41. Many children like to take a _____ to the beach.
- Ⓐ pail and shovel
- Ⓑ play house
- Ⓒ swing set
- Ⓓ train set

42. My daughter likes to ride her _____.
- Ⓐ hula hoop
- Ⓑ pool
- Ⓒ tricycle
- Ⓓ matchbox car

43. My son likes to build with his _____ .
- Ⓐ kiddie pool
- Ⓑ construction set
- Ⓒ action figure
- Ⓓ paint set

Ⓓ CLOZE READING

Paulo is buying holiday gifts for his family. His wife likes to take pictures, so he's going to buy her a digital | machine Ⓐ camera Ⓑ disk Ⓒ | ⁴⁴. His older son likes to play computer games. He's going to buy him a | joystick Ⓐ tripod Ⓑ scanner Ⓒ | ⁴⁵. His younger son likes to build things. He's going to buy him | a walkie-talkie Ⓐ markers Ⓑ a model kit Ⓒ | ⁴⁶. His older daughter likes music, so he's going to buy her a | boombox Ⓐ calculator Ⓑ modem Ⓒ | ⁴⁷. His younger daughter always plays outside, so he's going to buy her a | puzzle Ⓐ wagon Ⓑ doll Ⓒ | ⁴⁸. And he's going to buy his parents a | turntable Ⓐ slide projector Ⓑ DVD player Ⓒ | ⁴⁹ because they like to watch movies. Paulo is happy because he has a store coupon for 25% | on Ⓐ off Ⓑ for Ⓒ | ⁵⁰ the regular price.

Ⓔ WRITING SAMPLE

Choose one of these topics and write a paragraph. Use a separate sheet of paper.

- Do you like to shop in department stores? What are your favorite stores? How often do you shop there? What departments do you usually shop in? What do you buy? Do they often have things on sale?

- What electronic equipment do you have? Make a list. Which are your favorites? Where did you buy them? What new electronic item do you want to buy? Where will you buy it?

Name _____

Date _____

A BANKING ACTIONS

balance the checkbook	cash a check	use the ATM machine
bank online	open an account	write a check

1. _____   2. _____   3. _____

4. _____   5. _____   6. _____

B WHO ARE THEY?

activities director	emergency operator	mayor	paramedic	sanitation worker

7. The _____ answers phones at the police station.

8. The _____ works at city hall.

9. The _____ helps people at a senior center.

10. The _____ rides in an ambulance.

11. The _____ works at the dump.

C USING THE ATM

Enter	Insert	Remove	Select	Transfer	Withdraw

12. _____ your ATM card.   15. _____ cash.

13. _____ your PIN number.   16. _____ funds.

14. _____ a transaction.   17. _____ your card.

D WHAT HAPPENED?

accident	burglary	drunk driver	fire
bank robbery	downed power line	explosion	vandalism

18. _____

19. _____

20. _____

21. _____

22. _____

23. _____

24. _____

25. _____

E WHAT'S THE WORD?

26. I pay the _____ to my landlord every month.
    Ⓐ mail
    Ⓑ account
    Ⓒ rent
    Ⓓ slip

27. I own a house. Every month I have to pay the _____ payment.
    Ⓐ checkbook
    Ⓑ mortgage
    Ⓒ passbook
    Ⓓ money

28. I need to make a _____ at the bank.
    Ⓐ deposit
    Ⓑ bankbook
    Ⓒ deposit box
    Ⓓ deposit slip

29. I get a monthly _____ from my bank.
    Ⓐ checkbook
    Ⓑ statement
    Ⓒ bill
    Ⓓ credit card

30. You can pay by _____ or by check.
    Ⓐ loan
    Ⓑ letter
    Ⓒ stamp
    Ⓓ cash

31. A _____ watches customers in the store.
    Ⓐ mayor
    Ⓑ security guard
    Ⓒ city manager
    Ⓓ fire fighter

32. Your credit card _____ is on the front of the card.
    Ⓐ bill
    Ⓑ payment
    Ⓒ number
    Ⓓ order

33. I'd like to buy _____ of stamps.
    Ⓐ an envelope
    Ⓑ a card
    Ⓒ a package
    Ⓓ a roll

34. Every address in the U.S. has _____.
    Ⓐ a zip code
    Ⓑ an apartment number
    Ⓒ a return address
    Ⓓ a letter

35. I want to send this express _____.
    Ⓐ post
    Ⓑ mail
    Ⓒ service
    Ⓓ class

(continued)

36. I need a passport application _____.
    (A) stamp
    (B) order
    (C) form
    (D) card

37. My two-year old son goes to a _____ center.
    (A) senior
    (B) child-care
    (C) emergency
    (D) game

38. The recreation center has _____.
    (A) a swimming pool and game room
    (B) an emergency room
    (C) a post office
    (D) a church

39. I saw a terrible car _____ on Main Street this morning.
    (A) spill
    (B) break
    (C) accident
    (D) robbery

40. Call the police! There's a _____!
    (A) passport
    (B) firefighter
    (C) safe deposit box
    (D) water main break

41. I'm calling to report a gas _____!
    (A) outage
    (B) leak
    (C) derailment
    (D) line

F) CLOZE READING

There are many people at the community library today. A woman is giving her

| library | credit | book | 42 card to the clerk at the | teacher's | checkout | reference | 43 desk. |
| (A) | (B) | (C) | | (A) | (B) | (C) | |

Several people are looking at the | microfilm | online catalog | envelopes | 44 on the computers.
| (A) | (B) | (C) |

One man is looking for books on the | shelves | section | atlas | 45. People are reading
| (A) | (B) | (C) |

magazines and newspapers in the | audio | children's | periodical | 46 section. The reference
| (A) | (B) | (C) |

| librarian | clerk | author | 47 is answering questions. Nearby, several students are reading
| (A) | (B) | (C) |

| audiotapes | videotapes | encyclopedias | 48. People are looking at CDs and DVDs in the
| (A) | (B) | (C) |

| media | reference | checkout | 49 section. A father and his daughters are looking
| (A) | (B) | (C) |

for books on | title | tape | film | 50.
| (A) | (B) | (C) |

G) WRITING SAMPLE

Choose one of these topics and write a paragraph. Use a separate sheet of paper.

• How often do you pay your bills? What kinds of bills do you usually receive? Do you pay by check, cash, or credit card? What is your most expensive monthly bill?

• How often do you go to the bank? What do you usually do there? Do you use the ATM, or do you talk with a teller? What do other people do there?

Name _____

Date _____

(A) PARTS OF THE BODY

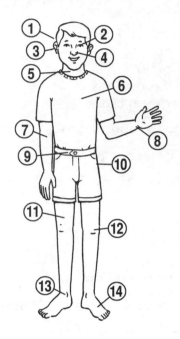

ankle	eye	knee	nose
arm	foot	leg	waist
chest	head	neck	wrist
ear	hip		

1. _____   8. _____
2. _____   9. _____
3. _____   10. _____
4. _____   11. _____
5. _____   12. _____
6. _____   13. _____
7. _____   14. _____

(B) WHAT'S THE WORD?

blisters	cavity	fever	laryngitis	sunburn	stomachache

15. I ate too much food. I have a _____ .

16. I got a _____ at the beach.

17. Marie is going to the dentist. She has a _____ .

18. I'm very hot. I have a _____ .

19. My shoes are too tight. I have _____ .

20. I can't talk. I have _____ .

(C) WHAT FIRST AID DO THESE PEOPLE NEED?

CPR	the Heimlich maneuver	rescue breathing	a splint	a tourniquet

21. He isn't breathing. _____   24. He's bleeding badly. _____

22. She broke her leg. _____   25. She has no pulse. _____

23. She's choking. _____

26. He _____ his finger with a knife.
  Ⓐ cut
  Ⓑ bruised
  Ⓒ broke
  Ⓓ twisted

27. She _____ her hand on the stove.
  Ⓐ wheezed
  Ⓑ vomited
  Ⓒ burned
  Ⓓ sprained

28. I have a bad cold. I'm very _____.
  Ⓐ bloated
  Ⓑ congested
  Ⓒ nauseous
  Ⓓ itchy

29. I didn't sleep last night. I'm _____.
  Ⓐ swollen
  Ⓑ short of breath
  Ⓒ exhausted
  Ⓓ fine

30. I have a _____ in my mouth.
  Ⓐ cavity
  Ⓑ fever
  Ⓒ cough
  Ⓓ bruise

31. She dislocated her _____.
  Ⓐ lip
  Ⓑ shoulder
  Ⓒ palm
  Ⓓ heel

32. I cut my toe. I need _____.
  Ⓐ tweezers
  Ⓑ antihistamine cream
  Ⓒ antibiotic ointment
  Ⓓ a splint

33. I have a headache. I need _____.
  Ⓐ gauze
  Ⓑ hydrogen peroxide
  Ⓒ a sterile pad
  Ⓓ aspirin

34. Someone hit me. My nose is _____.
  Ⓐ bleeding
  Ⓑ burned
  Ⓒ twisted
  Ⓓ running

35. My father fell and broke his _____.
  Ⓐ ear
  Ⓑ hip
  Ⓒ heart
  Ⓓ kidneys

36. Each person has two _____.
  Ⓐ toes
  Ⓑ fingers
  Ⓒ gums
  Ⓓ thumbs

37. A person with _____ always feels sad.
  Ⓐ heatstroke
  Ⓑ hiccups
  Ⓒ depression
  Ⓓ a splint

38. It's very cold outside. Don't get _____.
  Ⓐ frostbite
  Ⓑ an infection
  Ⓒ measles
  Ⓓ mumps

39. He sprained his ankle. It's _____.
  Ⓐ itchy
  Ⓑ swollen
  Ⓒ bloated
  Ⓓ dizzy

40. Insect bites are very _____.
  Ⓐ nauseous
  Ⓑ hot
  Ⓒ itchy
  Ⓓ unconscious

41. I have chills and a fever. I have _____.
  Ⓐ the flu
  Ⓑ asthma
  Ⓒ diabetes
  Ⓓ heart disease

At the Southside Clinic, many people are waiting to see doctors. Mrs. Yamamoto

checked	hurt	closed
(A)	(B)	(C)

⁴² her back yesterday. A nine-year-old boy has a rash. He had

an allergic
reaction	overdose	injection
(A)	(B)	(C)

⁴³ to some medicine. Mr. Thomas has high

heart attack	disease	blood pressure
(A)	(B)	(C)

⁴⁴. The nurse will check him soon. Maria's

baby is crying and holding his ear. He probably has an ear
fever	infection	shock
(A)	(B)	(C)

⁴⁵.

Angelo Lopez has a
wart	scratch	fingernail
(A)	(B)	(C)

⁴⁶ on his hand. The doctor needs to remove it.

Carol has asthma. She's
sneezing	vomiting	wheezing
(A)	(B)	(C)

⁴⁷ badly. Alexander has his

hand over his eye. He
broke	scratched	twisted
(A)	(B)	(C)

⁴⁸ his eye during a baseball game.

Amanda
scraped	dislocated	sprained
(A)	(B)	(C)

⁴⁹ her shin. She covered it with

tweezers	aspirin	gauze
(A)	(B)	(C)

⁵⁰ and adhesive tape.

F WRITING SAMPLE

Choose one of these topics and write a paragraph. Use a separate sheet of paper.

- Write about a time you had a medical emergency. What happened? Describe the emergency. What were your injuries? Did you use first-aid supplies? Did you call a doctor?

- Write about a time you didn't feel well. What was the matter? Did you have a temperature? What were your symptoms? What did you do to feel better? How long were you sick?

A STAYING HEALTHY

check your blood pressure	give a shot	take a chest X-ray
draw blood	measure your weight	take vitamins
examine your eyes	rest in bed	talk with a counselor

1. _____

2. _____

3. _____

4. _____

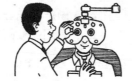

5. _____

6. _____

7. _____

8. _____

9. _____

B WHAT'S THE WORD?

cast	cough syrup	injection	walker
cold tablets	crutches	nasal spray	wheelchair

10. _____

11. _____

12. _____

13. _____

14. _____

15. _____

16. _____

17. _____

C) WHO ARE THEY?

cardiologist	lab technician	pediatrician	therapist
dentist	orthopedist	surgeon	X-ray technician

18. The _____ draws blood in the laboratory.

19. The _____ examines your teeth.

20. The _____ helps people with their problems.

21. The _____ can put a cast on a broken leg.

22. The _____ takes care of children.

23. The _____ helps people with heart disease.

24. The _____ operates in the operating room.

25. The _____ works in the radiology department.

D) WHAT'S THE WORD?

26. Use a _____ to take your temperature.
    - Ⓐ syringe
    - Ⓑ prescription
    - Ⓒ capsule
    - Ⓓ thermometer

27. You should _____ your teeth every day.
    - Ⓐ listen to
    - Ⓑ floss
    - Ⓒ draw
    - Ⓓ wash

28. The dentist will _____ the cavity.
    - Ⓐ inject
    - Ⓑ brush
    - Ⓒ drill
    - Ⓓ put on

29. Throat _____ are good for a sore throat.
    - Ⓐ lozenges
    - Ⓑ drops
    - Ⓒ tablets
    - Ⓓ ointments

30. He's losing weight. He's on a _____.
    - Ⓐ gauge
    - Ⓑ diet
    - Ⓒ chart
    - Ⓓ test

31. Take _____ for your sprained wrist.
    - Ⓐ a cane
    - Ⓑ an antacid tablet
    - Ⓒ a pain reliever
    - Ⓓ an I.V.

32. The dental hygienist wears _____.
    - Ⓐ a hospital gown
    - Ⓑ a mask and gloves
    - Ⓒ gauze
    - Ⓓ gloves and a brace

33. I had a bad cut. I got ten _____.
    - Ⓐ stitches
    - Ⓑ fillings
    - Ⓒ casts
    - Ⓓ canes

34. The nurse used a _____ to check my heart.
    - Ⓐ humidifier
    - Ⓑ drill
    - Ⓒ stethoscope
    - Ⓓ thermometer

35. The ambulance took the man to the _____.
    - Ⓐ X-ray machine
    - Ⓑ receptionist
    - Ⓒ humidifier
    - Ⓓ emergency room

(continued)

36. The father is feeding the baby with a _____.
- (A) bottle
- (B) cotton swab
- (C) cubby
- (D) wipe

37. The physician is reading the patient's _____.
- (A) hospital bed
- (B) call button
- (C) medical chart
- (D) bed control

38. The _____ is checking the pregnant woman.
- (A) gerontologist
- (B) orthodontist
- (C) audiologist
- (D) obstetrician

39. The mother is _____ the baby's diaper.
- (A) dressing
- (B) nursing
- (C) changing
- (D) bathing

40. Children should wear _____ outside.
- (A) sunscreen
- (B) bandages
- (C) ointment
- (D) nail polish

41. The child-care worker is _____ the baby in the rocking chair.
- (A) bathing
- (B) rocking
- (C) flossing
- (D) measuring

E) CLOZE READING

Every weekday, Mr. and Mrs. Wilson wake up early and get ready for work. Mr. Wilson

cleans	brushes	polishes
(A)	(B)	(C)

⁴² his teeth. He

takes	does	bathes
(A)	(B)	(C)

⁴³ a shower and then

he shaves with shaving

soap	powder	cream
(A)	(B)	(C)

⁴⁴ and a

razor	comb	clipper
(A)	(B)	(C)

⁴⁵. After

that, he puts on

toothpaste	mouthwash	deodorant
(A)	(B)	(C)

⁴⁶ and gets dressed. Mrs. Wilson

always washes her hair with

cologne	shampoo	bubble bath
(A)	(B)	(C)

⁴⁷ and uses a

conditioner	foundation	lotion
(A)	(B)	(C)

⁴⁸. After her shower, she gets dressed. Then she

puts	brushes	dries
(A)	(B)	(C)

⁴⁹ her hair with a blow dryer and styles her hair with a

bobby pin	curling iron	nail brush
(A)	(B)	(C)

⁵⁰.

F) WRITING SAMPLE

Choose one of these topics and write a paragraph. Use a separate sheet of paper.

- Describe your morning routine. What do you do for personal hygiene? Do you take a shower? Do you floss your teeth? Do you shave or put on makeup? Write about what you do and what things you use.

- How often do you have a medical exam? What does the nurse usually do? What does the doctor usually do? What tests do you have?

A SCHOOLS AND PLACES

adult school	hallway	medical school	science lab
cafeteria	gymnasium	music class	track
classroom	main office	principal's office	vocational school

1. _____

2. _____

3. _____

4. _____

5. _____

6. _____

7. _____

8. _____

9. _____

10. _____

11. _____

12. _____

B WHAT'S THE ORDER?

college	graduate school	middle school
elementary school	high school	nursery school

13. ⬚1 _____   16. ⬚4 _____

14. ⬚2 _____   17. ⬚5 _____

15. ⬚3 _____   18. ⬚6 _____

C   WHAT'S THE SUBJECT?

art	driver's education	geography	history
computer science	English	government	

19. We're studying maps in our _____ class.

20. Students are painting in their _____ class today.

21. Our instructor is explaining grammar in _____ class today.

22. Students are studying democracy and elections in their _____ class.

23. The teacher is talking about new software in the _____ class.

24. This week we're learning about China in the 1600s in our _____ class.

25. We're learning how to park a car in our _____ class.

D   WHAT'S THE WORD?

26. May I go to the ____? I have a stomachache.
    Ⓐ library
    Ⓑ gym
    Ⓒ principal's office
    Ⓓ nurse's office

27. I enjoy languages. I like my ____ class.
    Ⓐ home economics
    Ⓑ French
    Ⓒ science
    Ⓓ history

28. The counselor works in the ____ office.
    Ⓐ guidance
    Ⓑ main
    Ⓒ nurse's
    Ⓓ secretary's

29. The ____ teacher is teaching tennis.
    Ⓐ biology
    Ⓑ physical education
    Ⓒ shop
    Ⓓ music

30. Students go to their lockers in the ____.
    Ⓐ field
    Ⓑ cafeteria
    Ⓒ hallway
    Ⓓ library

31. I have ____ practice after school.
    Ⓐ band
    Ⓑ student government
    Ⓒ newspaper
    Ⓓ community service

32. Students learn chemistry in the ____.
    Ⓐ auditorium
    Ⓑ locker room
    Ⓒ cafeteria
    Ⓓ science lab

33. Students make furniture in ____.
    Ⓐ home economics
    Ⓑ industrial arts
    Ⓒ drama
    Ⓓ chorus

34. Six hundred people are sitting in the ____.
    Ⓐ hallway
    Ⓑ main office
    Ⓒ bleachers
    Ⓓ lab

35. Students should be very quiet in the ____.
    Ⓐ band
    Ⓑ library
    Ⓒ field
    Ⓓ classroom

(continued)

36. The _____ is sweeping the hallway.
  Ⓐ custodian
  Ⓑ teacher
  Ⓒ security guard
  Ⓓ clerk

37. Students study plants and animals in _____.
  Ⓐ math
  Ⓑ health
  Ⓒ biology
  Ⓓ business education

38. Students are cooking soup in _____.
  Ⓐ P.E.
  Ⓑ shop
  Ⓒ English
  Ⓓ home economics

39. In _____, students do problems with numbers.
  Ⓐ math
  Ⓑ the chess club
  Ⓒ driver's education
  Ⓓ chorus

40. The _____ has a photo of every student.
  Ⓐ literary magazine
  Ⓑ yearbook
  Ⓒ pep squad
  Ⓓ newspaper

41. Students are singing in the _____.
  Ⓐ science class
  Ⓑ orchestra
  Ⓒ chorus
  Ⓓ band

Ⓔ CLOZE READING

Evergreen [Adult Ⓐ / University Ⓑ / Community Ⓒ] ⁴² College welcomes all new students! This

Friday, there will be a meeting for new students in the [auditorium Ⓐ / locker room Ⓑ / hallway Ⓒ] ⁴³.

Come and meet your teachers and guidance [coaches Ⓐ / counselors Ⓑ / instructors Ⓒ] ⁴⁴.

There will be information about our [extracurricular Ⓐ / subject Ⓑ / office Ⓒ] ⁴⁵ activities. For

example, learn about student government, the international [crew Ⓐ / squad Ⓑ / club Ⓒ] ⁴⁶, and

community [service Ⓐ / help Ⓑ / computer Ⓒ] ⁴⁷. Do you play a musical instrument? Sign up for the

[pep squad Ⓐ / band Ⓑ / A.V. crew Ⓒ] ⁴⁸ or the [orchestra Ⓐ / piano Ⓑ / debate club Ⓒ] ⁴⁹. Talk with our

coaches about our [cheerleading Ⓐ / pep Ⓑ / football Ⓒ] ⁵⁰ and basketball teams.

Ⓕ WRITING SAMPLE

Choose one of these topics and write a paragraph. Use a separate sheet of paper.

- Describe your school. What kind of school is it? What subjects are you studying? What is your favorite class? Why? What subjects do you want to study in the future?

- Do you have a son or daughter in school? Describe the school. Who is your child's teacher? Do you know the principal or the guidance counselor? What are your child's favorite subjects? What extracurricular activities does your child do?

Name _____

Date _____

A   WHAT IS IT?

circle	magnet	pyramid	scale
dropper	microscope	rectangle	square

1. _____   2. _____   3. _____   4. _____

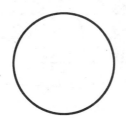
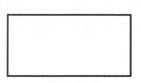
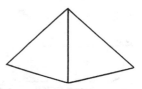

5. _____   6. _____   7. _____   8. _____

B   MATH SYMBOLS

divided by	equals	minus	percentage	plus	times

9. + _____   12. % _____

10. = _____   13. × _____

11. – _____   14. ÷ _____

C   LANGUAGE ARTS

article	noun	preposition	subject	verb

You know the parts of speech.

15   16   17   18   19

15. _____   18. _____

16. _____   19. _____

17. _____

| apostrophe | comma | exclamation mark | period | question mark | quotation marks |

"Are you going to Sue's party?" "Yes, I am." "That's great! Let's go together."
20   **21**   **22**   **23**   **24**   **25**

20. _____

21. _____

22. _____

23. _____

24. _____

25. _____

E **WHAT'S THE WORD?**

26. Algebra is a type of _____.
    Ⓐ geography
    Ⓑ math
    Ⓒ composition
    Ⓓ line

27. Please measure the _____ of the bookcase.
    Ⓐ inches
    Ⓑ meters
    Ⓒ height
    Ⓓ distance

28. My brother is 6 _____ tall.
    Ⓐ inches
    Ⓑ yards
    Ⓒ meters
    Ⓓ feet

29. Please draw a right _____.
    Ⓐ triangle
    Ⓑ rectangle
    Ⓒ square
    Ⓓ circle

30. Put a question mark at the end of _____ sentence.
    Ⓐ an exclamatory
    Ⓑ an imperative
    Ⓒ an interrogative
    Ⓓ a declarative

31. My essay has three _____.
    Ⓐ sentences
    Ⓑ paragraphs
    Ⓒ titles
    Ⓓ verbs

32. I corrected the _____ in my essay.
    Ⓐ compositions
    Ⓑ marks
    Ⓒ drafts
    Ⓓ mistakes

33. Did you get the _____ to my party?
    Ⓐ letter
    Ⓑ thank-you note
    Ⓒ invitation
    Ⓓ memo

34. I'm writing _____ to my friend.
    Ⓐ an e-mail
    Ⓑ an essay
    Ⓒ a magazine article
    Ⓓ an editorial

35. A history textbook is _____.
    Ⓐ fiction
    Ⓑ non-fiction
    Ⓒ a biography
    Ⓓ a novel

36. The _____ is very hot and dry.
    Ⓐ jungle
    Ⓑ shore
    Ⓒ desert
    Ⓓ brook

37. _____ is smaller than a lake.
    Ⓐ A bay
    Ⓑ A river
    Ⓒ An ocean
    Ⓓ A pond

(continued)

38. I need ____ for my science experiment.
- Ⓐ a triangle
- Ⓑ a beaker and a test tube
- Ⓒ an asteroid
- Ⓓ a U.F.O.

39. When you do an experiment, first you have to state the ____.
- Ⓐ problem
- Ⓑ conclusion
- Ⓒ scale
- Ⓓ chemicals

40. Mercury and Venus are ____.
- Ⓐ suns
- Ⓑ meteors
- Ⓒ planets
- Ⓓ comets

41. You can see the galaxy from the ____.
- Ⓐ woods
- Ⓑ valley
- Ⓒ jungle
- Ⓓ observatory

Ⓕ CLOZE READING

This weekend, our family is going to visit a national park. The distance is about

forty | meters Ⓐ | miles Ⓑ | feet Ⓒ | ⁴². It'll take an hour to get there. The weather report for the

weekend is good. There's a ten | percent Ⓐ | fraction Ⓑ | number Ⓒ | ⁴³ chance of rain. The park has

a beautiful | sand Ⓐ | forest Ⓑ | mountain Ⓒ | ⁴⁴ range. There are | valleys Ⓐ | streams Ⓑ | plains Ⓒ | ⁴⁵ with

fresh water and fish. The | forests Ⓐ | dunes Ⓑ | islands Ⓒ | ⁴⁶ are very quiet. On Saturday, we're

going to hike to the top of a mountain | valley Ⓐ | canyon Ⓑ | peak Ⓒ | ⁴⁷. At night, we'll look at the

| sun Ⓐ | stars Ⓑ | solar eclipse Ⓒ | ⁴⁸ in the sky with my | telescope Ⓐ | microscope Ⓑ | camera Ⓒ | ⁴⁹.

Maybe we'll see | an astronomer Ⓐ | a meteor Ⓑ | an astronaut Ⓒ | ⁵⁰ in the sky.

Ⓖ WRITING SAMPLE

Choose one of these topics and write a paragraph. Use a separate sheet of paper.

- What do you read during a typical day? Do you read a newspaper or magazine? Do you read in the morning? In the evening? What's your favorite kind of book? Do you like fiction or non-fiction?

- What's your favorite place to visit? Do you prefer the mountains or the seashore? Describe the geography of a special place. What do you like to do there?

A) WHAT'S YOUR OCCUPATION?

accountant	housekeeper	lawyer	pharmacist	store owner	travel agent
cashier	instructor	mechanic	postal worker	supervisor	truck driver

1. _____

2. _____

3. _____

4. _____

5. _____

6. _____

7. _____

8. _____

9. _____

10. _____

11. _____

12. _____

B) WHAT DO THEY DO?

assist	build	fly	grow	operate	prepare	translate

13. Pilots can _____ an airplane.

14. Carpenters _____ things.

15. Farmers _____ vegetables.

16. Cooks _____ dinner every night.

17. Pedro can _____ English into Spanish for his grandmother.

18. Construction workers often _____ heavy equipment.

19. The home health aide will _____ the elderly patient.

C. WHO ARE THEY?

| barber | butcher | factory worker | receptionist | reporter | tailor |

20. The _____ cuts meat and chicken.
21. The _____ is going to cut my son's hair.
22. The _____ answers the phone and helps visitors.
23. The _____ asked the police officer a lot questions.
24. The _____ will shorten your dress.
25. The _____ assembles computer components.

D. ON THE JOB

26. The ____ makes delicious cakes.
    - Ⓐ assembler
    - Ⓑ baker
    - Ⓒ courier
    - Ⓓ foreman

27. I'm a waiter. I ____ food in a restaurant.
    - Ⓐ wash
    - Ⓑ sell
    - Ⓒ serve
    - Ⓓ clean

28. A ____ takes care of my son after school.
    - Ⓐ babysitter
    - Ⓑ hairdresser
    - Ⓒ mason
    - Ⓓ security guard

29. I'd like to be a computer software ____.
    - Ⓐ clerk
    - Ⓑ carrier
    - Ⓒ server
    - Ⓓ engineer

30. The ____ is at our door with a pizza.
    - Ⓐ interpreter
    - Ⓑ delivery person
    - Ⓒ waiter
    - Ⓓ stock clerk

31. The ____ is cleaning the bedrooms.
    - Ⓐ housekeeper
    - Ⓑ cook
    - Ⓒ mover
    - Ⓓ serviceman

32. The secretary is ____ papers in the office.
    - Ⓐ using
    - Ⓑ filing
    - Ⓒ repairing
    - Ⓓ serving

33. The ____ is giving my cat an injection.
    - Ⓐ health-care attendant
    - Ⓑ gardener
    - Ⓒ veterinarian
    - Ⓓ assembler

34. A ____ calls you and tries to sell things.
    - Ⓐ telemarketer
    - Ⓑ stock clerk
    - Ⓒ teacher
    - Ⓓ mason

35. If you have a question, call a ____.
    - Ⓐ businessman
    - Ⓑ manager
    - Ⓒ customer service representative
    - Ⓓ secretary

36. A ____ wears a uniform.
    - Ⓐ secretary
    - Ⓑ serviceman
    - Ⓒ babysitter
    - Ⓓ photographer

37. The ____ will fix your dishwasher.
    - Ⓐ welder
    - Ⓑ architect
    - Ⓒ garment worker
    - Ⓓ repairperson

(continued)

38. The _____ workers collect trash every week.
- Ⓐ house
- Ⓑ construction
- Ⓒ sanitation
- Ⓓ fire

39. I'm a _____. I play the piano in a restaurant.
- Ⓐ chef
- Ⓑ mover
- Ⓒ dockworker
- Ⓓ musician

40. The architect is _____ a new building.
- Ⓐ painting
- Ⓑ selling
- Ⓒ designing
- Ⓓ washing

41. The _____ works on a boat in the ocean.
- Ⓐ interpreter
- Ⓑ fisher
- Ⓒ supervisor
- Ⓓ messenger

42. A _____ works outside every day.
- Ⓐ landscaper
- Ⓑ manager
- Ⓒ data entry clerk
- Ⓓ businesswoman

43. The _____ supervises the construction workers.
- Ⓐ secretary
- Ⓑ foreman
- Ⓒ customer service representative
- Ⓓ welder

E) CLOZE READING

There are many different types of jobs in a hospital. Of course, there are doctors,

nurses, and health-care | engineers Ⓐ aides Ⓑ operators Ⓒ |⁴⁴. But many other people also

work in a hospital. For example, on the first floor | patients Ⓐ servers Ⓑ receptionists Ⓒ |⁴⁵

help visitors. A | salesperson Ⓐ reporter Ⓑ courier Ⓒ |⁴⁶ works in the gift shop. Cooks and

| delivery people Ⓐ home health aides Ⓑ food-service workers Ⓒ |⁴⁷ work in the coffee shop or

cafeteria. | Housekeepers Ⓐ Hairdressers Ⓑ Sanitation workers Ⓒ |⁴⁸ and

| assemblers Ⓐ custodians Ⓑ chefs Ⓒ |⁴⁹ clean the rooms and floors. And medical equipment

managers | sell Ⓐ guard Ⓑ take Ⓒ |⁵⁰ inventory of all of the equipment and supplies. Most hospitals

have hundreds of employees.

F) WRITING SAMPLE

Choose one of these topics and write a paragraph. Use a separate sheet of paper.

- What is your occupation? What do you do? What are your skills? If you aren't working now, what occupation would you like to have? What skills do you need?

- What occupations do your friends and relatives have? List as many different people and occupations as you can. Describe what each person does.

A) IN THE OFFICE

adding machine	job notice	photocopier	swivel chair
coat rack	message board	rubber band	vending machine
file folder	paper clip	stapler	water cooler

1. _____

2. _____

3. _____

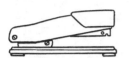

4. _____

5. _____

6. _____

7. _____

8. _____

9. _____

10. _____

11. _____

12. _____

B) AT THE FACTORY

conveyor	dolly	forklift	loading dock	time card

13. Take your _____ to the payroll office.

14. The factory worker is putting boxes on the _____ belt.

15. Who is driving the _____ to the warehouse?

16. The delivery truck is waiting at the _____.

17. I'm using the _____ to move a heavy box.

C WHICH GROUP?

| earplugs | goggles | mask | pickax | respirator | shovel | sledgehammer | trowel |

18–21. Safety Equipment

_____

_____

_____

_____

22–25. Construction Tools

_____

_____

_____

_____

D WHAT'S THE WORD?

26. The office assistant always _____ the mail.
- Ⓐ types
- Ⓑ responds
- Ⓒ sorts
- Ⓓ makes

27. The new postage meters are in the _____.
- Ⓐ mailbox
- Ⓑ mailroom
- Ⓒ employee lounge
- Ⓓ stacking tray

28. Please put these old letters into the _____.
- Ⓐ paper shredder
- Ⓑ organizer
- Ⓒ photocopier
- Ⓓ rotary card file

29. The _____ are in the supply cabinet.
- Ⓐ cubicles
- Ⓑ suggestion boxes
- Ⓒ shingles
- Ⓓ legal pads

30. The copier needs a new _____.
- Ⓐ ink cartridge
- Ⓑ ink pad
- Ⓒ pushpin
- Ⓓ staple

31. I cut my finger. I need the _____.
- Ⓐ latex gloves
- Ⓑ defibrillator
- Ⓒ first-aid kit
- Ⓓ glue

32. Cooks should wear _____.
- Ⓐ hairnets
- Ⓑ respirators
- Ⓒ earplugs
- Ⓓ goggles

33. Be careful! That material is _____.
- Ⓐ safety
- Ⓑ flammable
- Ⓒ latex
- Ⓓ concrete

34. The door has an electrical _____ sign.
- Ⓐ helmet
- Ⓑ support
- Ⓒ extinguisher
- Ⓓ hazard

35. During a fire, use the _____.
- Ⓐ emergency exits
- Ⓑ biohazard
- Ⓒ safety vest
- Ⓓ elevators

36. He keeps his tape measure in his _____.
- Ⓐ wheelbarrow
- Ⓑ toolbelt
- Ⓒ pipe
- Ⓓ mask

37. The painter is climbing the _____.
- Ⓐ backhoe
- Ⓑ drywall
- Ⓒ ladder
- Ⓓ wire

(continued)

38. The secretary is typing the job _____.
- Ⓐ interview
- Ⓑ salary
- Ⓒ classified
- Ⓓ announcement

39. The manager is giving a _____ in the conference room.
- Ⓐ work station
- Ⓑ presentation
- Ⓒ resume
- Ⓓ qualification

40. The office assistant is _____ a message.
- Ⓐ requesting
- Ⓑ listening
- Ⓒ taking
- Ⓓ sorting

41. I have a _____ job on the weekend.
- Ⓐ part-time
- Ⓑ full-time
- Ⓒ complete
- Ⓓ full

Ⓔ CLOZE READING

I saw an interesting job notice in the | clipboards (Ⓐ)   classified ads (Ⓑ)   qualifications (Ⓒ) | [42].

I want to | request (Ⓐ)   go (Ⓑ)   respond (Ⓒ) | [43] to the ad. First, I need to | file (Ⓐ)   prepare (Ⓑ)   fill out (Ⓒ) | [44] my

resume. In it, I'll give my | previous (Ⓐ)   future (Ⓑ)   available (Ⓒ) | [45] experience and education. I'm

going to send a letter and my resume tomorrow. I hope the company will call me for an interview.

If I go to an interview, I'll | wear (Ⓐ)   dress (Ⓑ)   ask (Ⓒ) | [46] appropriately. During the interview, I'll talk

about my | skills (Ⓐ)   hobbies (Ⓑ)   family (Ⓒ) | [47] and experience. I'll also ask about the job

| time (Ⓐ)   salary (Ⓑ)   paycheck (Ⓒ) | [48]. After the interview, I'll write

| a resume (Ⓐ)   an application (Ⓑ)   a thank-you note (Ⓒ) | [49]. I hope I get | hired (Ⓐ)   paid (Ⓑ)   asked (Ⓒ) | [50].

Ⓕ WRITING SAMPLE

Choose one of these topics and write a paragraph. Use a separate sheet of paper.

- What office supplies and equipment do you have in your home? Where do you keep these things? What supplies and equipment do you use every day? What do you rarely use?

- Describe the steps in a job search. What should you do first? Where can you look for a job? What should you do before an interview? During an interview? After an interview?

Name _____

Date _____

A) VEHICLES AND TRANSPORTATION

| hatchback | moving van | station wagon | S.U.V. | tow truck | train |
| motorcycle | sedan | subway | taxi | tractor trailer | van |

1. _____

2. _____

3. _____

4. _____

5. _____

6. _____

7. _____

8. _____

9. _____

10. _____

11. _____

12. _____

B) WHAT'S THE SIGN?

| handicapped parking only | pedestrian crossing | right turn only |
| no right turn | railroad crossing | school crossing |

13 14 15 16 17 18

13. _____

14. _____

15. _____

16. _____

17. _____

18. _____

C) IN THE CAR

| nozzle | oil | seat belt | tires | trunk | turn signal | windshield wipers |

19. You should always use your _____ when you drive.

20. The spare tire is often in the _____ of a car.

21. It's raining. Turn on the _____.

22. I always use the _____ when I make a right or left turn.

23. Check your _____ with a dipstick before a long trip.

24. Use an air pump to put air in your _____.

25. To pump gas, lift the _____ and select the gas.

D) WHAT'S THE WORD?

26. A bus driver collects fares from the ____.
    - Ⓐ drivers
    - Ⓑ passengers
    - Ⓒ conductors
    - Ⓓ pilots

27. The train's arrival time is on the ____.
    - Ⓐ timetable
    - Ⓑ meter
    - Ⓒ transfer
    - Ⓓ fare

28. Several people are standing on the ____.
    - Ⓐ station
    - Ⓑ counter
    - Ⓒ platform
    - Ⓓ booth

29. The bus driver is putting suitcases into the baggage ____.
    - Ⓐ window
    - Ⓑ desk
    - Ⓒ stand
    - Ⓓ compartment

30. Turn on your car ____ at night.
    - Ⓐ defroster
    - Ⓑ brake lights
    - Ⓒ headlights
    - Ⓓ warning lights

31. Cars must have a ____ on the back.
    - Ⓐ license plate
    - Ⓑ driver's license
    - Ⓒ jack
    - Ⓓ door handle

32. Open the ____ of the car to check the engine.
    - Ⓐ air filter
    - Ⓑ hood
    - Ⓒ sunroof
    - Ⓓ hubcap

33. The ____ tells how fast the car is going.
    - Ⓐ visor
    - Ⓑ odometer
    - Ⓒ metal detector
    - Ⓓ speedometer

34. What's wrong? The ____ is on!
    - Ⓐ horn
    - Ⓑ warning light
    - Ⓒ brake light
    - Ⓓ traffic signal

35. Put the key in the ____ to start the car.
    - Ⓐ ignition
    - Ⓑ gearshift
    - Ⓒ steering wheel
    - Ⓓ lock

(continued)

36. Put your foot on the _____ to stop the car.
- Ⓐ clutch
- Ⓑ brake
- Ⓒ engine
- Ⓓ accelerator

37. Take this entrance ramp _____ the interstate.
- Ⓐ in
- Ⓑ off
- Ⓒ onto
- Ⓓ out of

38. The pedestrian is walking _____ the street.
- Ⓐ over
- Ⓑ past
- Ⓒ out of
- Ⓓ across

39. I don't like to drive _____ high bridges.
- Ⓐ over
- Ⓑ up
- Ⓒ in
- Ⓓ down

40. We have to drive _____ a long tunnel.
- Ⓐ across
- Ⓑ down
- Ⓒ through
- Ⓓ around

41. Drivers stop and pay money at the _____.
- Ⓐ ticket counter
- Ⓑ tollbooth
- Ⓒ underpass
- Ⓓ intersection

Ⓔ CLOZE READING

I'm | fastening | towing | boarding |⁴² a plane at the airport. I'm showing my
 | Ⓐ | Ⓑ | Ⓒ

| transfer | boarding pass | pockets |⁴³ to the | flight attendant | pilot | customs officer |⁴⁴
| Ⓐ | Ⓑ | Ⓒ | | Ⓐ | Ⓑ | Ⓒ

at the front of the plane. I have | an emergency | a window | a chair |⁴⁵ seat. Before I sit
 | Ⓐ | Ⓑ | Ⓒ

down, I'll put my | carry-on bag | luggage cart | tray |⁴⁶ in the | glove | overhead | security |⁴⁷
 | Ⓐ | Ⓑ | Ⓒ | | Ⓐ | Ⓑ | Ⓒ

compartment. Then I'll relax. When I arrive in Miami, I'll take a taxi to my hotel. I'll check in at

the | ticket counter | gate | front desk |⁴⁸. The | security officer | bellhop | concierge |⁴⁹
 | Ⓐ | Ⓑ | Ⓒ | | Ⓐ | Ⓑ | Ⓒ

will help me with my luggage. I'll take the | elevator | cockpit | lobby |⁵⁰ up to my room.
 | Ⓐ | Ⓑ | Ⓒ

Ⓕ WRITING SAMPLE

Choose one of these topics and write a paragraph. Use a separate sheet of paper.

- How do you get to school? Do you take public transportation or do you drive? Describe what you do and give directions. How long does it usually take?

- Do you have a car or other vehicle? Describe it. How old is it? Does it have any problems? Does it have any special parts or equipment? What do you do for maintenance of your vehicle? What repairs does it need?

A **WHERE DO YOU LIKE TO GO?**

aquarium	fair	museum	playground
beach	historic site	national park	yard sale
concert	movies	play	zoo

1. _____ 2. _____ 3. _____

4. _____ 5. _____ 6. _____

7. _____ 8. _____ 9. _____

10. _____ 11. _____ 12. _____

B **AT THE BEACH**

lifeguard	sand castle	shells	sunscreen	surfer

13. A father is putting _____ on his son.

14. Children are picking up rocks and _____.

15. The _____ is watching the swimmers in the water.

16. Several children are building a _____,

17. The _____ is riding a big wave.

C) WHICH GROUP?

backpack   camping stove   canteen   compass   lantern   sleeping bag   tent   trail map

18–21. Hiking

_____

_____

_____

_____

22–25. Camping

_____

_____

_____

_____

D) WHAT'S THE WORD?

26. I like to _____ with watercolors.
- Ⓐ sew
- Ⓑ crochet
- Ⓒ paint
- Ⓓ draw

27. Students are making _____ in art class today.
- Ⓐ needlepoint
- Ⓑ pottery
- Ⓒ thimbles
- Ⓓ photography

28. I'm using the _____ to make a dress.
- Ⓐ easel
- Ⓑ potter's wheel
- Ⓒ model kit
- Ⓓ sewing machine

29. I have a lot of special stamps in my _____.
- Ⓐ coin collection
- Ⓑ stamp book
- Ⓒ stamp album
- Ⓓ magnifying glass

30. My family likes to play _____ games.
- Ⓐ origami
- Ⓑ coin
- Ⓒ embroidery
- Ⓓ board

31. I go _____ when I need to find information.
- Ⓐ online
- Ⓑ bird-watching
- Ⓒ climbing
- Ⓓ collecting

32. You need _____ when you build models.
- Ⓐ needles
- Ⓑ glue
- Ⓒ thread
- Ⓓ string

33. Very small children can play in a _____.
- Ⓐ rowing machine
- Ⓑ pond
- Ⓒ ramp
- Ⓓ sandbox

34. We're playing baseball on the _____.
- Ⓐ ballfield
- Ⓑ court
- Ⓒ bike path
- Ⓓ carousel

35. At the gym, I _____ on the treadmill.
- Ⓐ wrestle
- Ⓑ box
- Ⓒ exercise
- Ⓓ ride

36. My new jogging _____ is very comfortable.
- Ⓐ suit
- Ⓑ uniform
- Ⓒ saddle
- Ⓓ board

37. The gymnastics students are using the _____.
- Ⓐ target
- Ⓑ trampoline
- Ⓒ billiard balls
- Ⓓ weights

(continued)

38. I like my new golf _____ very much.
- Ⓐ rackets
- Ⓑ reins
- Ⓒ clubs
- Ⓓ paddles

39. You need a _____ when you play tennis or badminton.
- Ⓐ net
- Ⓑ ball
- Ⓒ birdie
- Ⓓ table

40. I always wear a _____ when I go biking or skateboarding.
- Ⓐ knee pad
- Ⓑ hat
- Ⓒ uniform
- Ⓓ helmet

41. You need special shoes for _____.
- Ⓐ badminton
- Ⓑ bowling
- Ⓒ the playground
- Ⓓ the planetarium

E) CLOZE READING

Every weekend in the summer, the Suarez family likes to have a

snack bar	kite	picnic
Ⓐ	Ⓑ	Ⓒ

⁴² in the park. They take a big

blanket	bench	bike rack
Ⓐ	Ⓑ	Ⓒ

⁴³

with them and put their picnic basket and

towel	cooler	stirrups
Ⓐ	Ⓑ	Ⓒ

⁴⁴ on it. Mr. and Mrs.

Suarez usually cook hamburgers on a

grill	pail	thermos
Ⓐ	Ⓑ	Ⓒ

⁴⁵. Their younger children

like to go to the

art gallery	playground	mat
Ⓐ	Ⓑ	Ⓒ

⁴⁶. They play on the slide and the

carnival	checkers	swings
Ⓐ	Ⓑ	Ⓒ

⁴⁷. Their oldest son likes to put on his skates and go

cycling	rollerblading	running
Ⓐ	Ⓑ	Ⓒ

⁴⁸. Before lunch, Mrs. Suarez sometimes goes

jogging	bowling	camping
Ⓐ	Ⓑ	Ⓒ

⁴⁹. Every weekend in the park, there's a

seesaw	Frisbee	craft fair
Ⓐ	Ⓑ	Ⓒ

⁵⁰. Everybody in the Suarez family likes to see what the

vendors are selling.

F) WRITING SAMPLE

Choose one of these topics and write a paragraph. Use a separate sheet of paper.

- What are your hobbies? Do you like to make things? Do you collect things? Do you like to play games? Tell about your hobbies and the supplies you use.

- Where do you like to go in your free time? What are your favorite places to visit? What do you do there? What individual sports and recreation activities do you enjoy doing? Where do you do them? How often?

A SPORTS EQUIPMENT

| baseball bat | basketball | football helmet | soccer ball |
| baseball glove | face guard | hockey stick | skis |

1. _____ 2. _____ 3. _____ 4. _____

5. _____ 6. _____ 7. _____ 8. _____

B MUSICAL INSTRUMENTS

| bass | clarinet | drums | flute | guitar | piano | trumpet | violin |

9. _____ 10. _____ 11. _____ 12. _____

13. _____ 14. _____ 15. _____ 16. _____

C MOVIES

| comedy | documentary | horror | musical | western |

17. The new _____ is about a young cowboy and his adventures.

18. You will laugh during this new _____.

19. This _____ is about New York City in the 1920s.

20. There's wonderful singing and dancing in this _____.

21. Children shouldn't watch _____ movies.

D TV PROGRAMS

cartoon	game show	nature	sports

22. In a _____, a person answers questions and can win money.

23. The soccer coach is talking about today's game on the _____ program.

24. Tonight's _____ program is about unusual jungle birds.

25. Many young children watch _____ shows on TV.

E WHAT'S THE WORD?

26. The softball team has new ____.
   Ⓐ skates
   Ⓑ masks
   Ⓒ uniforms
   Ⓓ shoulder pads

27. The volleyball team plays on a ____.
   Ⓐ court
   Ⓑ field
   Ⓒ rink
   Ⓓ net

28. You should wear a ____ on a sailboat.
   Ⓐ paddle
   Ⓑ towrope
   Ⓒ bathing cap
   Ⓓ life vest

29. You need an air tank when you go ____.
   Ⓐ rafting
   Ⓑ scuba diving
   Ⓒ sailing
   Ⓓ canoeing

30. He's going ____. He has his rod and bait.
   Ⓐ kayaking
   Ⓑ snorkeling
   Ⓒ fishing
   Ⓓ rowing

31. ____ is a popular winter sport.
   Ⓐ Surfing
   Ⓑ Canoeing
   Ⓒ Waterskiing
   Ⓓ Snowboarding

32. He ____ the ball and broke his bat.
   Ⓐ hit
   Ⓑ pitched
   Ⓒ passed
   Ⓓ kicked

33. She practices ____ at the town rink.
   Ⓐ windsurfing
   Ⓑ sledding
   Ⓒ figure skating
   Ⓓ baseball

34. ____ the ball!
   Ⓐ Dive
   Ⓑ Shoot
   Ⓒ Jump
   Ⓓ Bend

35. You should ____ before you run.
   Ⓐ reach
   Ⓑ shoot
   Ⓒ hop
   Ⓓ stretch

36. I use a baseball glove to ____ the ball.
   Ⓐ serve
   Ⓑ pass
   Ⓒ catch
   Ⓓ bounce

37. ____ music usually has a violin, guitar, and banjo.
   Ⓐ Classical
   Ⓑ Bluegrass
   Ⓒ Rock
   Ⓓ Rap

(continued)

38. This play is a _____, so it's very sad.
- Ⓐ comedy
- Ⓑ musical
- Ⓒ mystery
- Ⓓ tragedy

39. I like to watch _____ because I like to know what's happening in my community.
- Ⓐ sitcoms
- Ⓑ news programs
- Ⓒ soap operas
- Ⓓ shopping programs

40. The _____ is my favorite string instrument.
- Ⓐ cello
- Ⓑ tuba
- Ⓒ xylophone
- Ⓓ saxophone

41. The _____ danced beautifully.
- Ⓐ actresses
- Ⓑ conductors
- Ⓒ ballerinas
- Ⓓ musicians

F CLOZE READING

There are many types of | entertainment Ⓐ equipment Ⓑ percussion Ⓒ |⁴² to enjoy in our town

this Friday night. At the Civic Concert Hall, there will be a | mystery Ⓐ foreign Ⓑ classical Ⓒ |⁴³

music concert. | Conductor Ⓐ Comedian Ⓑ Opera singer Ⓒ |⁴⁴ Robert Stevens will lead the

| play Ⓐ orchestra Ⓑ team Ⓒ |⁴⁵ in music by Mozart. At the high school, there will be wonderful

singing and dancing. Students will present the famous | musical Ⓐ sitcom Ⓑ soap opera Ⓒ |⁴⁶,

West Side Story. The | screen Ⓐ musician Ⓑ theater Ⓒ |⁴⁷ will open for ticket sales at 7:00 P.M.

The city library will have a free movie night for families on Friday at 7:30 P.M. Everyone can enjoy

the adventure | play Ⓐ film Ⓑ club Ⓒ |⁴⁸ *Lost at Sea.* At the city park, there will be a free

| rock Ⓐ comedy Ⓑ drama Ⓒ |⁴⁹ music concert with a | recorder Ⓐ ballerina Ⓑ band Ⓒ |⁵⁰ from

the community college.

G WRITING SAMPLE

Choose one of these topics and write a paragraph. Use a separate sheet of paper.

- What is your favorite team sport? Do you like to play the sport? How often do you watch the sport? What is the name of your favorite team? Who are some of the best players on the team?

- What is your favorite TV program? What kind of program is it? When is it on? What is the program about? Why do you like it? Do you watch the program with your family?

A) ANIMALS

bat	dolphin	fox		kangaroo	parrot	rabbit
deer	eagle	hippopotamus		monkey	polar bear	seagull

1. _____ 2. _____ 3. _____ 4. _____

5. _____ 6. _____ 7. _____ 8. _____

9. _____ 10. _____ 11. _____ 12. _____

B) WHICH GROUP?

cow	giraffe	horse	pig	whale
crab	goat	jaguar	sea lion	
elephant	gorilla	octopus	shark	

13–16. In the Zoo   **17–21. In the Ocean**   **22–25. On the Farm**

_____   _____   _____

_____   _____   _____

_____   _____   _____

_____   _____   _____

                         _____

26. My favorite tree is the _____.
- Ⓐ geranium
- Ⓑ carnation
- Ⓒ daffodil
- Ⓓ dogwood

27. Careful! Don't touch the _____
- Ⓐ holly
- Ⓑ vine
- Ⓒ poison ivy
- Ⓓ oak

28. A tree has _____ on its trunk.
- Ⓐ roots
- Ⓑ bark
- Ⓒ stems
- Ⓓ pedals

29. _____ have thorns on their stems.
- Ⓐ Roses
- Ⓑ Tulips
- Ⓒ Flowers
- Ⓓ Ferns

30. That _____ has red berries.
- Ⓐ leaf
- Ⓑ bush
- Ⓒ bulb
- Ⓓ trunk

31. Many trees burned in the _____.
- Ⓐ tsunami
- Ⓑ hurricane
- Ⓒ environment
- Ⓓ wildfire

32. There's no school today because there's _____ outside.
- Ⓐ coal
- Ⓑ a blizzard
- Ⓒ a drought
- Ⓓ geothermal energy

33. _____ has very strong wind.
- Ⓐ A tornado
- Ⓑ A landslide
- Ⓒ An earthquake
- Ⓓ A mudslide

34. The sun is the source of solar _____.
- Ⓐ gas
- Ⓑ waste
- Ⓒ energy
- Ⓓ petroleum

35. _____ can come from cars and trucks.
- Ⓐ Air pollution
- Ⓑ Water pollution
- Ⓒ Radiation
- Ⓓ Hydroelectric power

36. There was a _____ eruption in Hawaii.
- Ⓐ water
- Ⓑ volcanic
- Ⓒ mud
- Ⓓ flood

37. My house has _____ for heating and cooking.
- Ⓐ trees
- Ⓑ wind
- Ⓒ natural gas
- Ⓓ global warming

38. We turn out lights to _____ energy.
- Ⓐ conserve
- Ⓑ make
- Ⓒ recycle
- Ⓓ use

39. We _____ newspapers, cans, and glass.
- Ⓐ prepare
- Ⓑ recycle
- Ⓒ return
- Ⓓ throw

40. _____ is an environmental problem.
- Ⓐ Solar energy
- Ⓑ Oil
- Ⓒ Conservation
- Ⓓ Global warming

41. _____ power uses water from big rivers.
- Ⓐ Coal
- Ⓑ Hydroelectric
- Ⓒ Nuclear
- Ⓓ Wind

D) CLOZE READING

It's a summer day on the farm. Turkeys, | baboons (A) roosters (B) panthers (C) | ⁴², and goats

are in the | barnyard (A) nest (B) coop (C) | ⁴³. The farmer is in the | crop (A) barn (B) shrub (C) | ⁴⁴.

He's feeding hay to the | hawks (A) pigeons (B) horses (C) | ⁴⁵. In the vegetable garden,

| bees (A) spiders (B) swans (C) | ⁴⁶ are flying around the plants. In front of the farmhouse,

the farmer's | gerbil (A) beaver (B) dog (C) | ⁴⁷ is sleeping under a big | maple (A) daisy (B) pansy (C) | ⁴⁸

tree. The hired hand is driving a | pasture (A) tractor (B) scarecrow (C) | ⁴⁹ in the field. Next to

the field, there's a large | stable (A) plant (B) orchard (C) | ⁵⁰ with fruit trees.

E) WRITING SAMPLE

Choose one of these topics and write a paragraph. Use a separate sheet of paper.

- What animals live in the area near your home? Tell about the animals, birds, and insects. What kinds of trees, bushes, and flowers grow in your area?

- Are you concerned about the environment? What are you worried about? How do you conserve energy? What do you recycle?

Word by Word Beginning Level
Unit 17 U.S. Edition Test:
PICTURE DICTIONARY PAGES 160–166

Name _____

Date _____

A) THE LEGAL SYSTEM AND CITIZENSHIP

| appear in court | be arrested | obey laws | pay taxes | serve on a jury | vote |

1. _____

2. _____

3. _____

4. _____

5. _____

6. _____

B) WHAT'S THE HOLIDAY?

| Halloween Independence Day | Martin Luther King, Jr. Day Memorial Day | New Year's Day Thanksgiving | Valentine's Day Veterans Day |

7. January 1 _____
8. January 19 _____
9. February 14 _____
10. May 31 _____
11. July 4 _____
12. October 31 _____
13. November 11 _____
14. November 25 _____

C) U.S. GOVERNMENT

| chief justice president | representatives senators | Supreme Court justices vice-president |

15–16. Legislative Branch   **17–18. Executive Branch**   **19–20. Judicial Branch**

_____   _____   _____

_____   _____   _____

D) U.S. HISTORY

| Civil War | Korean War | Revolutionary War | Vietnam War | World Wars I and II |

21. 1775–1783 _____

22. 1861–1865 _____

23. 1914–1945 _____

24. 1950–1953 _____

25. 1964–1973 _____

E) WHAT'S THE WORD?

26. The police officer asked to see my _____.
ⓐ birth certificate
ⓑ driver's license
ⓒ employee I.D. badge
ⓓ social security card

27. You must have _____ to enter the U.S.
ⓐ a work permit
ⓑ a social security card
ⓒ a passport
ⓓ an I.D. card

28. The president of the United States lives in the _____.
ⓐ Capitol Building
ⓑ House of Representatives
ⓒ Supreme Court
ⓓ White House

29. The first ten _____ to the Constitution are called the Bill of Rights.
ⓐ amendments
ⓑ laws
ⓒ branches
ⓓ freedoms

30. U.S. citizens can vote at age _____.
ⓐ 12
ⓑ 15
ⓒ 18
ⓓ 21

31. The U.S. _____ is often called "the supreme law of the land."
ⓐ flag
ⓑ president
ⓒ court
ⓓ Constitution

32. _____ was the first U.S. president.
ⓐ Thomas Jefferson
ⓑ George Washington
ⓒ Thomas Edison
ⓓ Abraham Lincoln

33. Christmas and _____ are on the same day every year.
ⓐ Valentine's Day
ⓑ Memorial Day
ⓒ Martin Luther King, Jr. Day
ⓓ Thanksgiving

34. The _____ saw the suspect steal the car.
ⓐ jury
ⓑ witness
ⓒ judge
ⓓ bailiff

35. The police officer put _____ on the prisoner.
ⓐ fines
ⓑ fingerprints
ⓒ handcuffs
ⓓ mug shots

(continued)

36. If you're arrested, you need to talk with a _____.
- Ⓐ court reporter
- Ⓑ prison guard
- Ⓒ bailiff
- Ⓓ lawyer

37. The jury decides if the suspect is _____.
- Ⓐ hired
- Ⓑ guilty
- Ⓒ booked
- Ⓓ arrested

38. _____ must live in a prison.
- Ⓐ Inmates
- Ⓑ Suspects
- Ⓒ Juries
- Ⓓ Defendants

39. He was _____ to three months in jail.
- Ⓐ arrested
- Ⓑ paid
- Ⓒ sentenced
- Ⓓ fined

40. If you're arrested for speeding, you have to pay a _____.
- Ⓐ fine
- Ⓑ bill
- Ⓒ bail
- Ⓓ witness

41. It's a citizen's responsibility to _____.
- Ⓐ go to school
- Ⓑ be part of community life
- Ⓒ have a passport
- Ⓓ recite the oath

F) CLOZE READING

When Ana came to the United States from Guatemala five years ago, she had a

social security card	passport	resident card
Ⓐ	Ⓑ	Ⓒ

⁴² from her country. Soon she got a

job and a
verdict	work certificate	work permit
Ⓐ	Ⓑ	Ⓒ

⁴³. She lived in the U.S., but she wasn't a

U.S.
resident	citizen	witness
Ⓐ	Ⓑ	Ⓒ

⁴⁴. Last month, she
applied for	took	attended
Ⓐ	Ⓑ	Ⓒ

⁴⁵

citizenship. Now she's taking a class and learning about U.S.
news	government	rights
Ⓐ	Ⓑ	Ⓒ

⁴⁶

and history. Next month, she'll take the citizenship
tax	application	test
Ⓐ	Ⓑ	Ⓒ

⁴⁷. She hopes she

passes it. After that, she'll go to a naturalization
interview	test	license
Ⓐ	Ⓑ	Ⓒ

⁴⁸. Finally, she'll

attend a naturalization
holiday	party	cermony
Ⓐ	Ⓑ	Ⓒ

⁴⁹. After she recites the Oath of

Residents	Allegiance	Citizenship
Ⓐ	Ⓑ	Ⓒ

⁵⁰, she'll receive her citizenship.

G) WRITING SAMPLE

Choose one of these topics and write a paragraph. Use a separate sheet of paper.

- Tell about all the forms of identification you have. When and where did you receive each one? When do you need each form of identification? When will you need a new one?

- Do you celebrate any of the U.S. holidays? Which ones are your favorites? Tell what you usually do on that holiday. Who do you see? What do you eat?

A **WHAT WILL THEY DO?**

exchange money	go to an Internet cafe	take a shuttle bus
get the baggage	mail some postcards	take a walking tour
go to a museum	rent a car	visit an historic site

1. _____

_____

2. _____

_____

3. _____

_____

4. _____

_____

5. _____

_____

6. _____

_____

7. _____

_____

8. _____

_____

9. _____

_____

B **TRAVEL**

business trip	cruise	expedition	study tour	travel agency

10. I like the ocean. I go on a _____ every summer.

11. I don't use a _____. I make my reservations online.

12. The students went on a _____ of historical cities.

13. The _____ in the mountains was difficult and cold.

14. I work for an international company. I go on a _____ every month.

| car rental counter | declaration form | traveler's checks |
| customs | souvenirs | |

15. When you enter a country, you must fill out a customs _____.

16. At _____, the agent will look through your luggage.

17. When I travel, I use _____. I don't carry very much cash.

18. Many tourists like to buy small _____.

19. We need to go to the _____ to pick up the keys.

D WHAT ARE THEY SAYING?

Can I pay with a credit card?	May I see your passport?
Can I take photographs here?	Please don't bother me!
I'd like to book a ski trip.	Please write that down for me.

20. _____

_____

21. _____

_____

22. _____

_____

23. _____

_____

24. _____

_____

25. _____

_____

26. We saw a lot of wild animals on the ____.
    Ⓐ guided tour
    Ⓑ museum tour
    Ⓒ safari
    Ⓓ sightseeing tour

27. The children will visit an important ____ with their class.
    Ⓐ club
    Ⓑ suite
    Ⓒ walking tour
    Ⓓ historic site

28. We're going on an eco-tour with a ____.
    Ⓐ tour company
    Ⓑ rental company
    Ⓒ concierge
    Ⓓ ticket

29. Every summer we take a ____ to visit our cousins.
    Ⓐ business trip
    Ⓑ family trip
    Ⓒ study tour
    Ⓓ guided tour

30. You must show your passport at ____.
    Ⓐ the baggage claim area
    Ⓑ the school
    Ⓒ immigration
    Ⓓ the taxi stand

31. At the hotel, you check out at the ____.
    Ⓐ front desk
    Ⓑ bell desk
    Ⓒ restaurant
    Ⓓ front door

32. ____ will help you order theater tickets.
    Ⓐ Room service
    Ⓑ Maintenance
    Ⓒ The waiter
    Ⓓ The concierge

33. ____ will clean the room after lunch.
    Ⓐ Housekeeping
    Ⓑ Room service
    Ⓒ Maintenance
    Ⓓ Gardeners

34. Let's call ____. The heat in our suite isn't working.
    Ⓐ the bell desk
    Ⓑ maintenance
    Ⓒ room service
    Ⓓ the gas company

35. I'd like a ____ at 6:00 A.M., please.
    Ⓐ phone call
    Ⓑ view
    Ⓒ telephone
    Ⓓ wake-up call

36. I need to wash my hands. Where's the ____?
    Ⓐ club
    Ⓑ museum
    Ⓒ restroom
    Ⓓ vehicle

37. ____. What did you say?
    Ⓐ Please
    Ⓑ I'm sorry
    Ⓒ Here
    Ⓓ Thank you

38. What do you ____ that in English?
    Ⓐ call
    Ⓑ say
    Ⓒ pronounce
    Ⓓ speak

39. I called the concierge and said, "____"
    Ⓐ I'd like to mail this to my country.
    Ⓑ Freeze!
    Ⓒ We need some towels.
    Ⓓ I'd like to get tickets for a show.

40. I didn't understand her. So I said, "____"
    Ⓐ Please go away!
    Ⓑ Please repeat that.
    Ⓒ Look out!
    Ⓓ Get away from me!

41. In an emergency, say, "____"
    Ⓐ Don't move!
    Ⓑ Good-bye!
    Ⓒ Help!
    Ⓓ Please speak slowly.

Last weekend, the Solanos and their children took a family | tour trip room |⁴².
                                                       Ⓐ   Ⓑ   Ⓒ

They went by train to visit an historic city in the mountains. They stayed in a very nice

| hotel cafe shop |⁴³ near the train station. The hotel manager gave them a large
 Ⓐ   Ⓑ   Ⓒ

| family suite non-smoking |⁴⁴ room with two | open double accessible |⁴⁵ beds.
 Ⓐ   Ⓑ   Ⓒ   Ⓐ   Ⓑ   Ⓒ

The room was on the sixth floor and had a nice | view sightseeing show |⁴⁶ of the city.
                                                         Ⓐ   Ⓑ   Ⓒ

After they relaxed in the room for a while, they went out for dinner. The next day they took

| a shuttle an eco-tour a bus tour |⁴⁷ of the city in the morning. In the afternoon, they
  Ⓐ   Ⓑ   Ⓒ

| took went made |⁴⁸ sightseeing and bought a few souvenirs. The concierge at the hotel
 Ⓐ   Ⓑ   Ⓒ

made | reservations tickets claims |⁴⁹ for them at a famous restaurant. She also got them
            Ⓐ   Ⓑ   Ⓒ

tickets for a | site fitness club concert |⁵⁰ in the evening.
              Ⓐ   Ⓑ   Ⓒ

G WRITING SAMPLE

Choose one of these topics and write a paragraph. Use a separate sheet of paper.

- Describe a recent family trip. Where did you go? How did you get there? Who went with you? Who did you visit? How long did you stay? What did you do?

- Tell about a special trip you would like to take someday. Where will you go? How will you get there? What exciting things will you do?

A) **WHAT'S THE WORD?**

1. Jose's _____ of birth is Miami.
   - Ⓐ date
   - Ⓑ place
   - Ⓒ state
   - Ⓓ street

2. What's your _____? I'll call you later.
   - Ⓐ middle initial
   - Ⓑ social security number
   - Ⓒ cell phone number
   - Ⓓ street name

3. I'd like to introduce my cousin Paul. He's my uncle's _____.
   - Ⓐ nephew
   - Ⓑ son-in-law
   - Ⓒ grandson
   - Ⓓ son

4. Surname is another word for _____ name.
   - Ⓐ family
   - Ⓑ middle
   - Ⓒ first
   - Ⓓ full

5. My date of birth is _____.
   - Ⓐ 045-32-4025
   - Ⓑ 6/19/91
   - Ⓒ Los Angeles, CA
   - Ⓓ junc5@ail.com

6. These are my children. Ben is my son, and Betsy is my _____.
   - Ⓐ granddaughter
   - Ⓑ niece
   - Ⓒ daughter
   - Ⓓ parent

7. My _____ and I have been married for ten years.
   - Ⓐ husband
   - Ⓑ uncle
   - Ⓒ aunt
   - Ⓓ brother

8. My mother's daughter is my _____.
   - Ⓐ aunt
   - Ⓑ niece
   - Ⓒ sister
   - Ⓓ cousin

9. Every _____ has nine numbers.
   - Ⓐ area code
   - Ⓑ zip code
   - Ⓒ phone number
   - Ⓓ social security number

10. I have one brother. He's my only _____.
    - Ⓐ cousin
    - Ⓑ parent
    - Ⓒ sibling
    - Ⓓ child

11. The area code is part of the _____ number.
    - Ⓐ telephone
    - Ⓑ street
    - Ⓒ apartment
    - Ⓓ social security

12. My father's sister is my _____.
    - Ⓐ niece
    - Ⓑ aunt
    - Ⓒ grandmother
    - Ⓓ sister-in-law

13. Let me introduce my _____. She's my son's wife.
    - Ⓐ granddaughter
    - Ⓑ daughter
    - Ⓒ daughter-in-law
    - Ⓓ son-in-law

14. My sister is getting married next week. I'm going to have a new _____.
    - Ⓐ sister-in-law
    - Ⓑ brother
    - Ⓒ father-in-law
    - Ⓓ brother-in-law

(continued)

15. When you send a letter, write the ____ after the city and state.
- Ⓐ last name
- Ⓑ zip code
- Ⓒ apartment number
- Ⓓ area code

16. My ____ is on my social security card.
- Ⓐ middle initial
- Ⓑ date of birth
- Ⓒ place of birth
- Ⓓ address

Ⓑ CLOZE READING

My husband and I have two [children Ⓐ   grandparents Ⓑ   parents Ⓒ] [17]—a son John and a

daughter Carol. My daughter is married. She and her husband have three daughters. My

[uncle Ⓐ   brother-in-law Ⓑ   son-in-law Ⓒ] [18] is a wonderful father. My son John and his

[wife Ⓐ   mother Ⓑ   sister-in-law Ⓒ] [19] have a new [nephew Ⓐ   baby Ⓑ   brother Ⓒ] [20] named Timmy.

He's my only [grandson Ⓐ   granddaughter Ⓑ   son Ⓒ] [21]. My

[grandmother Ⓐ   niece Ⓑ   daughter-in-law Ⓒ] [22] enjoys being a mother. My

[mother-in-law Ⓐ   daughter Ⓑ   grandson Ⓒ] [23] lives with my husband and me. She always likes

to tell my husband what to do. She says, "He's still my [uncle Ⓐ   husband Ⓑ   son Ⓒ] [24], you know.

And I'm still his [sister Ⓐ   mother Ⓑ   aunt Ⓒ] [25]."

Ⓒ WHAT'S THE WORD?

address	area code	e-mail address	social security number
apartment number	date of birth	phone number	zip code

26. My _____ is 408.

27. Our _____ is 555-917-5360.

28. His _____ is luke87@abc.com.

29. Her _____ is 227-12-3456.

30. My _____ is 10/25/90.

31. Our _____ is 5G.

32. Their _____ is 32904.

33. My _____ is 127 Central Avenue.

D · WHAT'S THE WORD?

brother	father	grandchildren	nephews	sister	uncle
cousin	father-in-law	grandfather	parents	sister-in-law	

34. My wife's father is my _____.
35. My mother's father is my _____.
36. My brother's wife is my _____.
37. My brother's sons are my _____.
38. My niece's mother is my _____.
39. My cousin's father is my _____.
40. My mother and father are my _____.
41. My husband's _____ is my father-in-law.
42. My nephew is my niece's _____.
43. My children are my parents' _____.
44. My uncle's son is my _____.

E · WHAT'S THE ANSWER?

45. What's your last name? _____
46. What's your street number? _____
47. What's your city and state? _____
48. What's your zip code? _____
49. What's your date of birth? _____
50. What's your place of birth? _____

F · WRITING SAMPLE

Choose one of these topics and write a paragraph. Write on a separate sheet of paper.

- Who are the people in your family? What are their names? How old are they?
- Describe your mother's family or your father's family. Who are your relatives? Where do they live? Where were they born?

A) WHAT'S THE WORD?

1. Do you like to write with _____ or a pencil?
- Ⓐ a ruler
- Ⓑ an eraser
- Ⓒ a pen
- Ⓓ a board

2. For the next ten minutes, please work _____.
- Ⓐ each other
- Ⓑ in a group
- Ⓒ the question
- Ⓓ the answers

3. Before I pass out the tests, please take out a _____.
- Ⓐ mouse
- Ⓑ keyboard
- Ⓒ monitor
- Ⓓ piece of paper

4. _____ has small squares on it.
- Ⓐ Notebook paper
- Ⓑ Graph paper
- Ⓒ A globe
- Ⓓ A screen

5. I'm trying to find Nigeria on the _____.
- Ⓐ paper
- Ⓑ answer
- Ⓒ bulletin board
- Ⓓ map

6. Come into the classroom and take your _____.
- Ⓐ answer
- Ⓑ seat
- Ⓒ light
- Ⓓ desk

7. What's the _____ of this word?
- Ⓐ definition
- Ⓑ dictionary
- Ⓒ question
- Ⓓ answer

8. The school principal spoke to students on the _____.
- Ⓐ bulletin board
- Ⓑ overhead projector
- Ⓒ notebook
- Ⓓ loudspeaker

9. Write your answers on a separate _____.
- Ⓐ screen
- Ⓑ desk
- Ⓒ sheet of paper
- Ⓓ homework

10. Remember! You can't use _____ during the math test.
- Ⓐ chalk
- Ⓑ a calculator
- Ⓒ paper
- Ⓓ a map

11. You can put those papers in your _____.
- Ⓐ homework
- Ⓑ chair
- Ⓒ binder
- Ⓓ monitor

12. I can't see the _____. What time is it?
- Ⓐ clock
- Ⓑ workbook
- Ⓒ calculator
- Ⓓ notebook

13. You can use this eraser to clean the _____.
- Ⓐ printer
- Ⓑ chalkboard
- Ⓒ wastebasket
- Ⓓ monitor

14. We need more paper for the _____.
- Ⓐ overhead projector
- Ⓑ pencil sharpener
- Ⓒ printer
- Ⓓ dictionary

(continued)

15. Please _____ so we can see the movie.
    Ⓐ lower the shades
    Ⓑ open the door
    Ⓒ turn on the lights
    Ⓓ turn off the monitor

16. If you know the answer, please _____.
    Ⓐ sign it
    Ⓑ collect it
    Ⓒ raise your hand
    Ⓓ turn on the lights

17. Read your papers again and _____ your mistakes.
    Ⓐ write
    Ⓑ correct
    Ⓒ answer
    Ⓓ take

18. How do I _____ this word?
    Ⓐ put
    Ⓑ answer
    Ⓒ hand in
    Ⓓ pronounce

19. It's important to _____ while you read.
    Ⓐ take notes
    Ⓑ fill in
    Ⓒ repeat
    Ⓓ bubble

20. Please stand _____ and go to the board.
    Ⓐ in
    Ⓑ on
    Ⓒ up
    Ⓓ down

21. _____ the question with other students.
    Ⓐ Match
    Ⓑ Help
    Ⓒ Work
    Ⓓ Discuss

22. We always _____ our homework at the beginning of class.
    Ⓐ pass out
    Ⓑ hand in
    Ⓒ cross out
    Ⓓ choose

23. Use a pencil to _____.
    Ⓐ look in the dictionary
    Ⓑ turn off the lights
    Ⓒ mark the answer sheet
    Ⓓ write on the board

24. Please _____ your books during the test.
    Ⓐ go over
    Ⓑ write on
    Ⓒ spell
    Ⓓ close

25. Don't talk with your classmates. Please _____.
    Ⓐ work alone
    Ⓑ work together
    Ⓒ discuss the questions
    Ⓓ repeat the words

B WHAT'S THE WORD?

Break up	Fill in	Help	Open	Put	Turn off

26. _____ the lights.

27. _____ your books.

28. _____ each other.

29. _____ the blank.

30. _____ into small groups.

31. _____ the words in order.

C WHAT'S THE ANSWER?

Look in the dictionary.	Print your name.	Share a book.
No. Work as a class.	Read page 27.	Write on a separate piece of paper.

32. What's today's homework?   _____

33. What does "resident" mean?   _____

34. I don't have my book today.   _____

35. Should we work with a partner?   _____

36. Where do I write the answers?   _____

37. What do I write at the top of the page?   _____

D CLOZE READING

board   out   over   overhead projector   partner   turned on   unscramble   write

Today our teacher passed _____ ³⁸ our tests from last week. We

went _____ ³⁹ the correct answers. He asked several students to

_____ ⁴⁰ the answers on the _____ ⁴¹. After we finished,

he gave us a worksheet. We had to _____ ⁴² the words to make

sentences. We worked with a _____ ⁴³. Finally, our teacher

_____ ⁴⁴ the _____ ⁴⁵ and explained our next writing

assignment.

E WHAT'S THE WORD?

above   in   of   on   to

46. The globe is _____ the table.

47. The clock is _____ the screen.

48. Put these papers _____ the wastebasket.

49. I'm sitting in front _____ the monitor.

50. The teacher's aide is standing next _____ the map.

F WRITING SAMPLE

Choose one of these topics and write a paragraph. Write on a separate sheet of paper.

• What do you see in your classroom? Describe where things are.

• What happened in your class yesterday? What did you do? What did your teacher do?

Name _____

Date _____

A WHAT'S THE WORD?

1. I have to ____ to the store to buy some milk.
Ⓐ leave
Ⓑ wash
Ⓒ take
Ⓓ go

2. It's ____. It's a good day to go to the park.
Ⓐ sunny
Ⓑ windy
Ⓒ cold
Ⓓ hailing

3. While I'm on vacation, my neighbor is going to ____ my cats.
Ⓐ make
Ⓑ practice
Ⓒ feed
Ⓓ leave

4. My children ____ the bus to school every day.
Ⓐ drive
Ⓑ take
Ⓒ sleep
Ⓓ walk

5. I ____ TV after I finish my homework.
Ⓐ do
Ⓑ see
Ⓒ listen
Ⓓ watch

6. My father usually ____ the dishes.
Ⓐ goes
Ⓑ washes
Ⓒ irons
Ⓓ makes

7. Yesterday I ____ some flowers.
Ⓐ washed
Ⓑ practiced
Ⓒ planted
Ⓓ walked

8. My grandparents like to ____ cards with their friends.
Ⓐ play
Ⓑ read
Ⓒ do
Ⓓ swim

9. I ____ my laundry last night.
Ⓐ went
Ⓑ did
Ⓒ came
Ⓓ used

10. Ten degrees Celsius is about 50 degrees ____
Ⓐ Fahrenheit
Ⓑ Centigrade
Ⓒ cold
Ⓓ weather

11. He ____ the guitar for an hour every day.
Ⓐ washes
Ⓑ listens
Ⓒ works
Ⓓ practices

12. It isn't raining very hard today. It's ____.
Ⓐ sunny
Ⓑ drizzling
Ⓒ windy
Ⓓ snowing

13. I usually ____ a sandwich for lunch.
Ⓐ feed
Ⓑ use
Ⓒ make
Ⓓ get up

14. During the summer, the weather is often hot and ____.
Ⓐ cold
Ⓑ freezing
Ⓒ cool
Ⓓ humid

(continued)

15. It's important to _____ every day.
- Ⓐ exercise
- Ⓑ feed
- Ⓒ use
- Ⓓ take

16. I usually _____ lunch at 12:00.
- Ⓐ go
- Ⓑ have
- Ⓒ get up
- Ⓓ come

17. I like to sit in the park and _____.
- Ⓐ drive
- Ⓑ go
- Ⓒ put on
- Ⓓ relax

18. Ivan always _____ dressed before breakfast.
- Ⓐ goes
- Ⓑ does
- Ⓒ gets
- Ⓓ makes

19. Elena usually _____ on makeup before she goes to a party.
- Ⓐ does
- Ⓑ puts
- Ⓒ makes
- Ⓓ turns

20. Carl _____ his teeth three times a day.
- Ⓐ washes
- Ⓑ combs
- Ⓒ brushes
- Ⓓ takes

21. I'm busy right now. I'm _____ a letter.
- Ⓐ making
- Ⓑ playing
- Ⓒ driving
- Ⓓ writing

22. Sam sometimes _____ to bed after midnight.
- Ⓐ goes
- Ⓑ puts
- Ⓒ leaves
- Ⓓ turns

23. My son doesn't like to _____ a bath.
- Ⓐ wash
- Ⓑ make
- Ⓒ take
- Ⓓ get up

24. My mother always tells me to _____ my bed.
- Ⓐ do
- Ⓑ make
- Ⓒ sleep
- Ⓓ go

25. Your hair is messy. You need to _____ it.
- Ⓐ take
- Ⓑ meet
- Ⓒ make
- Ⓓ comb

Ⓑ WHAT'S THE WORD?

| hot | smoggy | snowstorm | thunderstorm |

26. The _____ was very loud.

27. It's 90 degrees today. It's _____.

28. The schools closed at 11:00 A.M. because of the _____.

29. Our town is often _____ because there's a big factory nearby.

C WHAT'S THE ANSWER?

Fine, thanks.	It's sleeting.	Hold on a minute, please.
Not much.	Nice to meet you.	Of course. I'll speak more slowly.
See you later.		

30. What's new?   _____

31. May I please speak with Tom?   _____

32. How's the weather?   _____

33. Good bye.   _____

34. Hi. I'm Sandra.   _____

35. How are you doing?   _____

36. Can you please repeat that?   _____

D CLOZE READING

clear	cold	got	lightning	played	swim	walked
cloudy	drove	left	listened	read	used	weather

On Saturday the _____ ³⁷ was sunny and _____ ³⁸, so our family

decided to go to the beach. We _____ ³⁹ the computer to find directions to

get there. We _____ ⁴⁰ the house at 10:30 and _____ ⁴¹ to the beach.

We didn't _____ ⁴² because the water was _____ ⁴³. I _____ ⁴⁴

my book, the children _____ ⁴⁵ football, and my husband _____ ⁴⁶ our

dog along the water. In the afternoon, the weather was _____ ⁴⁷. We

_____ ⁴⁸ to the weather forecast on the radio. When we heard "There's going to be

_____ ⁴⁹ this afternoon," we left the beach very quickly. We _____ ⁵⁰

home at about 4:00.

E WRITING SAMPLE

Choose one of these topics and write a paragraph. Write on a separate sheet of paper.

- What is your daily routine? What time do you get up? What do you usually have for breakfast? Tell all the things you do on a typical day.

- What do you usually do on the weekend? Do you work? Do you relax? Do you do laundry? Describe what you have to do and what you like to do on the weekend.

Name _____

Date _____

A WHAT'S THE WORD?

1. Tom lives on the _____ floor.
- Ⓐ third
- Ⓑ three
- Ⓒ thirteen
- Ⓓ one-third

2. How _____ are you?
- Ⓐ age
- Ⓑ old
- Ⓒ many years
- Ⓓ years old

3. This shirt costs forty-nine _____.
- Ⓐ bills
- Ⓑ dollar bills
- Ⓒ pennies
- Ⓓ dollars

4. Today's _____ is June seventh.
- Ⓐ date
- Ⓑ day
- Ⓒ time
- Ⓓ month

5. I drink coffee _____ morning.
- Ⓐ this
- Ⓑ once
- Ⓒ every
- Ⓓ twice

6. Our test will be _____ afternoon.
- Ⓐ today
- Ⓑ tomorrow
- Ⓒ yesterday
- Ⓓ next

7. My guitar class is every Monday evening. It's once _____.
- Ⓐ a day
- Ⓑ an hour
- Ⓒ a time
- Ⓓ a week

8. Today is Emily's _____ birthday.
- Ⓐ twenty-one
- Ⓑ twenty-one years
- Ⓒ twenty-first
- Ⓓ twenty-first years

9. It's eleven _____ at night.
- Ⓐ A.M.
- Ⓑ o'clock
- Ⓒ clocks
- Ⓓ hours

10. She plays tennis _____ a week.
- Ⓐ twice
- Ⓑ second
- Ⓒ two
- Ⓓ times

11. It's a quarter _____ three.
- Ⓐ from
- Ⓑ before
- Ⓒ after
- Ⓓ behind

12. The concert begins _____ 8:00 P.M.
- Ⓐ on
- Ⓑ at
- Ⓒ in
- Ⓓ from

13. One million is less than _____.
- Ⓐ one hundred
- Ⓑ one hundred thousand
- Ⓒ nine hundred thousand
- Ⓓ one billion

14. It's very cold in New York in the _____.
- Ⓐ months
- Ⓑ winter
- Ⓒ autumn
- Ⓓ seasons

(continued)

15. My parents will celebrate their _____ next month.
- (A) year
- (B) appointment
- (C) date of birth
- (D) anniversary

16. Spring is my favorite _____.
- (A) week
- (B) month
- (C) season
- (D) summer

B) CLOZE READING

Tomorrow I have to go to the bakery to buy a | birth (A)   calendar (B)   birthday (C) | **17** cake for my

son. He's going to be four | years (A)   years old (B)   age (C) | **18** on | May (A)   date of birth (B)   Saturday (C) | **19**.

I've invited ten people to the party. We've never had a party for him before, so this will be his

| one (A)   first (B)   fourth (C) | **20** party. It will start at | noon (A)   morning (B)   midnight (C) | **21** and end at about

| second (A)   twelve (B)   two (C) | **22** in the | afternoon (A)   night (B)   evening (C) | **23**. I'm sure the weather

will be warm because it's the | autumn (A)   summer (B)   winter (C) | **24**. The children will probably play

outside for about | an hour (A)   a time (B)   a day (C) | **25** before we have cake inside the house.

C) WHAT TIME IS IT?

| a quarter after seven | half past seven | six fifteen |
| a quarter to seven | midnight | six thirty |

26. _____

27. _____

28. _____

29. _____

30. _____

31. _____

D) WHAT'S THE WORD?

July	March	Saturday	Tuesday
June	May	Sunday	Thursday

32.–33. _____, Wednesday, _____

34.– 35. Friday, _____, _____

36.– 37. _____, _____, August

38.– 39. _____, April, _____

E) WHAT'S THE WORD?

dime	half	penny	twenty
fifty	nickel	quarter	twenty-five

40. A quarter is worth _____ cents.

41. A _____ is worth ten cents.

42. A nickel is worth more than a _____.

43. I have $1.50. I have a _____ dollar and a silver dollar.

44. A _____ and two quarters is $.55.

45. A _____ and five ones is fifty-five dollars.

46. Fifteen pennies, two dimes, and a _____ is sixty cents.

47. Here are four five-dollar bills. It's change for a _____.

F) WHAT'S THE ANSWER?

48. What day of the week was yesterday? _____

49. What's today's date? _____

50. What's your date of birth? Write it in numbers. _____

G) WRITING SAMPLE

Choose one of these topics and write a paragraph. Write on a separate sheet of paper.

- What are the important dates for you during the year? When is your birthday? What other birthdays or anniversaries do you celebrate? List as many important dates as you can.

- Write about your daily schedule. What time do you get up? When do you go to work or to school? How many days a week do you work or go to school? What time do you usually eat breakfast, lunch, and dinner? What time do you do other activities?

- How much money do you usually spend during a day? What do you buy? How much do these things cost? Do you usually pay with cash?

A) WHAT'S THE WORD?

1. I heard the ____. I think someone is here.
- Ⓐ speaker
- Ⓑ doorbell
- Ⓒ stereo system
- Ⓓ DVD player

2. We keep our ____ in the tool shed.
- Ⓐ lawnmower
- Ⓑ VCR
- Ⓒ painting
- Ⓓ cutting board

3. Many senior citizens live in a ____.
- Ⓐ bureau
- Ⓑ mobile home
- Ⓒ nursing home
- Ⓓ dining room

4. There's a large mirror on the ____ above the dresser in our bedroom.
- Ⓐ floor
- Ⓑ headboard
- Ⓒ carpet
- Ⓓ wall

5. Let's eat lunch outside on the ____.
- Ⓐ village
- Ⓑ carpet
- Ⓒ deck
- Ⓓ stroller

6. We have a long white ____ around our house.
- Ⓐ fence
- Ⓑ bed frame
- Ⓒ gutter
- Ⓓ playpen

7. We have ____ on the window in our bedroom.
- Ⓐ a fitted sheet
- Ⓑ a quilt
- Ⓒ a shower curtain
- Ⓓ blinds

8. When it rains, water comes out of the ____.
- Ⓐ shutter
- Ⓑ drainpipe
- Ⓒ blender
- Ⓓ rug

9. College students often live in a ____.
- Ⓐ dormitory
- Ⓑ wall unit
- Ⓒ shelter
- Ⓓ buffet

10. We have several ____ on the mantel.
- Ⓐ lampshades
- Ⓑ throw pillows
- Ⓒ forks
- Ⓓ photographs

11. Twenty families live in our ____.
- Ⓐ duplex
- Ⓑ apartment building
- Ⓒ two-family house
- Ⓓ suburb

12. I have a small ____ next to my sofa.
- Ⓐ mattress
- Ⓑ dust ruffle
- Ⓒ end table
- Ⓓ spice rack

13. We have a ____ on our roof.
- Ⓐ satellite dish
- Ⓑ fireplace screen
- Ⓒ faucet
- Ⓓ storm door

14. Every Sunday, I wash my car in the ____.
- Ⓐ chimney
- Ⓑ shower
- Ⓒ canister
- Ⓓ driveway

(continued)

15. Let's buy the _____. It's bigger than the loveseat.
- Ⓐ armchair
- Ⓑ stroller
- Ⓒ couch
- Ⓓ booster seat

16. Marta likes to relax outside on the _____.
- Ⓐ box spring
- Ⓑ front porch
- Ⓒ back door
- Ⓓ cradle

Ⓑ CLOZE READING

Every evening after dinner, my children and I clean the kitchen together. First, we carry

the dirty | drapes   plates   blankets | ¹⁷ from the kitchen | table   towel   chair | ¹⁸ to the
            Ⓐ   Ⓑ   Ⓒ   Ⓐ   Ⓑ   Ⓒ

| range   sink   china cabinet | ¹⁹. My son puts them in the | disposal   oven   dishwasher | ²⁰.
  Ⓐ   Ⓑ   Ⓒ   Ⓐ   Ⓑ   Ⓒ

Then he washes the pots and pans and puts them in the | dish drainer   potholder   burner | ²¹.
                                                        Ⓐ   Ⓑ   Ⓒ

I put food into the | mixer   refrigerator   food processor | ²², and I put trash in the
                      Ⓐ   Ⓑ   Ⓒ

| tray   freezer   garbage pail | ²³. I also clean the stove and counters with a
  Ⓐ   Ⓑ   Ⓒ

| spoon   sponge   soap dish | ²⁴. My daughter takes the | placemats   pillows   bumpers | ²⁵
  Ⓐ   Ⓑ   Ⓒ   Ⓐ   Ⓑ   Ⓒ

off the table and puts them in a drawer. It doesn't take a long time to clean when everybody

helps.

Ⓒ WHAT IS IT?

| hamper | plunger | scale | wastebasket |
| medicine cabinet | rubber mat | soap | |

26. You use this to wash your hands. _____

27. People put their dirty clothes in this. _____

28. This tells you how much you weigh. _____

29. You use this to fix your toilet. _____

30. Many people keep aspirin and toothpaste here. _____

31. You put your trash here. _____

32. If you put this in the bathtub, you won't fall when you take a shower. _____

D WHAT'S THE WORD?

| alarm clock | comforter | napkin | pitcher | saucer | tablecloth |
| chandelier | mattress | nightstand | platter | serving bowl | vase |

33. We have a large glass _____ over our dining room table.

34. I put some fresh flowers in the _____.

35. Our _____ rings every morning at 6:30 A.M.

36. I just bought a striped yellow _____ to put on the dining room table.

37. There's a _____ of water on the buffet.

38. We have a small _____ next to our bed.

39. He put the meat on a large _____.

40. I need a _____ to put under my cup.

41. During the winter, I use a _____ on my bed.

42. Please put the green beans in a _____.

43. Could you give me a _____? I spilled some water.

44. A fitted sheet covers the _____.

E CLOZE READING

| baby monitor | crib | changing table | chest | playpen | stuffed animals |

My wife and I are going to have a new baby boy soon, so we're preparing his room. We bought a _____ ⁴⁵ for him to sleep in and a small _____ ⁴⁶ for his clothes. We also bought a _____ ⁴⁷ to use when we change his diapers and pajamas. When he's older, he can stand up in his _____ ⁴⁸ and play with his _____ ⁴⁹. At night, we can listen to him on the _____ ⁵⁰.

F WRITING SAMPLE

Choose one of these topics and write a paragraph. Write on a separate sheet of paper.

- What kind of community do you live in? Describe your neighborhood. Tell about the kinds of buildings and homes. Describe one building in detail.

- What's your favorite room in your home? Describe it. Include as many details as possible. Why do you enjoy this room?

- Describe the outside of your home. What kind of building is it? What's in the front, on the side, and in back? Give as many details as you can.

A WHAT'S THE WORD?

1. I always look through the _____ before I open my front door.
   Ⓐ door chain
   Ⓑ peephole
   Ⓒ smoke detector
   Ⓓ key

2. After dinner, my wife and I like to sit on our _____.
   Ⓐ storage locker
   Ⓑ trash bin
   Ⓒ balcony
   Ⓓ hedge

3. There are many apartments in the _____.
   Ⓐ classified ads
   Ⓑ vacancy sign
   Ⓒ superintendent
   Ⓓ moving van

4. Please put the garbage into the _____.
   Ⓐ swimming pool
   Ⓑ dustpan
   Ⓒ trash chute
   Ⓓ hand vacuum

5. There are several benches and trees in the _____ behind our building.
   Ⓐ fire escape
   Ⓑ courtyard
   Ⓒ sprinkler system
   Ⓓ lobby

6. I feel safe because we have a _____ in the basement of our building.
   Ⓐ chimney
   Ⓑ mousetrap
   Ⓒ laundry room
   Ⓓ security gate

7. We send a check for the rent to our _____ every month.
   Ⓐ landlord
   Ⓑ tenant
   Ⓒ neighbor
   Ⓓ doorman

8. In an apartment building, every floor must have two _____.
   Ⓐ keys
   Ⓑ fire exits
   Ⓒ signs
   Ⓓ elevators

9. Each tenant has two parking _____.
   Ⓐ lots
   Ⓑ meters
   Ⓒ garages
   Ⓓ spaces

10. I live on the twentieth floor, so I usually use the _____.
   Ⓐ buzzer
   Ⓑ elevator
   Ⓒ stairway
   Ⓓ whirlpool

11. Our front door key doesn't work. We need to call _____.
   Ⓐ a plumber
   Ⓑ a painter
   Ⓒ an appliance repairperson
   Ⓓ a locksmith

12. This room is very hot. It's too bad we don't have _____.
   Ⓐ a flyswatter
   Ⓑ an electrician
   Ⓒ an air conditioner
   Ⓓ a heating system

13. Call the exterminator! There are _____ in the house.
   Ⓐ fleas
   Ⓑ tiles
   Ⓒ steps
   Ⓓ weeds

14. I signed the _____ and paid a security deposit.
   Ⓐ level
   Ⓑ listing
   Ⓒ lease
   Ⓓ mailbox

(continued)

15. When it rains, our roof _____.
    Ⓐ cracks
    Ⓑ leaks
    Ⓒ breaks
    Ⓓ peels

16. _____ are small insects that eat wood.
    Ⓐ Mice
    Ⓑ Rats
    Ⓒ Termites
    Ⓓ Cockroaches

17. I _____ the furniture once a week.
    Ⓐ dust
    Ⓑ mop
    Ⓒ wash
    Ⓓ dry

18. Use this _____ to clean the sink.
    Ⓐ scraper
    Ⓑ scrub brush
    Ⓒ feather duster
    Ⓓ pail

19. Tim painted his room with a _____.
    Ⓐ wet mop
    Ⓑ whisk broom
    Ⓒ paint thinner
    Ⓓ spray gun

20. A _____ is a gardening tool.
    Ⓐ vise
    Ⓑ sponge
    Ⓒ rake
    Ⓓ recycling bin

21. Anna used _____ to fix her door.
    Ⓐ a hose
    Ⓑ a screwdriver
    Ⓒ a plunger
    Ⓓ an ax

22. I always keep pliers and a wrench in my
    _____.
    Ⓐ gas can
    Ⓑ yard waste bag
    Ⓒ toolbox
    Ⓓ nozzle

23. There are ants in the bathroom! Where's
    the _____?
    Ⓐ roofer
    Ⓑ oil
    Ⓒ glue
    Ⓓ insect spray

24. It's important to _____ the vegetable seeds
    we planted last week.
    Ⓐ mow
    Ⓑ water
    Ⓒ trim
    Ⓓ prune

25. All the houses in our neighborhood are
    dark. The _____ is out.
    Ⓐ heating system
    Ⓑ cable TV
    Ⓒ battery
    Ⓓ power

Ⓑ **WHAT THE WORD?**

blower	can	cord	electric	step	tape

26. watering _____

27. _____ drill

28. leaf _____

29. _____ measure

30. extension _____

31. _____ ladder

C WHAT'S THE WORD?

broom	hammer	saw	sprinkler	wheelbarrow
flashlight	plunger	shovel	trowel	

32. I use a _____ when I want to water the yard.

33. Where's the _____? I need to cut some wood.

34. You can use this _____ to sweep the floor.

35. If you want to fix this table, you'll need nails and a _____.

36. The toilet isn't working. Where's the _____?

37. Here! You can dig a big hole with this _____.

38. It's dark and I can't see. Where's the _____?

39. You can carry a lot of heavy things in a _____.

40. I use a _____ when I plant flowers.

D CLOZE READING

appliance	cracked	peeling	repairs
broken	dead-bolt lock	plumber	toilet
clogged	handyman		

I have many _____ ⁴¹ to do at my house. The paint on the outside is

_____ ⁴², so I'm sure I'll have to paint it soon. Also, the front steps are

_____ ⁴³, and the wall in the living room is _____ ⁴⁴. I need to call

a _____ ⁴⁵ to fix those things. Next, I need to put a new _____ ⁴⁶

on my front door. The oven isn't working very well, so I need to call the _____ ⁴⁷

repairperson. Also, the kitchen sink is _____ ⁴⁸ and the _____ ⁴⁹ leaks. I

can't fix those things myself, so I'm going to call the _____ ⁵⁰.

E WRITING SAMPLE

Choose one of these topics and write a paragraph. Write on a separate sheet of paper.

- Do you live in an apartment building? Describe the building, the lobby, the basement, and the outside areas. Include as many details as possible.

- What do you usually do to clean your home? Do you mop, vacuum, and dust? What else do you do? What do you do every week? every month? What cleaning supplies to you use?

- What repairs have you recently done in your home? What tools and supplies did you use?

Name _____

Date _____

A WHAT'S THE WORD?

1. Vinh bought medicine at the _____.
   - Ⓐ pharmacy
   - Ⓑ newsstand
   - Ⓒ florist
   - Ⓓ police station

2. There's a big sale on sofas at the _____.
   - Ⓐ clothing store
   - Ⓑ video store
   - Ⓒ furniture store
   - Ⓓ shoe store

3. I bought my grandson a stuffed animal at the _____.
   - Ⓐ electronics store
   - Ⓑ child-care center
   - Ⓒ office building
   - Ⓓ toy store

4. The man at the _____ fixed my watch.
   - Ⓐ nail salon
   - Ⓑ jewelry store
   - Ⓒ post office
   - Ⓓ taxi stand

5. I bought this hat from a _____.
   - Ⓐ street vendor
   - Ⓑ street light
   - Ⓒ meter maid
   - Ⓓ bus driver

6. Usually only men go to a _____.
   - Ⓐ car dealership
   - Ⓑ hair salon
   - Ⓒ barber shop
   - Ⓓ department store

7. I decided to use the _____ at the bank because it was raining.
   - Ⓐ library
   - Ⓑ drive-through window
   - Ⓒ sewer
   - Ⓓ street light

8. A _____ is a very large grocery store.
   - Ⓐ fast-food restaurant
   - Ⓑ convenience store
   - Ⓒ mall
   - Ⓓ supermarket

9. A taxi is also called a _____.
   - Ⓐ bus
   - Ⓑ curb
   - Ⓒ cab
   - Ⓓ taxi driver

10. Please get some ham and turkey at the _____.
    - Ⓐ donut shop
    - Ⓑ delicatessen
    - Ⓒ pizza shop
    - Ⓓ candy store

11. They can fix your car at the _____.
    - Ⓐ parking lot
    - Ⓑ taxi stand
    - Ⓒ bus stop
    - Ⓓ service station

12. A _____ carries water under the street.
    - Ⓐ sewer
    - Ⓑ street light
    - Ⓒ public telephone
    - Ⓓ subway

13. I'm going to the _____ today to get new glasses.
    - Ⓐ deli
    - Ⓑ optician
    - Ⓒ card store
    - Ⓓ restaurant

14. Margarita is pregnant so she shops at a _____.
    - Ⓐ clinic
    - Ⓑ hospital
    - Ⓒ maternity shop
    - Ⓓ shoe store

(continued)

15. A traffic light is also called a traffic _____.
  Ⓐ sign
  Ⓑ signal
  Ⓒ officer
  Ⓓ meter

16. Those men are putting the trash into the _____.
  Ⓐ hospital
  Ⓑ school
  Ⓒ fire hydrant
  Ⓓ garbage truck

B) CLOZE READING

Yesterday I drove downtown to go shopping. I needed to buy some CDs at the

copy center	music store	ice cream shop
Ⓐ	Ⓑ	Ⓒ

^{17}. I also had to pick up my plane tickets

at the

movie theater	train station	travel agency
Ⓐ	Ⓑ	Ⓒ

^{18}. I usually park my car in the

parking garage	crosswalk	police station
Ⓐ	Ⓑ	Ⓒ

^{19}, but it was full. After 10 minutes,

I found a parking space on the

subway station	street	mailbox
Ⓐ	Ⓑ	Ⓒ

^{20} in front of the

fire hydrant	fire station	courthouse
Ⓐ	Ⓑ	Ⓒ

^{21}. I put money in the parking

meter	lot	box
Ⓐ	Ⓑ	Ⓒ

^{22}.

After I did my errands, I had coffee at the

hardware store	donut shop	library
Ⓐ	Ⓑ	Ⓒ

^{23}.

Finally, I bought some flowers at the

florist	drug store	photo shop
Ⓐ	Ⓑ	Ⓒ

^{24}. Later, when

I was walking back to my car, I saw the meter

police	driver	maid
Ⓐ	Ⓑ	Ⓒ

^{25}. She was

giving me a ticket. It wasn't a good day for me.

C) WHAT'S THE WORD?

clinic	coffee shop	discount store	health club	hotel	laundromat

26. Sam exercises at the _____ after work every day.

27. Ana went to the _____ to see the doctor.

28. Do you prefer to stay in a motel or a _____?

29. A _____ has lower prices than a department store.

30. You can wash and dry your clothes at the _____.

31. On Saturdays, I have breakfast at a _____.

D   WHAT'S THE WORD?

crosswalk	manhole	stop
fire alarm box	public telephone	subway
intersection	sidewalk	trash container
jail		

32. There's a mailbox on the _____ in front of city hall.
33. You can call me from the _____ next to the bank.
34. Several children are waiting for the school bus at the bus _____.
35. If you see smoke, use the _____.
36. The _____ is the new building behind the courthouse.
37. I like to read the newspaper while I ride the _____ to work.
38. There's a gas station at the _____ of Pine Street and Main Street.
39. The city workers opened the _____ and climbed down into it.
40. Put your old newspaper in the _____.
41. Pedestrians should always cross the street at the _____.

E   MATCHING: *Where Are They?*

clothing store	electronics store	pet store
convenience store	hardware store	restaurant
day-care center	park	video store

42. birds and fish _____
43. waiters and cooks _____
44. TVs and radios _____
45. trees and flowers _____
46. hammers and nails _____

47. movies and DVDs _____
48. milk and bread _____
49. pants and suits _____
50. children and toys _____

F   WRITING SAMPLE

Choose one of these topics and write a paragraph. Write on a separate sheet of paper.

- Describe an area in your city or town. Tell about the stores and services that are there.
- Write about your favorite shopping mall. What department stores are in the mall? What other stores and restaurants are there?

A) WHAT'S THE WORD?

1. _____ are 13 to 19 years old.
  Ⓐ Boys
  Ⓑ Teenagers
  Ⓒ Toddlers
  Ⓓ Children

2. My niece is _____. She's two months old.
  Ⓐ an infant
  Ⓑ a boy
  Ⓒ a woman
  Ⓓ a senior citizen

3. Is your son's hair _____ or straight?
  Ⓐ thick
  Ⓑ shoulder length
  Ⓒ heavy
  Ⓓ curly

4. Armando isn't very tall. He's average _____.
  Ⓐ short
  Ⓑ age
  Ⓒ height
  Ⓓ weight

5. Please put the _____ clothes in the washer.
  Ⓐ soft
  Ⓑ neat
  Ⓒ little
  Ⓓ dirty

6. Your cup is _____. Would you like some more coffee?
  Ⓐ hot
  Ⓑ full
  Ⓒ empty
  Ⓓ clean

7. I couldn't sleep last night. The people next door were playing _____ music.
  Ⓐ loud
  Ⓑ soft
  Ⓒ inexpensive
  Ⓓ crooked

8. Uncle Charles can't walk. He's _____.
  Ⓐ hearing impaired
  Ⓑ physically challenged
  Ⓒ vision impaired
  Ⓓ bald

9. After I washed my car, it was _____.
  Ⓐ dull
  Ⓑ rich
  Ⓒ shiny
  Ⓓ light

10. I really don't want to go out tonight. I'm too _____.
  Ⓐ thin
  Ⓑ bored
  Ⓒ excited
  Ⓓ tired

11. I often have problems with my car because it's very _____.
  Ⓐ new
  Ⓑ old
  Ⓒ plain
  Ⓓ thin

12. I'm going to wear a _____ dress to my son's wedding.
  Ⓐ fancy
  Ⓑ wealthy
  Ⓒ thick
  Ⓓ tall

13. It's getting _____. Let's turn on the lights.
  Ⓐ early
  Ⓑ low
  Ⓒ dark
  Ⓓ black

14. Your room is very _____. Please clean it up.
  Ⓐ messy
  Ⓑ clean
  Ⓒ neat
  Ⓓ crooked

(continued)

15. This knife is too ____. I need a sharper one.
   Ⓐ thin
   Ⓑ smooth
   Ⓒ new
   Ⓓ dull

16. Eric was ____ because he didn't know many people.
   Ⓐ full
   Ⓑ lonely
   Ⓒ happy
   Ⓓ rich

17. Susan is ____ about her interview.
   Ⓐ nervous
   Ⓑ bad
   Ⓒ bored
   Ⓓ homesick

18. I'm ____. All my friends will be at my birthday party.
   Ⓐ worried
   Ⓑ sleepy
   Ⓒ excited
   Ⓓ disappointed

19. Marvin has a cough and a terrible headache. He's ____.
   Ⓐ rough
   Ⓑ miserable
   Ⓒ difficult
   Ⓓ empty

20. I'd like some water. I'm ____.
   Ⓐ cold
   Ⓑ dry
   Ⓒ thirsty
   Ⓓ hungry

21. Timothy feels ____ when he drives over high bridges.
   Ⓐ mad
   Ⓑ young
   Ⓒ disgusted
   Ⓓ scared

22. I was ____ when my boyfriend said he didn't love me.
   Ⓐ shocked
   Ⓑ honest
   Ⓒ sleepy
   Ⓓ comfortable

23. The shelf is too ____. You need a ladder.
   Ⓐ low
   Ⓑ short
   Ⓒ small
   Ⓓ high

24. I was ____ when I couldn't hit the tennis ball.
   Ⓐ noisy
   Ⓑ crooked
   Ⓒ frustrated
   Ⓓ wide

25. Tom was ____ when his brother didn't call him back.
   Ⓐ bored
   Ⓑ annoyed
   Ⓒ bad
   Ⓓ ill

Ⓑ WHAT THE OPPOSITE?

hard	rich	tall	thin	tight	young

26. _____ old

27. _____ short

28. _____ heavy

29. _____ poor

30. _____ soft

31. _____ loose

C WHAT'S THE WORD?

angry	dishonest	jealous	noisy	single
confused	homesick	narrow	proud	uncomfortable

32. When I was a child, I was always _____ when I stayed with my cousins.

33. Richard is _____. Someone stole his bicycle while he was in the library.

34. You're too _____! Please be quiet.

35. Sarah is an excellent student. Her parents are very _____ of her.

36. I'm _____. My friend's car is much nicer than mine.

37. It's _____ to take something that isn't yours.

38. I don't think we should buy this sofa. It's very _____.

39. Carlos is _____, but he wants to get married in the future.

40. I'm _____. Should I turn right or left?

41. This street is too _____ for such a wide truck.

D CLOZE READING

closed	embarrassed	hungry	surprised	worried
difficult	exhausted	sick	wet	

I had a busy day today. This morning, I went to a coffee shop with my friends.
I spilled my coffee on the table, and our books were all _____⁴². I was so
_____⁴³! At 9:00, I had a very _____⁴⁴ test. I'm
_____⁴⁵ about my grade. After the test, I went to my next class, but the door
was _____⁴⁶. I was _____⁴⁷ to learn that my instructor was
_____⁴⁸. We didn't have class, so I went to the library. At 1:00, I went to lunch
because I was very _____⁴⁹. After that, I went to the gym and exercised for two
hours. Now I'm _____⁵⁰.

E WRITING SAMPLE

Choose one of these topics and write a paragraph. Write on a separate sheet of paper.

- Describe the people in your family. Give as many details as possible.
- Describe a room in your home. Is it large or small? Is the furniture comfortable? Is it a quiet room? Give as many details as you can.

Name _____

Date _____

A) WHAT'S THE WORD?

1. My favorite fruit is _____.
- (A) bacon
- (B) zucchini
- (C) corn
- (D) cantaloupe

2. You can find apples in the _____ Section.
- (A) Meat
- (B) Poultry
- (C) Produce
- (D) Canned Goods

3. Please buy some _____ for a salad.
- (A) soup and crackers
- (B) lettuce and tomatoes
- (C) fish and lemons
- (D) milk and eggs

4. Would you like some _____ for a snack?
- (A) pretzels
- (B) onions
- (C) olive oil
- (D) parsley

5. The deli has very good _____.
- (A) frozen dinners
- (B) nuts
- (C) cole slaw
- (D) broccoli

6. _____ is a type of poultry.
- (A) Ham
- (B) Turkey
- (C) Ground beef
- (D) Trout

7. You can find _____ in the Condiments Section.
- (A) mustard and ketchup
- (B) ribs and sausages
- (C) rice and noodles
- (D) sugar and cake mix

8. _____ is usually green.
- (A) A carrot
- (B) A cucumber
- (C) An eggplant
- (D) A cauliflower

9. My mother's favorite meat is _____.
- (A) catfish
- (B) tofu
- (C) roast beef
- (D) macaroni

10. A _____ is a delicious fruit.
- (A) peach
- (B) pea
- (C) beet
- (D) garlic

11. You can find _____ in the household supplies aisle.
- (A) formula
- (B) cat food
- (C) aluminum foil
- (D) magazines

12. Please buy more _____ for the baby.
- (A) candy
- (B) coffee
- (C) chewing gum
- (D) diapers

13. We need two _____ of butter.
- (A) rolls
- (B) sticks
- (C) bottles
- (D) cans

14. _____ is not a dairy product.
- (A) Sour cream
- (B) Yogurt
- (C) Skim milk
- (D) Fruit punch

(continued)

15. I have a bad cold. Would you buy me some
_____?
Ⓐ jelly
Ⓑ tissues
Ⓒ coupons
Ⓓ paper towels

16. _____ are paper products.
Ⓐ Trash bags
Ⓑ Pickles
Ⓒ Napkins
Ⓓ Rolls

17. Provolone and mozzarella are kinds
of _____.
Ⓐ fruit
Ⓑ meat
Ⓒ fish
Ⓓ cheese

18. We need some _____ to bake cookies.
Ⓐ flour
Ⓑ relish
Ⓒ salsa
Ⓓ flounder

B) CLOZE READING

Carlos is 15 years old. He works at the supermarket downtown after school and on the

weekends. He's a | patron   bagger   manager | 19 at the checkout | counter   belt   aisle | 20.
　　　　　　　　　　　Ⓐ　　　　Ⓑ　　　　Ⓒ　　　　　　　　　　　　　　Ⓐ　　　Ⓑ　　Ⓒ

Before he starts to pack the groceries, he always asks if the | clerk   cashier   customer | 21 wants
　　　　　　　　　　　　　　　　　　　　　　　　　　　　　　　　　　Ⓐ　　　Ⓑ　　　Ⓒ

paper or | trash   plastic   aluminum | 22 bags. When a bag is full, he puts it into the
　　　　　　Ⓐ　　　Ⓑ　　　Ⓒ

| conveyor belt   scanner   shopping cart | 23. Carlos likes his job, but he hopes to become a
　Ⓐ　　　　　　　Ⓑ　　　　Ⓒ

| packer   cashier   shopper | 24 next year. He wants to learn how to use the
　Ⓐ　　　Ⓑ　　　Ⓒ

| cash register   checkout line   shopping basket | 25, and he wants to earn more money.
　Ⓐ　　　　　　Ⓑ　　　　　　Ⓒ

C) WHAT'S THE WORD?

| bag   bunch   can   carton   container   head   jar   loaf   roll   six-pack |

26. a _____ of bread
27. a _____ of milk
28. a _____ of jam
29. a _____ of tuna fish
30. a _____ of bananas

31. a _____ of cabbage
32. a _____ of soda
33. a _____ of yogurt
34. a _____ of rice
35. a _____ of paper towels

D) WHAT'S THE WORD?

fish	mix	soap	watermelon
margarine	scale	shellfish	wrap

36. The cashier is weighing a customer's produce on the _____.
37. Some people use _____ instead of butter.
38. A _____ is a large fruit.
39. Scallops and clams are _____.
40. Haddock and salmon are _____.
41. We need to buy liquid _____ at the supermarket.
42. It's easy to bake a cake when you use a cake _____.
43. May I have some plastic _____ to cover this food?

beef	cheese	salad	wings
butter	chops	sauce	

44. I like to put soy _____ on cooked vegetables.
45. You can find potato _____ in the Deli Section.
46. My children love peanut _____ sandwiches.
47. We need to buy some more Swiss _____.
48. My family has roast _____ for special dinners.
49. Chicken _____ are a popular appetizer.
50. I have an excellent recipe for pork _____.

E) WRITING SAMPLE

Choose one of these topics and write a paragraph. Write on a separate sheet of paper.

- What do you have in your refrigerator? What do you need to buy at the supermarket?
- What are your favorite foods? Write about your favorite fruit, vegetable, dairy product, snack food, baked good, and meat or fish.
- What do you usually have for breakfast? for lunch? for a snack? Tell about the foods you eat on a typical day.

(A) WHAT'S THE WORD?

1. You must _____ a banana before you eat it.
   - (A) chop
   - (B) serve
   - (C) peel
   - (D) grate

2. The recipe says to _____ three eggs into a bowl.
   - (A) break
   - (B) boil
   - (C) broil
   - (D) bake

3. I like to _____ chicken in a little oil.
   - (A) steam
   - (B) boil
   - (C) fry
   - (D) slice

4. I baked the cookies on a cookie _____.
   - (A) cutter
   - (B) sheet
   - (C) rack
   - (D) pot

5. Use some water to _____ the carrots.
   - (A) chop up
   - (B) cut
   - (C) add
   - (D) steam

6. Turn over the pancakes with a _____.
   - (A) spatula
   - (B) peeler
   - (C) beater
   - (D) rolling pin

7. Maria likes to _____ steak outside on the patio.
   - (A) bake
   - (B) grill
   - (C) simmer
   - (D) microwave

8. Would you please _____ some water for hot tea?
   - (A) saute
   - (B) stir
   - (C) bake
   - (D) boil

9. Do you have a can _____ for this can of soup?
   - (A) pan
   - (B) press
   - (C) opener
   - (D) strainer

10. Beat the eggs with a _____.
    - (A) whisk
    - (B) butter knife
    - (C) teaspoon
    - (D) straw

11. I need a _____ to cover the pot.
    - (A) tray
    - (B) wok
    - (C) ladle
    - (D) lid

12. I'd like some _____ on my sandwich.
    - (A) jello
    - (B) mustard
    - (C) soda
    - (D) french fries

13. Here's a _____ to peel the apples.
    - (A) dinner fork
    - (B) plastic spoon
    - (C) paring knife
    - (D) carving knife

14. After you boil the noodles, pour them into a _____.
    - (A) double boiler
    - (B) measuring spoon
    - (C) dinner plate
    - (D) colander

(continued)

15. A _____ is a popular breakfast food.
    Ⓐ hot dog
    Ⓑ BLT
    Ⓒ waffle
    Ⓓ chicken sandwich

16. _____ is a breakfast meat.
    Ⓐ Bacon
    Ⓑ A bagel
    Ⓒ Roast beef
    Ⓓ Shrimp cocktail

17. My favorite appetizer is _____.
    Ⓐ pudding
    Ⓑ nachos
    Ⓒ meatloaf
    Ⓓ baked potatoes

18. I don't eat meat, so I'd like _____.
    Ⓐ a hot dog
    Ⓑ a cheeseburger
    Ⓒ a corned beef sandwich
    Ⓓ an egg salad sandwich

19. What kind of bread do you want—white bread or _____?
    Ⓐ a danish
    Ⓑ whole wheat
    Ⓒ a taco
    Ⓓ biscuit

20. The waiter brought us a _____ with warm rolls.
    Ⓐ menu
    Ⓑ booth
    Ⓒ dessert cart
    Ⓓ bread basket

21. The waitress brought me a _____ of chili.
    Ⓐ bowl
    Ⓑ pot
    Ⓒ saucepan
    Ⓓ casserole dish

22. I'll have _____ for dessert.
    Ⓐ an antipasto
    Ⓑ a burrito
    Ⓒ a veal cutlet
    Ⓓ some apple pie

23. Today's special entree is _____.
    Ⓐ fruit cup
    Ⓑ broiled fish
    Ⓒ frozen yogurt
    Ⓓ mixed vegetables

24. Please pass me a _____ for my milkshake.
    Ⓐ check
    Ⓑ saucer
    Ⓒ straw
    Ⓓ knife

25. In a restaurant, diners usually leave a _____ for the server.
    Ⓐ menu
    Ⓑ tip
    Ⓒ tray
    Ⓓ check

Ⓑ WHAT THE OPPOSITE?

a cup	a gallon	a pound	a pint	a quart	a tablespoon

26. 3 teaspoons = _____

27. 16 ounces = _____

28. 8 fluid ounces = _____

29. 16 fluid ounces = _____

30. 32 fluid ounces = _____

31. 128 fluid ounces = _____

C WHAT'S THE WORD?

add	microwave	simmer
bake	mix	slice
grate	roast	stir-fry

32. Let's _____ some salt and pepper to the soup.

33. For the salad dressing, _____ together oil, vinegar, and spices.

34. My grandmother loves to _____ pies and cakes.

35. This muffin is frozen. We need to _____ it.

36. Would you please _____ this loaf of bread?

37. To cook something very slowly, _____ it on the stove.

38. The best way to cook a turkey is to _____ it in the oven.

39. I need to _____ cheese for the pizza.

40. For a healthy meal, I like to _____ vegetables and tofu in a wok.

D CLOZE READING

booster seats	cleared	hostess	poured	seat
chef	dining room	patrons	salad bar	set

Sandra is the _____ ⁴¹ at the Lakeview Restaurant. She is usually able to

_____ ⁴² customers at tables right away. But last night many _____ ⁴³

had to wait for tables. It was a very busy night, and Sandra had to do many jobs. To help the

servers, Sandra _____ ⁴⁴ water into the glasses and brought _____ ⁴⁵

for small children. Every busperson worked very hard. They _____ ⁴⁶ the dirty

dishes and _____ ⁴⁷ new tables. Sandra had to go to the kitchen several times to

tell the _____ ⁴⁸ that the _____ ⁴⁹ was out of lettuce and dressing.

At 9:30 P.M., the _____ ⁵⁰ was quiet and everything was going well.

E WRITING SAMPLE

Choose one of these topics and write a paragraph. Write on a separate sheet of paper.

• What can you cook or bake? Write the recipe: make a list of the ingredients and write the instructions.

• Describe your favorite restaurant. Does the restaurant have booths? a salad bar? a dessert cart? What do you usually order?

A WHAT'S THE WORD?

1. Pablo wore a _____ to his job interview at the First National Bank.
   - Ⓐ tunic
   - Ⓑ trench coat
   - Ⓒ coat and tie
   - Ⓓ jogging suit

2. I usually wear a _____ on a warm day.
   - Ⓐ short-sleeved shirt
   - Ⓑ blazer
   - Ⓒ V-necked sweater
   - Ⓓ long-sleeved shirt

3. I wear _____ on my hands when it's cold.
   - Ⓐ ear muffs
   - Ⓑ beads
   - Ⓒ loafers
   - Ⓓ mittens

4. My grandfather usually puts on his pajamas and _____ after dinner.
   - Ⓐ camisole
   - Ⓑ bathrobe
   - Ⓒ slip
   - Ⓓ leotard

5. Some men wear a _____ when they go to a wedding.
   - Ⓐ muffler
   - Ⓑ jumper
   - Ⓒ tuxedo
   - Ⓓ cover up

6. It's going to rain today. You should wear your _____.
   - Ⓐ poncho
   - Ⓑ ski mask
   - Ⓒ umbrella
   - Ⓓ pantyhose

7. Please hang the wet laundry on the _____.
   - Ⓐ drawer
   - Ⓑ clothesline
   - Ⓒ dryer
   - Ⓓ lint trap

8. I was cold, so I put on a _____.
   - Ⓐ tank top
   - Ⓑ camisole
   - Ⓒ sweatband
   - Ⓓ sweatshirt

9. I like to wear lycra _____ when I ride my bicycle.
   - Ⓐ boots
   - Ⓑ slacks
   - Ⓒ shorts
   - Ⓓ sunglasses

10. Ana is a high school principal. She usually wears a _____ to work.
    - Ⓐ suit
    - Ⓑ robe
    - Ⓒ running suit
    - Ⓓ jumpsuit

11. A _____ doesn't have any sleeves.
    - Ⓐ T-shirt
    - Ⓑ blanket sleeper
    - Ⓒ coat
    - Ⓓ vest

12. My doctor says I should always wear _____ when I go for a long walk.
    - Ⓐ moccasins
    - Ⓑ athletic shoes
    - Ⓒ flip-flops
    - Ⓓ slippers

13. Put on your _____. We're going to the beach today.
    - Ⓐ down jacket
    - Ⓑ ankle socks
    - Ⓒ overalls
    - Ⓓ bathing suit

14. I need to take this shirt to the cleaners. It's _____.
    - Ⓐ blue
    - Ⓑ stained
    - Ⓒ patterned
    - Ⓓ cotton

(continued)

15. My husband wears a _____ on his left hand.
- Ⓐ wedding band
- Ⓑ key ring
- Ⓒ cuff link
- Ⓓ wallet

16. _____ is a type of material.
- Ⓐ Floral
- Ⓑ Medium
- Ⓒ Silk
- Ⓓ Cardigan

17. Helen has a beautiful _____ on her wrist.
- Ⓐ ring
- Ⓑ pin
- Ⓒ barrette
- Ⓓ bracelet

18. Evelyn wears _____ around her neck.
- Ⓐ pumps
- Ⓑ beads
- Ⓒ high-tops
- Ⓓ high heels

B CLOZE READING

Tran is going to Chicago tomorrow to visit his cousin. The weather is going to be very

cold, so he's packing his suitcase with warm clothes. He's going to take three pairs of

straw	nylon	corduroy
Ⓐ	Ⓑ	Ⓒ

¹⁹ pants, two

flannel	sleeveless	short-sleeved
Ⓐ	Ⓑ	Ⓒ

²⁰ shirts,

and two turtleneck

coats	tights	shirts
Ⓐ	Ⓑ	Ⓒ

²¹. He's also going to pack his favorite wool

sweater	blouse	sock
Ⓐ	Ⓑ	Ⓒ

²². He wants to take his

sport	ski	linen
Ⓐ	Ⓑ	Ⓒ

²³ jacket, but

unfortunately it has a

broken	ripped	pierced
Ⓐ	Ⓑ	Ⓒ

²⁴ zipper. So he'll take his

tunic	jumpsuit	parka
Ⓐ	Ⓑ	Ⓒ

²⁵ and gloves instead.

C WHAT'S THE WORD?

bag	cap	crew	hiking	sport	three-piece	wedding	wrist

26. _____ boots

27. _____ coat

28. _____ ring

29. shoulder _____

30. _____ socks

31. _____ suit

32. baseball _____

33. _____ watch

hang up	iron	lengthen	let out	repair	sort	take in	unload	wide

34. I'm going to _____ the torn pocket on my jacket.

35. The laundry is dry. Could you please _____ the clothes from the dryer?

36. Bonnie needs to _____ these slacks. They're too tight.

37. Before I start the laundry, I _____ the clothes into light and dark clothing.

38. Would you please _____ these coats in the closet?

39. This shirt is very wrinkled. You need to _____ it before you wear it.

40. Those pants are too short. You should _____ them.

41. I have to _____ that dress. It's too loose.

color	jewelry	string
earring	pattern	suspenders
handbag	size	windbreaker

42. It's a little cool today, so I think I'll wear my _____.

43. This jacket is too large. I need a smaller _____.

44. Yellow is my favorite _____.

45. Marta keeps her car keys in her _____.

46. Rita is upset. She lost a clip-on _____ at the restaurant last night.

47. This brooch is my favorite piece of _____.

48. Walter doesn't use a belt with his pants. He uses _____.

49. Paisley is my favorite _____.

50. My grandmother gave me a beautiful _____ of pearls.

E) WRITING SAMPLE

Choose one of these topics and write a paragraph. Write on a separate sheet of paper.

- What are you wearing right now? Describe the colors, materials, and patterns. Do any of your clothes have problems? If they do, what are the problems? Are you wearing any jewelry or accessories? What are they?

- You're going to a very special party. What do you think you'll wear? Describe the colors, materials, and patterns. What shoes, jewelry, or accessories will you wear? Describe them.

A **WHAT'S THE WORD?**

1. Before you wash your sweater, read the ____.
   - Ⓐ sale price
   - Ⓑ receipt
   - Ⓒ price
   - Ⓓ care instructions

2. If you want to ____ information about an item, ask a salesperson.
   - Ⓐ get
   - Ⓑ tell
   - Ⓒ return
   - Ⓓ exchange

3. This price is 20% off the ____.
   - Ⓐ discount
   - Ⓑ regular price
   - Ⓒ sales tax
   - Ⓓ sale sign

4. The shirt label gives the ____.
   - Ⓐ total price
   - Ⓑ price tag
   - Ⓒ material and price
   - Ⓓ size and material

5. My daughter likes to do jigsaw ____.
   - Ⓐ stickers
   - Ⓑ figures
   - Ⓒ puzzles
   - Ⓓ blocks

6. A ____ has three wheels.
   - Ⓐ wagon
   - Ⓑ tricycle
   - Ⓒ bicycle
   - Ⓓ skateboard

7. Watch out! The ____ door is closing.
   - Ⓐ elevator
   - Ⓑ escalator
   - Ⓒ directory
   - Ⓓ water fountain

8. We're going to the beach today. Don't forget to take the ____!
   - Ⓐ paint set
   - Ⓑ playhouse
   - Ⓒ pail and shovel
   - Ⓓ modeling clay

9. My children like to sit and play in the ____ in our yard.
   - Ⓐ inflatable pool
   - Ⓑ matchbox cars
   - Ⓒ toy trucks
   - Ⓓ doll house furniture

10. My son likes to draw with ____.
    - Ⓐ blocks
    - Ⓑ crayons
    - Ⓒ board games
    - Ⓓ trading cards

11. Tom built an airplane with the ____.
    - Ⓐ science kit
    - Ⓑ swing set
    - Ⓒ bubble soap
    - Ⓓ model kit

12. I carry my camera in a camera ____.
    - Ⓐ film
    - Ⓑ lens
    - Ⓒ case
    - Ⓓ battery

13. A digital camera uses a ____.
    - Ⓐ joystick
    - Ⓑ memory disk
    - Ⓒ tripod
    - Ⓓ floppy disk

14. You can buy a ____ at a toy store or in the Electronics Department.
    - Ⓐ walkie-talkie
    - Ⓑ surge protector
    - Ⓒ track ball
    - Ⓓ voltage regulator

(continued)

15. You have a message on your ____.
 - Ⓐ adapter
 - Ⓑ answering machine
 - Ⓒ adding machine
 - Ⓓ modem

16. When my parents were young, they played records on a ____.
 - Ⓐ radio
 - Ⓑ DVD player
 - Ⓒ turntable
 - Ⓓ tape deck

17. I put a new ____ into the CD player.
 - Ⓐ DVD
 - Ⓑ compact disk
 - Ⓒ camera
 - Ⓓ LCD TV

18. The mayor used a ____ when he spoke.
 - Ⓐ microphone
 - Ⓑ boombox
 - Ⓒ CPU
 - Ⓓ video game system

19. Ana carries her ____ in her purse.
 - Ⓐ monitor
 - Ⓑ notebook computer
 - Ⓒ desktop computer
 - Ⓓ electronic personal organizer

20. What word-processing ____ do you use?
 - Ⓐ game
 - Ⓑ mouse
 - Ⓒ program
 - Ⓓ attachment

21. We videotaped the party with a ____.
 - Ⓐ camcorder
 - Ⓑ plasma TV
 - Ⓒ calculator
 - Ⓓ movie screen

22. I like to listen to my ____ while I jog in the park.
 - Ⓐ stereo system
 - Ⓑ shortwave radio
 - Ⓒ video game system
 - Ⓓ portable CD player

23. Please put this audiotape into the ____.
 - Ⓐ audiocassette
 - Ⓑ cassette deck
 - Ⓒ speakers
 - Ⓓ CD player

24. Donaldo put on his ____ to listen to music on the bus.
 - Ⓐ speakers
 - Ⓑ zoom lens
 - Ⓒ portable TV
 - Ⓓ headphones

25. If I don't answer my phone, call my ____.
 - Ⓐ disk drive
 - Ⓑ CD-ROM
 - Ⓒ pager
 - Ⓓ remote control

B WHAT'S THE WORD?

bought	exchanged	paid	return	tried

26. I went to the store and _____ the green sweater for a blue one.

27–28. After I _____ on the suit, I _____ for it with my credit card.

29–30. I _____ these shoes last week, but now I have to _____ them.

C CLOZE READING

| camera | charger | fax | game | notebook | phone | printer | radio | TV |

Frank owns a painting company, and he has an office in his home. In his office, he has a

cordless _____³¹ and the battery _____³² for his cell phone on his desk.

He uses a _____³³ computer. He has a _____³⁴ machine so that he can

receive important papers. He uses his _____³⁵ for customer bills and receipts. He

has a digital _____³⁶ because he takes pictures of houses he has painted. There's

a clock _____³⁷ on his desk and a plasma _____³⁸ in the corner of the

room. When he wants to relax, he likes to play a video _____³⁹.

D WHAT'S THE WORD?

Children's Clothing	Gift Wrap	Housewares	Perfume
Customer Service	Home Furnishings	Jewelry	Women's Clothing
Electronics	Household Appliances	Men's Clothing	

40. We went to the _____ Department to look for a coffee table.

41. The _____ Department has many different microwaves.

42. Alex and Sofia are looking at pots and pans in the _____ Department.

43. If you want to exchange something, you have to take it to the _____ Counter.

44. Maria bought everything for her sound system in the _____ Department.

45. After I paid for the blouse for my mother, I took it to the _____ Counter.

46. Pablo looked at watches at the _____ Counter.

47. Baby clothes are 20 percent off in the _____ Department.

48. The _____ Counter always smells wonderful.

49. I bought a tie for my uncle in the _____ Department.

50. The _____ Department has many different kinds of dresses.

E WRITING SAMPLE

Choose one of these topics and write a paragraph. Write on a separate sheet of paper.

- Do you like to shop in department stores? What is your favorite store? How often do you shop there? What departments do you usually shop in? What do you buy?

- What electronic equipment do you have? Which do you use the most? What new electronic equipment do you want to buy? Why?

Name _____

Date _____

A) WHAT'S THE WORD?

1. My bank sends me a monthly _____.
   - Ⓐ statement
   - Ⓑ checkbook
   - Ⓒ credit card
   - Ⓓ bill

2. I own my own house, so I have to make a monthly _____ payment.
   - Ⓐ vault
   - Ⓑ traveler's check
   - Ⓒ passbook
   - Ⓓ mortgage

3. Your credit card _____ is on the front of your card.
   - Ⓐ bill
   - Ⓑ address
   - Ⓒ number
   - Ⓓ signature

4. I keep important papers in my _____.
   - Ⓐ safe deposit box
   - Ⓑ bankbook
   - Ⓒ dictionary
   - Ⓓ certified mail

5. I receive a _____ at the beginning of every month.
   - Ⓐ bank account
   - Ⓑ gas bill
   - Ⓒ currency
   - Ⓓ deposit slip

6. You can get _____ at the post office.
   - Ⓐ an author
   - Ⓑ an atlas
   - Ⓒ a journal
   - Ⓓ a change-of-address form

7. I balance my _____ every month.
   - Ⓐ cash
   - Ⓑ checkbook
   - Ⓒ rent
   - Ⓓ currency

8. I went to the bank to _____ a check.
   - Ⓐ make
   - Ⓑ select
   - Ⓒ cash
   - Ⓓ insert

9. You should write information about every check in your _____.
   - Ⓐ check register
   - Ⓑ card catalog
   - Ⓒ withdrawal slip
   - Ⓓ transaction slip

10. Before we buy a house, we have to _____ a loan.
    - Ⓐ transfer
    - Ⓑ open
    - Ⓒ exchange
    - Ⓓ apply for

11. Please buy a _____ of stamps for me.
    - Ⓐ sheet
    - Ⓑ magazine
    - Ⓒ box
    - Ⓓ slip

12. Every day the _____ delivers my mail.
    - Ⓐ mail clerk
    - Ⓑ teller
    - Ⓒ letter carrier
    - Ⓓ paramedic

13. The _____ on this letter is May 15.
    - Ⓐ postage
    - Ⓑ postmark
    - Ⓒ title
    - Ⓓ zip code

14. I want to send this letter by express _____.
    - Ⓐ post
    - Ⓑ class
    - Ⓒ mail
    - Ⓓ service

(continued)

15. Call the police! There's a _____ on Second Avenue!
- Ⓐ passport
- Ⓑ firefighter
- Ⓒ paramedic
- Ⓓ water main break

16. I saw a terrible car _____ on Main Street this morning.
- Ⓐ spill
- Ⓑ break
- Ⓒ accident
- Ⓓ robbery

Ⓑ CLOZE READING

I needed to get some cash this morning, so I took the bus downtown to the

| bank Ⓐ | library Ⓑ | emergency room Ⓒ | **17**. First, I went to the | card Ⓐ | ATM Ⓑ | copy Ⓒ | **18** |

and I | removed Ⓐ | opened Ⓑ | inserted Ⓒ | **19** my card. After I entered my | account Ⓐ | PIN Ⓑ | check Ⓒ | **20**

number, I | selected Ⓐ | got Ⓑ | applied Ⓒ | **21** a transaction. When I tried to

| apply Ⓐ | withdraw Ⓑ | make Ⓒ | **22** cash, the machine didn't work. I went inside and waited in line to

see a | teller Ⓐ | security guard Ⓑ | city manager Ⓒ | **23**. She helped me with my transaction. I also

| took Ⓐ | wrote Ⓑ | made Ⓒ | **24** a deposit. Finally, I got a money | slip Ⓐ | order Ⓑ | check Ⓒ | **25** to pay my rent.

Ⓒ WHAT THE WORD?

| activities director | derailment | hall | nursery | senior center |
| ambulance | dump | mugging | outage | |

26. Ivan is an eldercare worker at the _____.

27. Monica is the new _____ at the recreation center.

28. The _____ in the child-care center is usually very noisy.

29. If you see a _____, call the police department immediately.

30. The EMT took the man out of the _____.

31. The mayor is working in his office at city _____.

32. The police got a phone call about a train _____.

33. The sanitation workers unload the trash at the _____.

34. After the big storm, there was a large power _____ in the city.

D) CLOZE READING

checkout	library card	on tape	periodical
encyclopedias	media	online catalog	reference

There are many people at the community library today. A man is giving his

_____³⁵ to the clerk at the _____³⁶ desk. Several people are

looking at the _____³⁷ on the computers. People are reading magazines and

newspapers in the _____³⁸ section. The _____³⁹ librarian

is answering questions. Nearby, several students are reading _____⁴⁰. In the

_____⁴¹ section, people are looking for CDs and DVDs. A mother and her sons

are looking for books _____⁴².

E) WHAT'S THE WORD?

drunk driving	gas leak	playroom	spill
fire	gym	recycling center	vandalism

43. The explosion at the factory started a big _____.

44. At the recreation center, the teenagers were playing basketball in the _____.

45. I smell something strange in the kitchen. Do you think we have a _____?

46. They collect bottles and cans at the _____.

47. The driver ahead of us is driving very badly. He could be arrested for _____.

48. The store owner called to report _____ at his store—broken windows
    and signs.

49. The child-care worker is teaching the children a game in the _____.

50. There was a chemical _____ on the highway, and it took five hours to
    clean up.

F) WRITING SAMPLE

Choose one of these topics and write a paragraph. Write on a separate sheet of paper.

- How often do you pay your bills? What kinds of bills do you usually receive? Do you pay by
  check, cash, or credit card? What is your most expensive monthly bill?

- What emergency happened in your city or neighborhood recently? Was the fire department
  there? the police department? What happened?

A) WHAT'S THE WORD?

1. I _____ my ankle yesterday.
ⓐ sneezed
ⓑ vomited
ⓒ twisted
ⓓ burped

2. After he drank two cans of soda, Jonathan felt _____.
ⓐ bloated
ⓑ faint
ⓒ swollen
ⓓ congested

3. Careful! This pan is hot. Don't _____ yourself.
ⓐ break
ⓑ scrape
ⓒ bruise
ⓓ burn

4. I called the dentist about my _____.
ⓐ wart
ⓑ headache
ⓒ toothache
ⓓ earache

5. My new shoes gave me a _____.
ⓐ blister
ⓑ cramp
ⓒ pelvis
ⓓ tourniquet

6. _____ is a common adult disease.
ⓐ A cough
ⓑ Diabetes
ⓒ Frostbite
ⓓ Heimlich

7. If someone is having _____, call an ambulance right away.
ⓐ a pulse
ⓑ a splint
ⓒ an ear infection
ⓓ a heart attack

8. I have a _____. I think I'm getting a cold.
ⓐ cavity
ⓑ runny nose
ⓒ backache
ⓓ stiff neck

9. The baseball hit Tommy in his face and broke his _____.
ⓐ jaw
ⓑ hip
ⓒ neck
ⓓ back

10. I need _____ for this insect bite.
ⓐ tweezers
ⓑ sterile pads
ⓒ antihistamine cream
ⓓ CPR

11. If you have _____, drink a lot of water.
ⓐ a rash
ⓑ hiccups
ⓒ an iris
ⓓ a headache

12. Jim can't talk because he has _____.
ⓐ hypertension
ⓑ heart disease
ⓒ a sunburn
ⓓ laryngitis

13. When I run, I have _____.
ⓐ shortness of breath
ⓑ the chills
ⓒ depression
ⓓ an infection

14. Most of the _____ in your body are under your skin.
ⓐ gums
ⓑ teeth
ⓒ measles
ⓓ nerves

(continued)

15. The ____ is part of your eye.
    (A) heel
    (B) pupil
    (C) esophagus
    (D) small intestine

16. It's freezing outside. Don't get ____!
    (A) influenza
    (B) chicken pox
    (C) frostbite
    (D) mumps

17. Alex has big eyes and long ____.
    (A) corneas
    (B) eyelashes
    (C) eyelids
    (D) cheeks

18. The player dislocated his ____.
    (A) shoulder
    (B) tongue
    (C) chest
    (D) liver

19. The ____ is a muscle in the leg.
    (A) arm
    (B) knee
    (C) calf
    (D) gallbladder

20. Your ____ are inside your ribcage.
    (A) lips
    (B) shins
    (C) hands
    (D) lungs

21. He has a cut on his forehead, above his ____.
    (A) eyebrow
    (B) brain
    (C) neck
    (D) chin

22. I have a fever and a sore throat. I might have ____.
    (A) asthma
    (B) strep throat
    (C) an electric shock
    (D) depression

23. Hold the pen between your ____ and your fingers.
    (A) thumb
    (B) palm
    (C) toe
    (D) wrist

24. The ____ carry blood to the heart.
    (A) bones
    (B) knuckles
    (C) veins
    (D) kidneys

25. Your ____ is inside your skull.
    (A) abdomen
    (B) bladder
    (C) pancreas
    (D) brain

B) WHAT'S THE WORD?

| antiseptic | aspirin | bandage | gauze | kit |

26. I need to take some _____ for my headache.

27. Every family should have a first-aid _____.

28. Use this _____ cleansing wipe to clean your cut.

29. The nurse wrapped my ankle with an elastic _____.

30. The doctor covered the cut with _____ and adhesive tape.

C WHAT'S THE WORD?

infection	measles	poison	reaction	shock	unconscious
maneuver	pains	pulse	rescue	tuberculosis	

31. After the car accident, several people were in _____.

32. Keep cleaning supplies away from children so that they don't swallow _____.

33. Some people can have an allergic _____ to peanuts.

34. The man wasn't breathing, so the EMT started _____ breathing.

35. My daughter is sick. She has a bad ear _____.

36. The boy's eyes were closed, but he was breathing. He was _____.

37. If someone is choking, you should do the Heimlich _____.

38. Christopher has _____, a disease of the lungs.

39. The woman had no _____, so the paramedic did CPR.

40. The man upstairs had bad chest _____, so his son called the ambulance.

41. Timmy is getting red spots all over his body. I think he has _____.

D CLOZE READING

bandage	bloody	dizzy	fell	heatstroke	ointment	temperature	throw	tooth

There are a lot of children in the school nurse's office. Tomas got hit by a baseball, and he has a _____ ⁴² nose. Tina _____ ⁴³ down, so she needs a _____ ⁴⁴ for her knee. The nurse is putting antibiotic _____ ⁴⁵ on her knee. Suzy feels _____ ⁴⁶ and has a _____ ⁴⁷. One girl is holding her stomach. She looks like she's going to _____ ⁴⁸ up. Two children are lying down on the beds. They have _____ ⁴⁹ after they played in the hot sun. A six-year-old boy is pointing to his mouth and crying. He has his first loose _____ ⁵⁰.

E WRITING SAMPLE

Choose one of these topics and write a paragraph. Write on a separate sheet of paper.

- Write about a time you or a family member had a medical emergency. What happened? Were there any injuries? Did you use first-aid supplies? Did you call a doctor?

- Write about a time when you were sick. What was the matter? Did you have a temperature? What were your symptoms? How long were you sick? What did you do to feel better?

A WHAT'S THE WORD?

1. Several patients were sitting in the ____ at the doctor's office.
   - Ⓐ nurse's station
   - Ⓑ operating room
   - Ⓒ exam room
   - Ⓓ waiting room

2. I'm going to use this ____ to listen to your heart.
   - Ⓐ call button
   - Ⓑ stethoscope
   - Ⓒ I.V.
   - Ⓓ X-ray

3. Put this ____ on your swollen ankle.
   - Ⓐ ice pack
   - Ⓑ scale
   - Ⓒ gauze
   - Ⓓ perfume

4. It's important to keep your ____ clean and dry.
   - Ⓐ cavity
   - Ⓑ cotton ball
   - Ⓒ wound
   - Ⓓ cane

5. It was a deep cut, so I got ten ____.
   - Ⓐ caplets
   - Ⓑ stitches
   - Ⓒ drops
   - Ⓓ gurneys

6. The ____ will relax your muscles.
   - Ⓐ humidifier
   - Ⓑ bed control
   - Ⓒ heating pad
   - Ⓓ drill

7. The allergist gave me a ____ for a stronger antihistamine.
   - Ⓐ pacifier
   - Ⓑ teaspoon
   - Ⓒ fluid
   - Ⓓ prescription

8. After I broke my leg, I used ____.
   - Ⓐ crutches
   - Ⓑ a rocking chair
   - Ⓒ a sling
   - Ⓓ shoelaces

9. The ____ helped me use the walker.
   - Ⓐ audiologist
   - Ⓑ physical therapist
   - Ⓒ patient
   - Ⓓ lab technician

10. After the dentist ____ the tooth, he'll fill it.
    - Ⓐ drills
    - Ⓑ closes
    - Ⓒ takes
    - Ⓓ draws

11. The orthodontist put ____ on the young boy.
    - Ⓐ dental floss
    - Ⓑ lipstick
    - Ⓒ braces
    - Ⓓ tape

12. If you have a cold, drink a lot of ____.
    - Ⓐ cough syrup
    - Ⓑ tablespoons
    - Ⓒ bottles
    - Ⓓ fluids

13. Susan is ____ the baby's diaper.
    - Ⓐ changing
    - Ⓑ bathing
    - Ⓒ dressing
    - Ⓓ nursing

14. The baby is crying, so his father is ____ him.
    - Ⓐ playing
    - Ⓑ rocking
    - Ⓒ flossing
    - Ⓓ measuring

(continued)

15. I'm _____. I work in the radiology department.
- Ⓐ a chiropractor
- Ⓑ an anesthesiologist
- Ⓒ a dental hygienist
- Ⓓ an X-ray technician

16. An orderly is pushing a patient in _____.
- Ⓐ a mask
- Ⓑ a hospital gown
- Ⓒ a wheelchair
- Ⓓ an examination table

Ⓑ CLOZE READING

Ken woke up very late this morning, and he only had 15 minutes to get ready for work.

Usually he takes a long, hot | rinse Ⓐ shower Ⓑ bus Ⓒ | 17 and washes his hair with

| shampoo Ⓐ toothpaste Ⓑ powder Ⓒ | 18. But this morning, he just washed his face and hands with

| conditioner Ⓐ foundation Ⓑ soap Ⓒ | 19. He shaved with shaving | cream Ⓐ cologne Ⓑ scissors Ⓒ | 20 and

a razor and put on a little aftershave | gel Ⓐ lipstick Ⓑ lotion Ⓒ | 21. Then he put some water on

his hair, styled it with a | nail brush Ⓐ blow dryer Ⓑ shower cap Ⓒ | 22, and put some

| deodorant Ⓐ perfume Ⓑ lotion Ⓒ | 23 under his arms. He | combed Ⓐ washed Ⓑ brushed Ⓒ | 24

his teeth, but he was in a hurry so he didn't | floss Ⓐ gargle Ⓑ polish Ⓒ | 25 them. Finally, he got

dressed quickly and ran out the door to catch the bus.

Ⓒ WHAT THE WORD?

| counselor | gerontologist | ophthalmologist | pediatrician |
| ENT specialist | obstetrician | orthopedist | |

26. The _____ examined the man's broken leg.

27. If you have depression, it's helpful to talk with a _____.

28. I took my baby to the _____ because he had a fever.

29. The _____ checked my ear, nose, and throat.

30. The _____ gave the new baby to the mother in the delivery room.

31. A _____ helps elderly people with their health problems.

32. The _____ asked me to read the eye chart.

dressed	drew	examined	measured	rested	took	went

33. The nurse _____ my height and weight.

34. The doctor _____ my throat, and then she ordered a lab test.

35. The baby seemed sick, so I _____ his temperature.

36. Ramona had the flu last week, so she _____ in bed for several days.

37. Richard _____ on a diet after he got on the scale and saw his weight.

38. The lab technician _____ blood from the patient.

39. After my mother cleaned my wound, she _____ it with gauze and tape.

antacid	formula	mascara	vitamin
clipper	lotion	pill	wipes
conditioner	lozenges	sunscreen	

40. For this prescription, I have to take one _____ every four hours.

41. Children should put on _____ if they're going to play outside.

42. When I have a stomachache, I take one or two _____ tablets.

43. My teenage daughter likes to wear _____ and eyeliner.

44. My doctor says I should take a _____ every day.

45. After I wash my hair, I put _____ on it.

46. I need to cut my nails. Do you have a nail _____?

47. When I change the baby's diaper, I use baby _____.

48. My throat is very sore. Do you have any throat _____?

49. The baby drinks _____ out of a bottle.

50. This body _____ will feel very good on your sunburn.

E WRITING SAMPLE

Choose one of these topics and write a paragraph. Write on a separate sheet of paper.

- Describe your morning routine. What do you do for personal hygiene? Do you take a shower? Do you floss your teeth? Write about what you do and what things you use.

- How often do you have a medical exam? What does the nurse usually do? What does the doctor do? What tests do you have?

Name _____

Date _____

A WHAT'S THE WORD?

1. Timmy is four years old. He goes to ____.
   - Ⓐ trade school
   - Ⓑ elementary school
   - Ⓒ preschool
   - Ⓓ law school

2. The students' lockers are in the ____.
   - Ⓐ hallway
   - Ⓑ cafeteria
   - Ⓒ library
   - Ⓓ main office

3. In ____, students learn how to cook.
   - Ⓐ shop
   - Ⓑ geography
   - Ⓒ chemistry
   - Ⓓ home economics

4. The ____ teacher is going to show us how to play the game.
   - Ⓐ P.E.
   - Ⓑ art
   - Ⓒ driver's ed
   - Ⓓ chemistry

5. The ____ manages all the teachers and school employees.
   - Ⓐ school clerk
   - Ⓑ principal
   - Ⓒ custodian
   - Ⓓ librarian

6. I like to learn languages, so I think I'll take ____ next year.
   - Ⓐ science
   - Ⓑ industrial arts
   - Ⓒ geography
   - Ⓓ French

7. Miguel is one of the best singers in the ____.
   - Ⓐ chorus
   - Ⓑ orchestra
   - Ⓒ pep squad
   - Ⓓ art class

8. The ____ makes sure that students aren't too noisy in the cafeteria.
   - Ⓐ coach
   - Ⓑ vice-principal
   - Ⓒ lunchroom monitor
   - Ⓓ secretary

9. We're studying writing and grammar in in our ____ class.
   - Ⓐ business education
   - Ⓑ English
   - Ⓒ history
   - Ⓓ physics

10. The ____ class meets in the science lab twice a week.
    - Ⓐ biology
    - Ⓑ computer science
    - Ⓒ government
    - Ⓓ driver's education

11. Students are changing into their gym clothes in the ____.
    - Ⓐ classroom
    - Ⓑ bleachers
    - Ⓒ locker
    - Ⓓ locker room

12. Ana felt sick so she went to the ____.
    - Ⓐ guidance office
    - Ⓑ nurse's office
    - Ⓒ principal's office
    - Ⓓ main office

13. The soccer ____ met with the team.
    - Ⓐ teacher
    - Ⓑ counselor
    - Ⓒ coach
    - Ⓓ monitor

14. ____ practices twice a week after school.
    - Ⓐ The band
    - Ⓑ Student government
    - Ⓒ The newspaper
    - Ⓓ Community service

(continued)

15. In P.E., we sometimes run around the _____ for exercise.
    Ⓐ guidance office
    Ⓑ hallway
    Ⓒ locker room
    Ⓓ track

16. The _____ served lunch to the students.
    Ⓐ coaches
    Ⓑ secretaries
    Ⓒ cafeteria workers
    Ⓓ lunchroom monitors

17. The _____ sets up lights for the play.
    Ⓐ orchestra
    Ⓑ security guard
    Ⓒ debate club
    Ⓓ A.V. crew

18. The team played soccer on the _____.
    Ⓐ lockers
    Ⓑ field
    Ⓒ track
    Ⓓ bleachers

19. The _____ performed a play last night in the auditorium.
    Ⓐ drama club
    Ⓑ choir
    Ⓒ pep squad
    Ⓓ A.V. crew

20. The _____ helps students check out books.
    Ⓐ computer science teacher
    Ⓑ assistant principal
    Ⓒ driver's education teacher
    Ⓓ school librarian

21. We sat outside in the _____ and watched the football game.
    Ⓐ gymnasium
    Ⓑ bleachers
    Ⓒ auditorium
    Ⓓ lunchroom

22. Marie likes to write. Her favorite extracurricular activity is _____.
    Ⓐ the school newspaper
    Ⓑ the debate club
    Ⓒ the chess club
    Ⓓ cheerleading

23. The _____ talked with Sam about his class schedule and his grades.
    Ⓐ custodian
    Ⓑ nurse
    Ⓒ counselor
    Ⓓ assistant principal

24. In _____, we're studying continents, oceans, and rivers.
    Ⓐ government
    Ⓑ geography
    Ⓒ health
    Ⓓ biology

25. Alice painted a wonderful picture in her _____ class.
    Ⓐ physics
    Ⓑ history
    Ⓒ art
    Ⓓ music

Ⓑ **WHAT'S THE ORDER?**

| college | graduate school | middle school |
| elementary school | high school | nursery school |

26. 1 _____

27. 2 _____

28. 3 _____

29. 4 _____

30. 5 _____

31. 6 _____

C WHAT'S THE WORD?

adult	health	law	math	vocational
government	international	literary	medical	yearbook

32. The school _____ has a photo of every student and teacher.

33. In our _____ class, we're studying nutrition and good eating habits.

34. There are some good stories and poems in this month's _____ magazine.

35. The _____ club is planning a dinner with foods from around the world.

36. Alexis is studying to be a chef at a _____ school.

37. Luisa wants to be a lawyer, so she's going to apply to _____ school next fall.

38. We're studying democracy and elections in our _____ class.

39. Richard is excellent at _____. He hopes to be an accountant.

40. Keiko plans to go to _____ school to become a physician.

41. The _____ school in our community has language, dance, and art classes.

D CLOZE READING

community	education	guidance	service	university
club	extracurricular	high	subjects	

Jose is 16 years old and is in 11th grade in _____ 42 school. His favorite _____ 43 are business _____ 44 and computer science. He's a good student and does several _____ 45 activities. He loves to fix computers, so of course he's in the computer _____ 46. Also, for community _____ 47, he volunteers at a preschool twice a week. Yesterday, he had an appointment with his _____ 48 counselor to talk about his college plans. They discussed the local _____ 49 college and a state _____ 50.

E WRITING SAMPLE

Choose one of these topics and write a paragraph. Write on a separate sheet of paper.

- Describe your school. What kind of school is it? What subjects are you studying? What is your favorite class? Why? What subjects do you want to study in the future?

- Do you have a son or daughter in school? Describe the school. Who is your child's teacher? Do you know the principal or the guidance counselor? What are your child's favorite subjects? What extracurricular activities does your child do?

Name _____

Date _____

A) WHAT'S THE WORD?

1. Geometry is a type of _____.
Ⓐ math
Ⓑ physics
Ⓒ geography
Ⓓ subtraction

2. The length of the sofa is 58 _____.
Ⓐ feet
Ⓑ meters
Ⓒ inches
Ⓓ yards

3. Please draw a right _____.
Ⓐ apex
Ⓑ pyramid
Ⓒ rectangle
Ⓓ triangle

4. The _____ 1/2 is equal to 50 percent.
Ⓐ half
Ⓑ third
Ⓒ fraction
Ⓓ forecast

5. A _____ is a solid figure.
Ⓐ curved line
Ⓑ cube
Ⓒ square
Ⓓ centimeter

6. My _____ is 6 feet.
Ⓐ height
Ⓑ width
Ⓒ depth
Ⓓ apex

7. The _____ of a circle is the measurement across the middle.
Ⓐ acute angle
Ⓑ diameter
Ⓒ circumference
Ⓓ hypotenuse

8. One mile equals 1.6 _____.
Ⓐ feet
Ⓑ yards
Ⓒ kilometers
Ⓓ meters

9. When I revise my writing, I correct my _____.
Ⓐ marks
Ⓑ feedback
Ⓒ speech
Ⓓ mistakes

10. I like non-fiction, so I rarely read _____.
Ⓐ history books
Ⓑ novels
Ⓒ biographies
Ⓓ autobiographies

11. Before you do a scientific experiment, you need to carefully plan the _____.
Ⓐ conclusion
Ⓑ paragraph
Ⓒ procedure
Ⓓ problem

12. An _____ is a punctuation mark.
Ⓐ oval
Ⓑ adverb
Ⓒ imperative
Ⓓ apostrophe

13. I had to write _____ about recycling.
Ⓐ a report
Ⓑ an invitation
Ⓒ an instant message
Ⓓ a letter

14. The manager sent _____ about sales to all of the employees.
Ⓐ a plateau
Ⓑ a memo
Ⓒ an exclamation point
Ⓓ a postcard

15. I'm taking a _____ course.
Ⓐ division
Ⓑ multiplication
Ⓒ calculus
Ⓓ subtraction

16. The Big Dipper is a _____.
Ⓐ planet
Ⓑ moon
Ⓒ star
Ⓓ constellation

B) CLOZE READING

When I was a child, I lived in a city near the Atlantic | Rainforest (A)   Waterfall (B)   Ocean (C) | [17].

The city is on a | bay (A)   brook (B)   galaxy (C) | [18], and many boats sailed in and out. I often went with

my family to swim at the | plateau (A)   seashore (B)   canyon (C) | [19] and play on the sand

| dunes (A)   islands (B)   plains (C) | [20]. Now I live in a town with very different geography. My town

is in a | river (A)   pond (B)   valley (C) | [21] with a mountain | jungle (A)   range (B)   peninsula (C) | [22] on one side.

I enjoy hiking up to the mountain | peaks (A)   pyramids (B)   shores (C) | [23]. There's a large

| stream (A)   forest (B)   lake (C) | [24] close to my town, and I often sail there on weekends.

Around the town there are many green | comets (A)   meadows (B)   deserts (C) | [25] and small hills.

C) WHAT THE WORD?

| adjective   adverb   article   noun   preposition   pronoun   verb |

The **astronomer saw** a meteor **in the** sky. **It** was **yellow** and disappeared **quickly.**
      26   27   28   29   30   31   32

26. _____

27. _____

28. _____

29. _____

30. _____

31. _____

32. _____

D) PUNCTUATION

| colon   exclamation point   period   question mark   quotation marks   semi-colon |

33. [?] _____

34. [:] _____

35. [;] _____

36. [.] _____

37. [" "] _____

38. [!] _____

divided	minus	percent	plus	times

39. Twenty-seven _____ ten equals seventeen.

40. Sixty _____ by two equals thirty.

41. Thirty _____ thirty equals sixty.

42. Nine _____ three equals twenty-seven.

43. Fifty _____ of sixty is thirty.

funnel	hypothesis	magnet	microscope	satellites	telescope	test tube

44. The student poured the liquid through the _____ into the beaker.

45. The strong _____ easily picked up the nails from the floor.

46. In the scientific method, you state the problem and then form a _____.

47. _____ that fly around the Earth can help scientists forecast weather.

48. Ed used a dropper to put a small amount of the chemical into each _____.

49. The astronomers used a powerful _____ at the observatory.

50. The students used a _____ to study the water from the pond.

F) **WRITING SAMPLE**

Choose one of these topics and write a paragraph. Write on a separate sheet of paper.

• What do you read during a typical day? Do you read a newspaper or magazine? Do you read in the morning? in the evening? What's your favorite kind of book? Do you like fiction or non-fiction?

• What's your favorite place to visit? Do you prefer the mountains or the seashore? Describe the geography of a special place. What do you like to do there?

A WHAT'S THE WORD?

1. My husband is _____. He writes articles for a newspaper.
   - Ⓐ a tailor
   - Ⓑ a welder
   - Ⓒ an actor
   - Ⓓ a journalist

2. The _____ are putting soup cans on the shelves in the supermarket.
   - Ⓐ fishers
   - Ⓑ stock clerks
   - Ⓒ truck drivers
   - Ⓓ housekeepers

3. The _____ gave my cat an injection.
   - Ⓐ baker
   - Ⓑ salesperson
   - Ⓒ veterinarian
   - Ⓓ travel agent

4. I'm a _____. I wear a uniform every day.
   - Ⓐ servicewoman
   - Ⓑ secretary
   - Ⓒ photographer
   - Ⓓ babysitter

5. Rachel is a _____. She often delivers important papers to people's offices.
   - Ⓐ teacher
   - Ⓑ store clerk
   - Ⓒ courier
   - Ⓓ carpenter

6. The post office has a job opening for a _____.
   - Ⓐ lawyer
   - Ⓑ firefighter
   - Ⓒ factory worker
   - Ⓓ mail carrier

7. The _____ polished Carol's fingernails.
   - Ⓐ manicurist
   - Ⓑ barber
   - Ⓒ security guard
   - Ⓓ photographer

8. The _____ gave me 3 pounds of beef.
   - Ⓐ attendant
   - Ⓑ butcher
   - Ⓒ supervisor
   - Ⓓ instructor

9. All of our _____ must speak four languages.
   - Ⓐ interpreters
   - Ⓑ firefighters
   - Ⓒ letter carriers
   - Ⓓ garment workers

10. The _____ is supervising the construction workers.
    - Ⓐ mason
    - Ⓑ janitor
    - Ⓒ foreman
    - Ⓓ mechanic

11. Rita is _____ in a toy factory.
    - Ⓐ a medical assistant
    - Ⓑ a musician
    - Ⓒ a shopkeeper
    - Ⓓ an assembler

12. My cable TV isn't working, so I called _____.
    - Ⓐ an architect
    - Ⓑ a customer service representative
    - Ⓒ a computer software engineer
    - Ⓓ a trash collector

13. A _____ sells things on the telephone.
    - Ⓐ telemarketer
    - Ⓑ data entry clerk
    - Ⓒ postal worker
    - Ⓓ receptionist

14. A _____ needs to be able to lift heavy garbage cans.
    - Ⓐ babysitter
    - Ⓑ delivery person
    - Ⓒ sanitation worker
    - Ⓓ messenger

(continued)

15. My uncle is ____. He plays the guitar in a band.
    Ⓐ a waiter
    Ⓑ a musician
    Ⓒ a server
    Ⓓ an actor

16. I'm busy. I'm ____ inventory of everything in the supply room.
    Ⓐ taking
    Ⓑ making
    Ⓒ drawing
    Ⓓ writing

17. The waitress ____ the meal.
    Ⓐ cooked
    Ⓑ baked
    Ⓒ served
    Ⓓ washed

18. A garment worker ____ dresses.
    Ⓐ sings
    Ⓑ cleans
    Ⓒ uses
    Ⓓ sews

19. The bricklayer ____ the old fireplace.
    Ⓐ played
    Ⓑ repaired
    Ⓒ grew
    Ⓓ filed

20. A police officer is ____ the entrance to the bank.
    Ⓐ guarding
    Ⓑ building
    Ⓒ operating
    Ⓓ assisting

21. I'm not employed, but I take care of my house and my children. I'm a ____.
    Ⓐ physician assistant
    Ⓑ child day-care worker
    Ⓒ businesswoman
    Ⓓ homemaker

22. A secretary must be able to ____ very quickly.
    Ⓐ speak
    Ⓑ mow
    Ⓒ type
    Ⓓ paint

23. I'm learning how to ____ accounting software.
    Ⓐ do
    Ⓑ use
    Ⓒ take
    Ⓓ assemble

24. The dockworkers are ____ new cars onto the large ships.
    Ⓐ putting
    Ⓑ selling
    Ⓒ repairing
    Ⓓ constructing

25. ____ must complete many difficult college courses.
    Ⓐ A truck driver
    Ⓑ A tailor
    Ⓒ An engineer
    Ⓓ A server

B) WHAT'S THE WORD?

| barber | cashier | hairdresser | landscaper | painter | pharmacist |

26–27. The _____ mowed while the _____ worked on the house.

28–29. My father goes to a _____, but my mother goes to a _____.

30–31. The _____ prepared the prescription. Then I paid the _____

at the counter.

C WHAT'S THE WORD?

assisted	built	file	flew	grow	operate	prepared	sold	take

32. Construction workers _____ the bridge in six months.

33. The pilot _____ the plane through a very bad storm.

34. The farmers _____ corn and tomatoes every summer.

35. The home-health aide _____ the elderly man with his meal.

36. The chef _____ a beautiful dinner for the wedding party.

37. I'm an assembly worker. I _____ equipment in a factory.

38. A babysitter is going to _____ care of my son while I go out today.

39. Sonya has to _____ letters in her office every afternoon.

40. Ramon _____ the most cars last year at the dealership.

D CLOZE READING

accountants	cashier	data entry	housekeepers	secretaries
aides	custodians	food-service	receptionists	translators

In addition to doctors, nurses, and health-care _____ 41, there are many other

employees in a hospital. For example, on the first floor _____ 42 greet visitors and

give them information. A _____ 43 works in the gift shop. _____ 44

workers and cooks are in the coffee shop or cafeteria. _____ 45 clean the patients'

rooms and _____ 46 clean the hallways. There are many office workers too, including

managers and _____ 47. In the medical records department, _____ 48

clerks work on computers and make sure that all information is correct. There are many

_____ 49 to check patients' bills and accounts. Also, many hospitals employ

_____ 50 to help patients who don't speak English.

E WRITING SAMPLE

Choose one of these topics and write a paragraph. Write on a separate sheet of paper.

- Describe your occupation. If you aren't working now, what occupation would you like to have?
- What occupations do your friends and relatives have? Describe what each person does.

Name _____

Date _____

A **WHAT'S THE WORD?**

1. The _____ is usually at the entrance to an office.
   - Ⓐ mailroom
   - Ⓑ conference table
   - Ⓒ employee lounge
   - Ⓓ reception area

2. There are more _____ in the supply cabinet.
   - Ⓐ file folders
   - Ⓑ swivel chairs
   - Ⓒ computer workstations
   - Ⓓ receptionists

3. The copier needs a new _____.
   - Ⓐ coat rack
   - Ⓑ file cabinet
   - Ⓒ ink cartridge
   - Ⓓ mailroom

4. Please put the old bank statements in the _____.
   - Ⓐ mailbox
   - Ⓑ typewriter
   - Ⓒ adding machine
   - Ⓓ paper shredder

5. I can cover up this mistake with _____.
   - Ⓐ thumbtacks
   - Ⓑ correction fluid
   - Ⓒ glue
   - Ⓓ legal pads

6. I need a _____ to put this note on the message board.
   - Ⓐ clipboard
   - Ⓑ rubber band
   - Ⓒ pushpin
   - Ⓓ mask

7. Keito put the book in _____ and sent it to his friend.
   - Ⓐ an index card
   - Ⓑ a mailer
   - Ⓒ a mailing label
   - Ⓓ an organizer

8. Tina gave a _____ in the conference room.
   - Ⓐ presentation
   - Ⓑ coffee machine
   - Ⓒ postal scale
   - Ⓓ letter

9. May I have some _____ to close up this box?
   - Ⓐ paper clips
   - Ⓑ work areas
   - Ⓒ packing tape
   - Ⓓ supply rooms

10. The _____ is the administrative assistant's boss.
    - Ⓐ file clerk
    - Ⓑ office assistant
    - Ⓒ receptionist
    - Ⓓ office manager

11. The _____ in our office have very healthy snacks.
    - Ⓐ vending machines
    - Ⓑ coat closets
    - Ⓒ water coolers
    - Ⓓ desk pads

12. Keep these papers together with a staple or a _____.
    - Ⓐ paper cutter
    - Ⓑ paper clip
    - Ⓒ rubber stamp
    - Ⓓ memo pad

13. The clerk put the letters in the _____.
    - Ⓐ personal planner
    - Ⓑ rotary card file
    - Ⓒ stacking tray
    - Ⓓ stapler

14. You can use _____ to glue things.
    - Ⓐ envelopes
    - Ⓑ Post-It note pads
    - Ⓒ desk calendars
    - Ⓓ rubber cement

(continued)

15. I need to look in my _____ to check the time of the meeting.
   Ⓐ letterhead
   Ⓑ postage meter
   Ⓒ appointment book
   Ⓓ presentation board

16. In my office, most employees work in _____.
   Ⓐ cubicles
   Ⓑ locker rooms
   Ⓒ storage closets
   Ⓓ photocopiers

Ⓑ CLOZE READING

For many years, Marco [sorted Ⓐ   gave Ⓑ   took Ⓒ] **17** the mail at a large company.

Several months ago, he saw a job [experience Ⓐ   announcement Ⓑ   full-time Ⓒ] **18** on the

message board in the employee [desk Ⓐ   cubicle Ⓑ   lounge Ⓒ] **19**. It was a position for an office

[message Ⓐ   assistant Ⓑ   planner Ⓒ] **20**. He decided to [respond Ⓐ   ask Ⓑ   talk Ⓒ] **21** to the job notice.

A person from Human Resources called him, and he went to an [application Ⓐ   ink Ⓑ   interview Ⓒ] **22**.

The manager asked him quetions about his [qualifications Ⓐ   family Ⓑ   health Ⓒ] **23**. A few days

later, he got [prepared Ⓐ   hired Ⓑ   requested Ⓒ] **24**. He started in his new position last month. He

types letters, [takes Ⓐ   makes Ⓑ   prepares Ⓒ] **25** phone messages, and files papers. He's very happy in

his new job.

Ⓒ WHAT THE WORD?

| earplugs | goggles | hairnets | helmets | respirators | safety vests |

26. All food preparation workers must wear _____.

27. Workers wear _____ when they use a jackhammer because it's so loud.

28. Construction inside the new shopping mall is very dusty, so some workers have decided to wear _____.

29. Welders use _____ to cover their eyes.

30. All equipment operators wear _____ on their heads.

31. Many construction workers on the highway wear _____ in bright colors so drivers can easily see them.

D WHAT'S THE WORD?

| benefits | interview | previous | resume | salary | search | skills |

32. Roberto learned many useful computer _____ in high school.

33. Kim's _____ experience includes four years as an accountant.

34. I mailed the completed application and my _____ to the store manager.

35. The _____ for this position starts at $20.00 an hour.

36. It's important to dress appropriately for your _____.

37. My employer offers excellent _____, such as medical and dental insurance.

38. I'm reading job notices, want ads, and calling companies for my job _____.

biohazard	corrosive	dump	payroll
clock	defibrillator	forklift	pickax
conveyor	dock	hand	shingles

39. The delivery truck parked at the loading _____.

40. When the _____ belt broke, the assembly line workers had to stop.

41. Bob put the boxes on the _____ truck and pushed it into the freight elevator.

42. Don't open that door! It has a _____ sign on it.

43. The shipping clerk drove the _____ to the warehouse.

44. Every morning the workers put their time cards into the time _____.

45. If you have a question about your check, go to the _____ office.

46. You must use heavy gloves because this liquid is _____.

47. The woman was having a heart attack, so the EMT used a _____.

48. The front-end loader dropped the old wood into the _____ truck.

49. The workers put new _____ on the roof of the house.

50. The landscaper used a _____ to break up the big rock.

E WRITING SAMPLE

Choose one of these topics and write a paragraph. Write on a separate sheet of paper.

- What office supplies and equipment do you have? Where do you keep them?
- Have you applied for a job? Have you gone to an interview? Describe your experience.

A WHAT'S THE WORD?

1. The taxi _____ shows how much your ride costs.
   - Ⓐ ticket
   - Ⓑ meter
   - Ⓒ route
   - Ⓓ antenna

2. The bus driver put my suitcase into the _____.
   - Ⓐ baggage compartment
   - Ⓑ vent
   - Ⓒ luggage
   - Ⓓ trunk

3. Put the subway token into the _____.
   - Ⓐ fare card
   - Ⓑ divider
   - Ⓒ turnstile
   - Ⓓ transfer

4. There's a new _____ under the river.
   - Ⓐ bridge
   - Ⓑ tunnel
   - Ⓒ overpass
   - Ⓓ underpass

5. People are standing on the _____ to wait for the train.
   - Ⓐ timetable
   - Ⓑ conductor
   - Ⓒ track
   - Ⓓ platform

6. Put your foot on the _____ when you want to stop the car.
   - Ⓐ brake
   - Ⓑ signal
   - Ⓒ clutch
   - Ⓓ gas pedal

7. We put down the top of our _____.
   - Ⓐ station wagon
   - Ⓑ van
   - Ⓒ limousine
   - Ⓓ convertible

8. A motorcycle is larger than _____.
   - Ⓐ a moving van
   - Ⓑ an S.U.V.
   - Ⓒ a moped
   - Ⓓ a tractor trailer

9. The biggest kind of truck is the _____.
   - Ⓐ pickup truck
   - Ⓑ semi
   - Ⓒ tow truck
   - Ⓓ hybrid

10. The mechanic opened the _____ of the car to check the engine.
    - Ⓐ dashboard
    - Ⓑ roof rack
    - Ⓒ hood
    - Ⓓ fender

11. The _____ shows how far the car has gone.
    - Ⓐ odometer
    - Ⓑ speedometer
    - Ⓒ accelerator
    - Ⓓ fuel gauge

12. A _____ was burning next to the car with a flat tire.
    - Ⓐ brake light
    - Ⓑ spark plug
    - Ⓒ defroster
    - Ⓓ flare

13. Six passengers can ride in a _____.
    - Ⓐ minivan
    - Ⓑ jeep
    - Ⓒ sports car
    - Ⓓ sedan

14. Drivers stop and pay money at the _____.
    - Ⓐ ticket window
    - Ⓑ tollbooth
    - Ⓒ intersection
    - Ⓓ route sign

(continued)

15. Take the interstate _____ to East Ave.
    (A) intersection
    (B) median
    (C) exit
    (D) divider

16. The _____ says 40 miles per hour.
    (A) temperature gauge
    (B) visor
    (C) stop sign
    (D) speed limit sign

17. Put the key in the _____ to start the car.
    (A) gearshift
    (B) ignition
    (C) power outlet
    (D) alternator

18. A man got _____ the taxi.
    (A) across
    (B) up
    (C) onto
    (D) out of

19. Sue walks her dog _____ the block.
    (A) around
    (B) under
    (C) on
    (D) in

20. I don't like to drive _____ high bridges.
    (A) at
    (B) through
    (C) over
    (D) into

21. Drivers had to take a _____ because of the road construction.
    (A) stop
    (B) detour
    (C) yield
    (D) corner

22. The sign says "no outlet." That means it's a _____.
    (A) dead end
    (B) one-way street
    (C) pedestrian crossing
    (D) railroad crossing

23. Carlos takes the _____ across the river to the city.
    (A) valet parking
    (B) barrier
    (C) ferry
    (D) visa

24. When you enter a country, the _____ may check your luggage.
    (A) flight attendant
    (B) pilot
    (C) immigration officer
    (D) customs officer

25. The bathroom on an airplane is called _____.
    (A) a lavatory
    (B) an aisle
    (C) a terminal
    (D) a carousel

B) WHAT'S THE WORD?

| brake | compartment | pipe | tank | wheel | wipers |

26. windshield _____

27. exhaust _____

28. gas _____

29. steering _____

30. glove _____

31. emergency _____

C   WHAT'S THE WORD?

down	off	onto	past	through

32. Slow down when you drive _____ a school.

33. Turn on your headlights when you drive _____ a tunnel.

34. I found a twenty-dollar bill while I was walking _____ the street.

35. I got _____ the train and found an empty seat.

36. Get _____ the bus at 10th Avenue and walk two blocks north.

bellhop	concierge	guests	housekeeper

37. When I arrived at the hotel, the _____ carried my luggage inside.

38. In the lobby, the _____ helped me buy tickets for the theater.

39. The _____ gave us some extra towels for our room.

40. Only _____ may use the swimming pool.

D   CLOZE READING

agent	carry-on	counter	metal	security
boarding	compartment	gate	seat belt	X-ray

When I got to the airport, I checked my suitcase at the ticket _____ ⁴¹.

After that, I waited in a long line at the _____ ⁴² checkpoint. I had to put my

_____ ⁴³ bag and shoes through the _____ ⁴⁴ machine. Then I

walked through the _____ ⁴⁵ detector. Next, I walked to the

_____ ⁴⁶. About 30 minutes before departure time, I showed my

_____ ⁴⁷ pass to the ticket _____ ⁴⁸ and I boarded the plane.

I put my bag in the overhead _____ ⁴⁹, sat down, and fastened my

_____ ⁵⁰.

E   WRITING SAMPLE

Choose one of these topics and write a paragraph. Write on a separate sheet of paper.

- How do you get to school or work? Do you take public transportation or do you drive? Describe what you do and give directions. How long does it usually take?

- Do you have a car or other vehicle? Describe it. How old is it? Does it have any problems? What do you do for maintenance of your vehicle? What repairs does it need?

Name _____

Date _____

A) WHAT'S THE WORD?

1. Isabel's favorite craft is _____.
- Ⓐ chess
- Ⓑ easels
- Ⓒ embroidery
- Ⓓ a deck of cards

2. If you give me _____, I'll sew the button on your shirt.
- Ⓐ some thread
- Ⓑ a safety pin
- Ⓒ some glue
- Ⓓ some pins

3. I made a bookshelf with a _____.
- Ⓐ thimble
- Ⓑ seesaw
- Ⓒ field guide
- Ⓓ woodworking kit

4. Which board game do you prefer— _____?
- Ⓐ crochet or cards
- Ⓑ checkers or Scrabble
- Ⓒ Monopoly or origami
- Ⓓ ping pong or backgammon

5. Jose goes _____ to read the news.
- Ⓐ swimming
- Ⓑ to the museum
- Ⓒ to a fair
- Ⓓ online

6. My uncle _____ stamps and coins.
- Ⓐ collects
- Ⓑ draws
- Ⓒ builds
- Ⓓ does

7. You can see very small things clearly with a _____.
- Ⓐ camera
- Ⓑ magnifying glass
- Ⓒ target
- Ⓓ shuttlecock

8. You use a saddle when you go _____.
- Ⓐ weightlifting
- Ⓑ cycling
- Ⓒ horseback riding
- Ⓓ bowling

9. A _____ is a safe place for small children to play.
- Ⓐ skateboard ramp
- Ⓑ sandbox
- Ⓒ canteen
- Ⓓ treadmill

10. Parents watched the two teams play on the _____.
- Ⓐ bikeway
- Ⓑ picnic area
- Ⓒ ballfield
- Ⓓ trampoline

11. We cooked food outside on the _____.
- Ⓐ thermos
- Ⓑ lantern
- Ⓒ paddle
- Ⓓ grill

12. Children like going down a _____.
- Ⓐ slide
- Ⓑ kite
- Ⓒ swing
- Ⓓ playground

13. When I go camping, I sleep in a _____.
- Ⓐ net
- Ⓑ tent
- Ⓒ mat
- Ⓓ fountain

14. I follow a _____ when I go hiking.
- Ⓐ trail map
- Ⓑ harness
- Ⓒ climber
- Ⓓ backpack

(continued)

15. It's raining. Let's go _____!
- Ⓐ jogging
- Ⓑ rock climbing
- Ⓒ to the movies
- Ⓓ on a picnic

16. I used a _____ to cut the wood.
- Ⓐ shovel
- Ⓑ harness
- Ⓒ kite
- Ⓓ hatchet

Ⓑ CLOZE READING

Last summer I worked as a | sunbather lifeguard vendor |[17]at the beach near
                            | Ⓐ   Ⓑ   Ⓒ |

my home. I sat for hours and watched the | swimmers painters riders |[18] and surfers.
                                           | Ⓐ   Ⓑ   Ⓒ |

I always wore a hat and | rope elbow pads sunglasses |[19], and of course I put on
                         | Ⓐ   Ⓑ   Ⓒ |

| sunscreen clay glue |[20]. In the mornings, it was usually quiet. Children played with their
| Ⓐ   Ⓑ   Ⓒ |

| grills swings pails |[21] and built sand | fairs castles matches |[22]. Adults sat under
| Ⓐ   Ⓑ   Ⓒ | | Ⓐ   Ⓑ   Ⓒ |

beach | umbrellas chairs balls |[23]. I bought my lunch at the | rock snack shell |[24] bar.
      | Ⓐ   Ⓑ   Ⓒ | | Ⓐ   Ⓑ   Ⓒ |

In the afternoon, the | towels coolers waves |[25] often became big and dangerous. I had to
                      | Ⓐ   Ⓑ   Ⓒ |

tell people to get out of the water.

Ⓒ WHAT'S THE WORD?

| aquarium | beach | concert | historic | mountains | park | yard sales |

26. Every weekend I go to _____. I always buy something useful.

27. My cousin is a surfer. She goes to the _____ almost every day.

28. Many people go running in the city _____.

29. The class visited the _____ site to learn about the Revolutionary War.

30. The music was so relaxing that I fell asleep at the _____.

31. We saw many different types of fish at the _____.

32. Joan likes to go rock climbing in the _____.

D WHAT'S THE WORD?

botanical	carnival	gallery	national	planetarium	play

33. We could see many stars very clearly from the _____.

34. People visit the _____ gardens in the spring to see the beautiful flowers.

35. Dan is a great actor. He's going to be in the school _____ next week.

36. Many people visit this _____ park for a day, but some go camping here.

37. There were some beautiful new watercolor paintings at the art _____.

38. Every August, our town has a _____ with rides and games

arrows	clubs	martial	rowing
beam	helmet	pool	telescope
binoculars	knee pads	racquetball	weights

39. I use _____ when I go bird-watching.

40. The children must be careful with their bows and _____.

41. Omar uses the _____ machine at his health club.

42. Elena practiced on the balance _____ during gymnastics.

43. You need to wear a _____ when you go mountain biking.

44. Cindy learned about astronomy after her parents gave her a _____.

45. Ray lifts _____ at the gym three times a week. He's getting very strong.

46. You have to wear safety goggles when you play _____.

47. "Billiards" is another word for _____.

48. It's a good idea to wear _____ when you go inline skating.

49. I bought some new golf _____. I hope my game gets better.

50. Van has studied _____ arts for five years. He has his black belt.

E WRITING SAMPLE

Choose one of these topics and write a paragraph. Write on a separate sheet of paper.

- What are your hobbies? Do you like to make things? Do you collect things? Do you like to play games? Tell about your hobbies and the supplies you use.

- Where do you like to go in your free time? What are your favorite places to visit? What do you do there? What individual sports and recreation activities do you enjoy doing?

Name _____

Date _____

A) WHAT'S THE WORD?

1. Do you like downhill or _____ skiing?
   - (A) cross-country
   - (B) ice
   - (C) figure
   - (D) snowboard

2. When you go canoeing, you should wear a _____.
   - (A) face guard
   - (B) glove
   - (C) life vest
   - (D) raft

3. Ice hockey players play on a _____.
   - (A) mountain
   - (B) field
   - (C) band
   - (D) rink

4. Volleyball teams play on a _____.
   - (A) cymbal
   - (B) court
   - (C) ballfield
   - (D) net

5. In basketball, players _____ the ball while they are running.
   - (A) dribble
   - (B) walk
   - (C) reach
   - (D) jump

6. The lacrosse team has new _____.
   - (A) poles
   - (B) bindings
   - (C) oars
   - (D) uniforms

7. My favorite type of music is _____ music.
   - (A) drama
   - (B) jazz
   - (C) sitcom
   - (D) soap opera

8. The winner of the _____ won $40,000.
   - (A) comedy
   - (B) bluegrass
   - (C) quiz show
   - (D) nature program

9. I watched an interesting _____ about early American history
   - (A) science fiction film
   - (B) western
   - (C) reality show
   - (D) documentary

10. This river is very fast and strong. It's perfect for _____.
    - (A) swimming
    - (B) surfing
    - (C) white-water rafting
    - (D) bobsledding

11. I put _____ on the end of my fishing line.
    - (A) bait
    - (B) a net
    - (C) fins
    - (D) a blade

12. The _____ danced beautifully.
    - (A) ballet
    - (B) ballerinas
    - (C) musicians
    - (D) conductors

13. Ana _____ the ball and broke her bat.
    - (A) swung
    - (B) caught
    - (C) threw
    - (D) hit

14. There are a lot of _____ on television for young children.
    - (A) cartoons
    - (B) news programs
    - (C) horror movies
    - (D) war movies

(continued)

15. This play is a _____. It has a sad ending.
   Ⓐ sports program
   Ⓑ comedy
   Ⓒ tragedy
   Ⓓ screen

16. _____ will make your stomach strong.
   Ⓐ Hip hop
   Ⓑ Sit-ups
   Ⓒ Shinguards
   Ⓓ Deep knee bends

17. You use your mouth to play a _____.
   Ⓐ harmonica
   Ⓑ drum
   Ⓒ xylophone
   Ⓓ harp

18. The _____ is a keyboard instrument.
   Ⓐ trombone
   Ⓑ organ
   Ⓒ piccolo
   Ⓓ viola

19. _____ music is popular with teenagers.
   Ⓐ Action
   Ⓑ Tuba
   Ⓒ Opera
   Ⓓ Rap

20. A cello is bigger than a _____.
   Ⓐ theater
   Ⓑ piano
   Ⓒ violin
   Ⓓ bass

21. The catcher uses a catcher's _____ to catch the ball.
   Ⓐ paddle
   Ⓑ mitt
   Ⓒ mask
   Ⓓ helmet

22. It's a good idea to _____ before you run.
   Ⓐ stretch
   Ⓑ swim
   Ⓒ shoot
   Ⓓ pitch

23. My brother is very funny. He should become _____.
   Ⓐ a musician
   Ⓑ a ballet dancer
   Ⓒ an opera singer
   Ⓓ a comedian

24. _____ music usually has drums and electric guitars.
   Ⓐ Folk
   Ⓑ Rock
   Ⓒ Reggae
   Ⓓ Bluegrass

25. Keep your eye on the baseball when you _____ your bat.
   Ⓐ throw
   Ⓑ run
   Ⓒ swing
   Ⓓ swim

Ⓑ **WHAT'S THE EQUIPMENT?**

glove	net	paddles	rod	shoulder pads	towrope

26. fishing _____
27. kayaking _____
28. softball _____
29. volleyball _____
30. football _____
31. waterskiing _____

C WHAT'S THE WORD?

bend	bounce	dive	hop	kicked	lift	pitched	served	shot

32. When I _____ the tennis ball, it hit the net.

33. I used to jump into the swimming pool, but now I _____.

34. The football game started when our player _____ the ball.

35. In ping pong, the ball must _____ on the table before you hit it.

36. Barbara _____ the basketball, and it went into the basket.

37. When I _____ over, I can touch my toes.

38. When my children play, they like to _____ like rabbits.

39. Luis _____ a very fast ball. The other player couldn't hit it.

40. Frank is trying to _____ a very heavy weight.

D CLOZE READING

band	concert	entertainment	film	orchestra
classical	conductor	field	musical	soccer

There are many types of _____ 41 to enjoy in our town this Friday night.

At the Civic Auditorium, there will be a _____ 42 music concert. Lydia Markova,

a guest _____ 43, will lead the _____ 44 in music by Mozart.

At the high school, there will be wonderful singing and dancing. Students will present the famous

_____ 45 *West Side Story.* The public library will have a free movie night at

7:30 P.M. Everyone can enjoy the adventure _____ 46 *Lost at Sea.* At the city

park, there will be a free rock music _____ 47 with a _____ 48

from the community college. For sports fans, the adult _____ 49 team will play

the Lakeville team. The game will start at 7:00 P.M. at the town _____ 50.

E WRITING SAMPLE

Choose one of these topics and write a paragraph. Write on a separate sheet of paper.

- What is your favorite team sport? How often do you watch it? What is your favorite team? Who are some of the best players on the team? Do you like to play the sport?

- What is your favorite TV program? What kind of program is it? What is the program about? Why do you like it? When is it on? Do you watch it with your family?

A WHAT'S THE WORD?

1. The farmer is giving hay to the _____.
   - (A) turkeys
   - (B) horses
   - (C) scarecrows
   - (D) anteaters

2. In my state, many farmers grow _____.
   - (A) soybeans and roosters
   - (B) fields and corn
   - (C) wheat and cotton
   - (D) alfalfa and barns

3. At night, chickens sleep in the _____.
   - (A) farmhouse
   - (B) hen house
   - (C) stable
   - (D) pig pen

4. Cows are eating grass in the _____.
   - (A) pasture
   - (B) tractor
   - (C) bushes
   - (D) pansy

5. My eight-year-old sister has two pet _____.
   - (A) otters
   - (B) gophers
   - (C) hyenas
   - (D) hamsters

6. _____ can make a terrible smell.
   - (A) Canaries
   - (B) Slugs
   - (C) Skunks
   - (D) Rabbits

7. The farmers use _____ to water their fields.
   - (A) irrigation systems
   - (B) stables
   - (C) leaves
   - (D) acid rain

8. Sheep have baby _____ in the spring.
   - (A) hens
   - (B) kittens
   - (C) ponies
   - (D) lambs

9. A tree has _____ that covers its trunk.
   - (A) cocoons
   - (B) bark
   - (C) roots
   - (D) bulbs

10. _____ have thorns on their stems.
    - (A) Daffodils
    - (B) Carnations
    - (C) Roses
    - (D) Irises

11. Watch out for poison _____!
    - (A) ivy
    - (B) tulips
    - (C) holly
    - (D) pine

12. During the storm, a big _____ fell down from the maple tree.
    - (A) orchard
    - (B) crocus
    - (C) branch
    - (D) pine cone

13. The marigold flower has many _____.
    - (A) buds
    - (B) needles
    - (C) twigs
    - (D) petals

14. Many kinds of _____ grow in the desert.
    - (A) berries
    - (B) cacti
    - (C) ferns
    - (D) orchids

(continued)

15. There was a _____ because of the very heavy rain.
- Ⓐ mudslide
- Ⓑ drought
- Ⓒ tornado
- Ⓓ blizzard

16. If you turn off your lights, you will _____ energy.
- Ⓐ warn
- Ⓑ concern
- Ⓒ recycle
- Ⓓ conserve

Ⓑ CLOZE READING

I'm with my family at the zoo today. We're having a wonderful time. It's fun to look at all

the | crops Ⓐ   animals Ⓑ   insects Ⓒ |¹⁷. | Chimpanzees Ⓐ   Lizards Ⓑ   Camels Ⓒ |¹⁸ are swinging from

branches in their cages. A male | deer Ⓐ   moose Ⓑ   lion Ⓒ |¹⁹ with a big mane and a beautiful

striped | tiger Ⓐ   bear Ⓑ   gorilla Ⓒ |²⁰ are resting near some rocks. Nearby, zookeepers are giving

an | eel Ⓐ   owl Ⓑ   elephant Ⓒ |²¹ a bath. The animal is using its trunk to spray water on its back. In

another area, pink | flamingos Ⓐ   turtles Ⓑ   seals Ⓒ |²² are standing on their long legs and eating

from the pond. In a separate pond, several big | coyotes Ⓐ   alligators Ⓑ   rats Ⓒ |²³ are sleeping in

the sun. In a big field, tall | beavers Ⓐ   panthers Ⓑ   giraffes Ⓒ |²⁴ are eating leaves from the tops of

the trees. Also, several black and white | zebras Ⓐ   sea horses Ⓑ   parrots Ⓒ |²⁵ are eating grass.

Ⓒ WHAT'S THE WORD?

air	geothermal	hydroelectric	solar
earthquake	hurricanes	natural	warming

26. The sun is the source for _____ energy.

27. Cars and trucks add to _____ pollution in large cities.

28. Typhoons and _____ are similar types of storms.

29. Global _____ is a serious environmental problem.

30. The new _____ energy plant uses energy from deep in the earth.

31. Many people use _____ gas to heat their homes.

32. A powerful _____ under the ocean started a tsunami.

33. This plant uses water from rivers to make _____ power.

bats	bees	porcupine	spider	ticks
bear	jaguar	puppy	squirrel	worms

34. At night, _____ fly around and catch insects.

35. The _____ ran down from the tree and buried the nuts in the ground.

36. A _____ has many sharp quills on its back.

37. Our big black dog used to be a very cute little _____.

38. The _____ is a rare animal. It lives in jungle areas.

39. Robins like to eat _____ from the ground.

40. I found a big _____ in our garage. It was building a web.

41. The _____ are making honey in their hive.

42. The _____ used its sharp claws to catch fish in the stream.

43. After you go hiking, check your legs for _____. These small insects
carry diseases.

cobra	crabs	flounder	frogs	gills	octopus	shark

44. The _____ usually has eight long tentacles.

45. Most fresh water ponds have turtles and _____.

46. Fish have scales and _____.

47. Some _____ dig homes in the dry sand on the seashore.

48. The _____ is a poisonous snake.

49. Tuna and _____ are popular fish for eating.

50. When the lifeguard saw the _____, she told everyone to get out of
the water.

E WRITING SAMPLE

Choose one of these topics and write a paragraph. Write on a separate sheet of paper.

• What animals live in the area near your home? Tell about the animals, birds, and insects. What
kinds of trees, bushes, and flowers grow in your area?

• Are you concerned about the environment? What are you worried about? How do you
conserve energy? What do you recycle?

A) WHAT'S THE WORD?

1. When the police officer stopped me, I had to show my _____.
   Ⓐ taxes
   Ⓑ driver's license
   Ⓒ fingerprints
   Ⓓ proof of residence

2. You have to send a copy of your _____ with your passport application.
   Ⓐ laws
   Ⓑ visa
   Ⓒ work permit
   Ⓓ birth certificate

3. I have to show my employee I.D. _____ at the office entrance.
   Ⓐ badge
   Ⓑ license
   Ⓒ permit
   Ⓓ sentence

4. You must show your _____ for a job in the United States.
   Ⓐ citizenship
   Ⓑ social security card
   Ⓒ police photo
   Ⓓ passport

5. Senators are part of the _____ branch.
   Ⓐ judicial
   Ⓑ executive
   Ⓒ legislative
   Ⓓ criminal

6. Congressmen are also called _____.
   Ⓐ representatives
   Ⓑ senators
   Ⓒ justices
   Ⓓ citizens

7. The _____ explains the laws in the U.S.
   Ⓐ state
   Ⓑ judicial branch
   Ⓒ police department
   Ⓓ president

8. The _____ began in 1954.
   Ⓐ March on Washington
   Ⓑ Great Depression
   Ⓒ Persian Gulf War
   Ⓓ civil rights movement

9. The first person landed on the moon in _____.
   Ⓐ 1969
   Ⓑ 1991
   Ⓒ 1879
   Ⓓ 1929

10. The vice-president works in the _____
    Ⓐ stock market
    Ⓑ Capital Building
    Ⓒ White House
    Ⓓ Supreme Court Building

11. _____ got the right to vote in 1920.
    Ⓐ Pilgrims
    Ⓑ Senators
    Ⓒ Colonists
    Ⓓ Women

12. Amendments are changes to the _____.
    Ⓐ Bill of Rights
    Ⓑ Constitution
    Ⓒ cabinet
    Ⓓ Supreme Court

13. The 1st Amendment guarantees freedom of _____.
    Ⓐ speech
    Ⓑ women
    Ⓒ slavery
    Ⓓ voting

14. The 16th Amendment established _____.
    Ⓐ the Senate
    Ⓑ freedom of the press
    Ⓒ income taxes
    Ⓓ the Preamble

(continued)

15. Freedom of ____ means that large groups can get together in public.
- Ⓐ assembly
- Ⓑ religion
- Ⓒ speech
- Ⓓ movement

16. A. U.S. citizen can vote at age ____.
- Ⓐ 16
- Ⓑ 18
- Ⓒ 21
- Ⓓ 25

17. ____ attacked the U.S. in 2001.
- Ⓐ Slavery
- Ⓑ Civil rights
- Ⓒ Colonists
- Ⓓ Terrorists

18. ____ was the first U.S. president.
- Ⓐ George Washington
- Ⓑ Abraham Lincoln
- Ⓒ Thomas Edison
- Ⓓ Neil Armstrong

19. A citizen must obey ____.
- Ⓐ votes
- Ⓑ news
- Ⓒ laws
- Ⓓ events

20. I had to pay a $50 parking ____.
- Ⓐ proof
- Ⓑ mug shot
- Ⓒ bail
- Ⓓ fine

21. The verdict was that the woman was ____.
- Ⓐ evidence
- Ⓑ innocent
- Ⓒ arrested
- Ⓓ registered

22. Several ____ saw the man steal the car.
- Ⓐ suspects
- Ⓑ bailiffs
- Ⓒ witnesses
- Ⓓ inmates

23. The man was ____, so he went to jail.
- Ⓐ convicted
- Ⓑ released
- Ⓒ acquitted
- Ⓓ booked

24. After my uncle was arrested, he ____ an attorney.
- Ⓐ sentenced
- Ⓑ went
- Ⓒ stood
- Ⓓ hired

25. The ____ asked the defendant several additional questions.
- Ⓐ police officer
- Ⓑ judge
- Ⓒ prisoner
- Ⓓ jury

Ⓑ U.S. HISTORY

Civil War	Korean War	Revolutionary War	Vietnam War	World War II

26. 1861–1865 _____

27. 1950–1953 _____

28. 1939–1945 _____

29. 1775–1783 _____

30. 1964–1973 _____

C WHAT'S THE HOLIDAY?

| Halloween | Martin Luther King, Jr. Day | New Year's Day | Valentine's Day |
| Independence Day | Memorial Day | Thanksgiving | Veterans Day |

31. January 1 _____

32. The 3rd Monday in January _____

33. February 14 _____

34. The last Monday in May _____

35. July 4 _____

36. October 31 _____

37. November 11 _____

38. The 4th Tuesday in November _____

D CLOZE READING

| Allegiance | citizen | government | jury | passport | student |
| ceremony | citizenship | I.D. | naturalization | permit | test |

When Chet came to the United States from Thailand five years ago, he had a

_____ ^39 from his country. He was studying English, so he had a student

_____ ^40 card and a _____ ^41 visa. Later he got a full-time job

and a work _____ ^42. Even though he lived in the U.S. and paid taxes,

he wasn't a U.S. _____ ^43. Last month, he applied for _____ ^44.

Now he's taking a class and learning about U.S. _____ ^45. Next year, he'll

take the citizenship _____ ^46 and have a _____ ^47 interview. If

he passes, he'll attend a naturalization _____ ^48. After he recites the Oath

of _____ ^49, he'll become a citizen. Then he'll have the right to vote and serve

on a _____ ^50.

E WRITING SAMPLE

Choose one of these topics and write a paragraph. Write on a separate sheet of paper.

- Tell about all the forms of identification you have. When and where did you receive each one? When do you need each form of identification? When will you need a new one?

- Do you celebrate any of the U.S. holidays? Which ones are your favorites? Tell what you usually do on each holiday. Who do you see? What do you eat?

A   WHAT'S THE WORD?

1. I called a _____ to make plans for my trip.
   - Ⓐ guided tour
   - Ⓑ museum
   - Ⓒ travel agent
   - Ⓓ shuttle bus

2. Alicia wants to go on a _____ because she loves the ocean.
   - Ⓐ ski trip
   - Ⓑ safari
   - Ⓒ train trip
   - Ⓓ cruise

3. This _____ company has great sightseeing trips in Canada.
   - Ⓐ tour
   - Ⓑ historic
   - Ⓒ car
   - Ⓓ cell phone

4. Our class visited an important _____.
   - Ⓐ concierge
   - Ⓑ family trip
   - Ⓒ historic site
   - Ⓓ concert

5. I called _____ to order breakfast.
   - Ⓐ housekeeping
   - Ⓑ room service
   - Ⓒ the front desk
   - Ⓓ the chef

6. Only strong hikers should go on this _____ in the mountains.
   - Ⓐ train
   - Ⓑ sightseeing
   - Ⓒ bus
   - Ⓓ expedition

7. Our _____ will give you a free ride.
   - Ⓐ taxi
   - Ⓑ hotel courtesy vehicle
   - Ⓒ rental car
   - Ⓓ bus tour

8. I made my reservations over _____.
   - Ⓐ the phone
   - Ⓑ an agency
   - Ⓒ a credit card
   - Ⓓ a suite

9. You can pick up your luggage at the _____.
   - Ⓐ single room
   - Ⓑ shuttle bus
   - Ⓒ baggage claim area
   - Ⓓ baggage claim check

10. May I cash this _____?
    - Ⓐ money
    - Ⓑ traveler's check
    - Ⓒ exchange
    - Ⓓ credit card

11. The officer will inspect your bags at _____.
    - Ⓐ the travel agency
    - Ⓑ the restaurant
    - Ⓒ customs
    - Ⓓ the taxi stand

12. We studied the environment during our _____ on the island.
    - Ⓐ eco-tour
    - Ⓑ ski trip
    - Ⓒ business trip
    - Ⓓ airplane trip

13. Many guests were checking out at the _____.
    - Ⓐ restroom
    - Ⓑ passport control
    - Ⓒ bell desk
    - Ⓓ front desk

14. _____ will order show tickets for you.
    - Ⓐ Maintenance
    - Ⓑ The concierge
    - Ⓒ The Internet cafe
    - Ⓓ The waiter

(continued)

15. Every summer, we take a _____ to visit our cousins.
    Ⓐ study tour
    Ⓑ guided tour
    Ⓒ family trip
    Ⓓ business trip

16. If you need help with your bags, call the _____.
    Ⓐ bell desk
    Ⓑ tour company
    Ⓒ fitness club
    Ⓓ concierge

17. _____ will clean your room after lunch.
    Ⓐ Room service
    Ⓑ Housekeeping
    Ⓒ The hotel manager
    Ⓓ Gardeners

18. May I have a 5:00 A.M. _____?
    Ⓐ wake-up call
    Ⓑ telephone
    Ⓒ view
    Ⓓ taxi stand

19. _____. What did you say?
    Ⓐ Please
    Ⓑ Excuse
    Ⓒ Repeat
    Ⓓ I'm sorry

20. A single room usually has _____.
    Ⓐ a view
    Ⓑ one bed
    Ⓒ double beds
    Ⓓ three beds

21. You must show your _____ to enter another country.
    Ⓐ postcard
    Ⓑ plane ticket
    Ⓒ passport
    Ⓓ credit card

22. I called maintenance and said, "_____"
    Ⓐ The heat in our suite isn't working.
    Ⓑ We need four more towels.
    Ⓒ I'd like to mail this to my country.
    Ⓓ I need to check out.

23. In an emergency, say, "_____"
    Ⓐ Good-bye!
    Ⓑ Please go away!
    Ⓒ Freeze!
    Ⓓ Help!

24. I didn't understand her. So I said, "_____"
    Ⓐ Please repeat that.
    Ⓑ Look out!
    Ⓒ What's your name?
    Ⓓ Don't move!

25. If someone is bothering you, say, "_____"
    Ⓐ Please write that down!
    Ⓑ Help!
    Ⓒ Get away from me!
    Ⓓ Fire!

Ⓑ WHAT'S THE WORD?

business	cafe	club	exchange	room	tour

26. non-smoking _____

27. Internet _____

28. health _____

29. guided _____

30. _____ trip

31. money _____ counter

C WHAT'S THE WORD?

| car rental | customs | declaration | souvenirs | traveler's checks | visa |

32. Before you enter a country, you must fill out a customs _____ form.

33. Some countries require visitors to have a _____.

34. At _____, the agent will look through your luggage.

35. When you travel, _____ are safer than cash.

36. After we get our bags, we need to go to the _____ counter to pick up keys.

37. During my trip, I bought some small _____ to bring home as gifts.

| book | exchange | pay | use |

38. It isn't polite to _____ a cell phone in a restaurant.

39. Most customers _____ for their hotels with a credit card.

40. I went to the bank to _____ my dollars.

41. I usually go online to _____ my hotel reservation.

D CLOZE READING

| double | hotel | reservations | show | sightseeing | suite | tour | trip | view |

Last weekend, the Cardozas took a family _____ ^{42} to an historic city in the mountains. They stayed in a very nice _____ ^{43}. The manager gave them a large _____ ^{44} with _____ ^{45} beds. The room was on the sixth floor and had a nice _____ ^{46} of the city. The next morning they took a walking _____ ^{47} of the city. In the afternoon, they went _____ ^{48} and bought a few souvenirs. The concierge at the hotel made _____ ^{49} for them at a famous restaurant. She also got them tickets for a _____ ^{50} in the evening.

E WRITING SAMPLE

Choose one of these topics and write a paragraph. Write on a separate sheet of paper.

- Describe a recent family trip. Where did you go? How did you get there? Who went with you? How long did you stay? What did you do? Did you visit anybody? Who?

- Tell about a special trip you would like to take someday. Where will you go? How will you get there? What exciting things will you do?

WORD BY WORD PICTURE DICTIONARY, 2ND ED.
LITERACY-LEVEL TESTS ANSWER KEY

UNIT 1 TEST: Picture Dictionary Pages 1–3

A. What Is It?
1. B
2. A
3. D
4. C

B. What's the Word?
5. B
6. D
7. A
8. C
9. B
10. C

C. Who Are They?
11. grandfather
12. grandmother
13. father
14. mother
15. aunt
16. son
17. daughter

D. What's the Word?
18. uncle
19. cousins
20. aunt
21. baby

E. Personal Information
22–25. (Answers will vary.)

UNIT 2A TEST: Picture Dictionary Pages 4–8

A. What Is It?
1. C
2. D
3. A
4. B

B. What's the Word?
5. D
6. B
7. A
8. B
9. D
10. C

C. What's the Word?
11. Raise
12. Read
13. Write
14. Go
15. Stand

D. Where Is It?
16. under
17. in front of
18. on
19. in
20. behind

E. What's the Action?
21. Work with a partner.
22. Put away your book.
23. Spell your name.
24. Turn off the lights.
25. Circle the correct answer.

UNIT 2B TEST: Picture Dictionary Pages 9–14

A. What's the Action?
1. B
2. D
3. C
4. B

B. What's the Action?
5. A
6. D
7. B
8. C
9. B
10. D

C. What Do You Say?
11. Good morning.
12. See you later.
13. Excuse me.
14. I don't understand.

D. Everyday Conversation
15. Not much.
16. Fine, thanks.
17. You're welcome.
18. Nice to meet you, too.
19. Yes. Hold on a moment.

E. Weather
20. sunny
21. raining
22. cloudy
23. snowing
24. windy
25. lightning

UNIT 3 TEST: Picture Dictionary Pages 15–19

A. What Is It?
1. B
2. C
3. B
4. A

B. What's the Word?
5. D
6. B
7. A
8. D
9. C
10. B

C. What Time Is It?
11. 9:15
12. 8:45
13. 5:10
14. 10:05

D. How Much Is It?
15. $.65
16. $.18
17. $10.25
18. $6.50

E. What's Missing?
19. March
20. May
21. September
22. December
23. Tuesday
24. Thursday
25. Sunday

UNIT 4A TEST: Picture Dictionary Pages 20–27

A. What Is It?
1. A
2. D
3. B
4. D

B. What's the Word?
5. B
6. C
7. A
8. C
9. B
10. D

C. What Is It?
11. couch
12. rug
13. window
14. wall
15. fireplace
16. coffee table
17. mirror
18. lamp

D. What Is It?
19. medicine cabinet
20. shower
21. tub
22. microwave
23. stove
24. oven
25. toaster

UNIT 4B TEST: Picture Dictionary Pages 28–35

A. What Is It?
1. D
2. C
3. A
4. C

B. What's the Word?
5. B
6. D
7. A
8. C
9. D
10. B

C. What Is It?
11. glue
12. oil
13. window cleaner
14. flashlight

D. Who Is It?
15. exterminator
16. plumber
17. appliance repairperson
18. locksmith
19. electrician

E. What's the Word?
20. floor
21. lock
22. security deposit
23. lobby
24. basement
25. smoke detector

UNIT 5 TEST: Picture Dictionary Pages 36–41

A. What Is It?
1. B
2. C
3. B
4. D

B. What's the Word?
5. D
6. A
7. C
8. D
9. B
10. A

C. What Is It?
11. movie theater
12. shopping mall
13. clinic
14. restaurant
15. cleaners
16. supermarket
17. department store

D. What Is It?
18. deli
19. pizza shop
20. donut shop
21. bakery
22. mailbox
23. sidewalk
24. parking meter
25. fire alarm box

UNIT 6 TEST: Picture Dictionary Pages 42–47

A. What Is It?
1. A
2. C
3. D
4. A

B. What's the Word?
5. C
6. B
7. A
8. C
9. D
10. B

C. What's the Word?
11. confused
12. surprised
13. nervous
14. scared

D. What's the Answer?
15. old
16. soft
17. dirty
18. open
19. full

E. What's the Word?
20. tall
21. short
22. wet
23. dry
24. loose
25. tight

UNIT 7A TEST: Picture Dictionary Pages 48–56

A. What Is It?
1. C
2. A
3. B
4. D

B. What's the Word?
5. A
6. C
7. B
8. D
9. C
10. B

C. What Is It?
11. straws
12. tissues
13. paper towels
14. shopping basket
15. liquid soap
16. paper bag
17. plastic wrap
18. shopping cart

D. What's the Word?
19. loaf
20. pound
21. box
22. bottle
23. head
24. jar
25. dozen

UNIT 7B TEST: Picture Dictionary Pages 57–64

A. What Is It?
1. C
2. D
3. A
4. D

B. What's the Word?
5. B
6. C
7. A
8. B
9. D
10. C

C. What Is It?
11. ounce
12. quart
13. tablespoon
14. gallon

D. Who Is It?
15. server
16. customer
17. hostess
18. busperson

E. What Is It?
19. salad
20. pancakes
21. milkshake
22. sandwich
23. baked potato
24. cheeseburger
25. apple pie

UNIT 8 TEST: Picture Dictionary Pages 65–73

A. What Is It?
1. C
2. D
3. B
4. A

B. What's the Word?

5. C
6. D
7. B
8. A
9. C
10. B

C. What Is It?

11. dress
12. socks
13. jacket
14. blouse
15. sunglasses
16. umbrella
17. raincoat
18. pajamas

D. Which Group?

19–22. gloves, parka, scarf, sweater
23–25. shorts, swimsuit, T-shirt

UNIT 9 TEST: Picture Dictionary Pages 74–79

A. What Is It?

1. D
2. B
3. A
4. C

B. What's the Word?

5. A
6. C
7. D
8. C
9. B
10. C

C. What Is It?

11. printer
12. cable
13. mouse
14. monitor
15. headphones
16. cassette
17. remote control

D. What Is It?

18. receipt
19. label
20. sale sign
21. price tag

E. What's the Word?

22. return
23. try on
24. exchange
25. pay for

UNIT 10 TEST: Picture Dictionary Pages 80–85

A. What Is It?

1. D
2. A
3. C
4. D

B. What's the Word?

5. B
6. C
7. A
8. B
9. A
10. D

C. What Is It?

11. fire
12. bank robbery
13. vandalism
14. car accident
15. burglary
16. gas leak
17. chemical spill
18. gang violence

D. What's the Word?

19. bank
20. police station
21. senior center
22. ambulance
23. nursery
24. city hall
25. dump

UNIT 11A TEST: Picture Dictionary Pages 86–91

A. What Is It?

1. B
2. C
3. A
4. C

B. What's the Word?

5. A
6. C
7. B
8. C
9. D
10. A

C. What Is It?

11. insect bite
12. runny nose
13. cough
14. stiff neck
15. bandage
16. allergic reaction
17. splint
18. rescue breathing

D. What Is It?

19. asthma
20. high blood pressure
21. influenza
22. diabetes
23. heart attack
24. heatstroke
25. Heimlich maneuver

UNIT 11B TEST: Picture Dictionary Pages 92–100

A. What Is It?

1. B
2. A
3. D
4. B

B. What's the Word?

5. C
6. D
7. C
8. A
9. B
10. D

C. What Is It?

11. examine your eyes
12. listen to your heart
13. take your temperature
14. change the diaper
15. drink fluids
16. check your blood pressure

D. What Is It?

17. prescription
18. sling
19. cast
20. stitches

E. What's the Word?

21. razor
22. shampoo
23. blow dryer
24. bottle
25. deodorant

UNIT 12A TEST: Picture Dictionary Pages 101–104

A. What Is It?

1. A
2. C
3. B
4. C

B. What's the Word?

5. D
6. B
7. A
8. B
9. C
10. D

C. What Is It?

11. band
12. coach
13. auditorium
14. guidance office
15. adult school
16. university
17. elementary school
18. vocational school

D. What Is It?
19. chorus
20. football
21. drama
22. orchestra
23. yearbook
24. community service
25. international club

UNIT 12B TEST: Picture Dictionary Pages 105–111

A. What Is It?
1. C
2. B
3. A
4. D

B. What's the Word?
5. D
6. C
7. B
8. C
9. A
10. B

C. What Is It?
11. period
12. comma
13. question mark
14. exclamation point
15. preposition
16. noun
17. verb
18. pronoun

D. What's the Word?
19. plus
20. times
21. minus
22. divided by

E. What Is It?
23. three quarters
24. fifty percent
25. one third

UNIT 13A TEST: Picture Dictionary Pages 112–117

A. What Is It?
1. B
2. A
3. D
4. B

B. What's the Word?
5. C
6. D
7. A
8. B
9. C
10. D

C. Who Is It?
11. carpenter
12. firefighter
13. hairdresser
14. artist
15. barber
16. delivery person
17. babysitter
18. businessman

D. What's the Word?
19. mows lawns
20. serves food
21. flies airplanes
22. speaks Spanish and English
23. teaches students
24. prepares food
25. builds houses

UNIT 13B TEST: Picture Dictionary Pages 118–123

A. What Is It?
1. C
2. A
3. D
4. B

B. What's the Word?
5. B
6. C
7. D
8. A
9. C
10. A

C. What's the Word?
11. full-time
12. part-time
13. hour
14. evenings
15. excellent
16. experience

D. What Is It?
17. take a message
18. make copies
19. fill out an application
20. go to an interview

E. What Is It?
21. hard hat
22. goggles
23. safety vest
24. fire extinguisher
25. first-aid kit

UNIT 14 TEST: Picture Dictionary Pages 124–133

A. What Is It?
1. B
2. D
3. C
4. B

B. What's the Word?
5. B
6. D
7. A
8. C
9. D
10. B

C. What Is It?
11. no right turn
12. school crossing
13. no left turn
14. pedestrian crossing
15. passport
16. security officer
17. ticket counter
18. baggage
19. customs officer
20. boarding pass

D. What's the Word?
21. in front of
22. in
23. into
24. behind
25. under

UNIT 15A TEST: Picture Dictionary Pages 134–141

A. What Is It?
1. B
2. D
3. B
4. A

B. What's the Word?
5. C
6. D
7. A
8. D
9. B
10. A

C. What's the Word?
11. jogging
12. swimmer
13. boxing
14. surfer
15. gymnastics
16. historic site
17. national park
18. skateboarding

D. What Is It?
19. cooler
20. tent
21. grill
22. sun hat
23. kite
24. backpack
25. picnic table

UNIT 15B TEST: Picture Dictionary Pages 142–150

A. What Is It?
1. B
2. D
3. C
4. A

B. What's the Word?
5. C
6. B
7. A
8. C
9. D
10. B

C. What Is It?
11. rock music
12. comedy
13. western
14. musical
15. game show
16. classical music
17. cartoon
18. talk show

D. Which Group?
19–22. canoeing, sailing, snorkeling, swimming
23–25. ice skating, skiing, sledding

UNIT 16 TEST: Picture Dictionary Pages 151–159

A. What Is It?
1. A
2. C
3. D
4. B

B. What's the Word?
5. B
6. D
7. C
8. A
9. C
10. B

C. What Is It?
11. flood
12. tornado
13. hurricane
14. earthquake
15. global warming
16. solar energy
17. recycle
18. air pollution

D. Which Group?
19–21. chicken, horse, turkey
22–25. bear, elephant, ostrich, tiger

UNIT 17 TEST (US EDITION): Picture Dictionary Pages 160–166

A. What Is It?
1. B
2. C
3. A
4. C

B. What's the Word?
5. B
6. D
7. A
8. C
9. D
10. A

C. What Is It?
11. the Constitution
12. freedom of speech
13. freedom of the press
14. freedom of religion
15. the right to vote
16. Civil War
17. Vietnam War
18. World War II
19. Revolutionary War

D. What Is It?
20. vote
21. follow the news
22. pay taxes
23. apply for citizenship
24. take a citizenship test
25. serve on a jury

UNIT 17 TEST (INTERNATIONAL EDITION): Picture Dictionary Pages 160–165

A. What Is It?
1. C
2. B
3. D
4. A

B. What's the Word?
5. C
6. D
7. A
8. D
9. C
10. B

C. What Is It?
11. taxi stand
12. non-smoking room
13. shuttle bus
14. Internet cafe

D. What's the Word?
15. tickets
16. towels
17. dinner
18. days
19. city

E. What Do You Say?
20. Help!
21. Fire!
22. Look out!
23. Please go away!
24. Please write that down.
25. What did you say?

WORD BY WORD BEGINNING-LEVEL TESTS ANSWER KEY

UNIT 1 TEST: Picture Dictionary Pages 1–3

A. Personal Information
1. first name
2. middle initial
3. last name
4. street number
5. street
6. apartment number
7. city
8. state
9. zip code

B. What's the Word?
10. address
11. area code
12. telephone number
13. e-mail address
14. social security number
15. date of birth

C. Who Are They?
16. parents
17. aunt
18. mother
19. cousin
20. brother-in-law

D. What's the Answer?
21–25. (Answers will vary.)

E. What's the Word?
26. C   29. A
27. A   30. D
28. B   31. B

F. The Jackson Family
32. B   37. D
33. C   38. B
34. D   39. D
35. A   40. C
36. A   41. B

G. Who Are They?
42. C   47. C
43. B   48. B
44. A   49. D
45. D   50. C
46. B

H. Writing Sample
(Answers will vary.)

UNIT 2A TEST: Picture Dictionary Pages 4–8

A. What's the Word?
1. calculator
2. pencil sharpener
3. binder
4. globe
5. thumbtack
6. graph paper
7. wastebasket
8. eraser

B. Which Group?
9–12. bulletin board, chalkboard, clock, loudspeaker
13–16. keyboard, monitor, mouse, printer
17–20. chalk, marker, pen, pencil

C. What's the Word?
21. hand
22. mistakes
23. listen
24. book
25. Put

D. Classroom Actions
26. A   30. A
27. D   31. D
28. B   32. B
29. C   33. A

E. Cloze Reading
34. B   39. B
35. A   40. A
36. C   41. C
37. A   42. B
38. C

F. The Classroom
43. B   47. D
44. D   48. B
45. C   49. C
46. B   50. A

G. Writing Sample
(Answers will vary.)

UNIT 2B TEST: Picture Dictionary Pages 9–14

A. What Are You Doing?
1. studying   7. combing
2. walking   8. feeding
3. doing   9. going
4. cleaning   10. exercising
5. taking   11. relaxing
6. driving   12. ironing

B. What Do They Do?
13. uses
14. brushes
15. puts
16. washes
17. gets

C. What's the Weather?
18. foggy
19. drizzling
20. windy
21. cloudy
22. lightning
23. snowing
24. humid
25. hailing

D. What's the Answer?
26. C   30. A
27. A   31. B
28. B   32. A
29. C

E. Cloze Reading
33. C   39. B
34. B   40. A
35. A   41. A
36. B   42. C
37. C   43. B
38. B   44. A

F. What's the Answer?
45. C   48. D
46. A   49. A
47. B   50. D

G. Writing Sample
(Answers will vary.)

UNIT 3 TEST: Picture Dictionary Pages 15–19

A. What's the Next Word?
1. eleven
2. sixth
3. third
4. fifteenth
5. ninety

B. How Much Is It?
6. $1.39
7. $5.07
8. $ .50

C. What Time Is It?
9. half past seven
10. a quarter after seven
11. noon
12. a quarter to seven
13. three ten
14. ten to three

D. It's Tuesday
15. Monday
16. April
17. the fifth
18. Wednesday
19. 4/3
20. 4/4

E. What's the Answer?
21–25. (Answers will vary.)

F. What's the Word?
26. A   29. B
27. D   30. D
28. C   31. C

G. Check the Facts
32. C   35. C
33. D   36. A
34. B   37. D

H. What's the Answer?

38. C		41. D	
39. A		42. B	
40. C		43. D	

I. Cloze Reading

44. C		48. A	
45. A		49. C	
46. B		50. A	
47. C			

J. Writing Sample
(Answers will vary.)

UNIT 4A TEST: Picture Dictionary Pages 20–27

A. Where Do They Live?

1. town
2. apartment building
3. duplex
4. city
5. house
6. suburbs
7. nursing home
8. condominium

B. What's the Word?

9. vase	13. bed
10. armchair	14. plant
11. cabinet	15. dishwasher
12. bed	

C. What's the Next Word?

16. table	21. lamp
17. radio	22. box
18. player	23. frame
19. sheet	24. system
20. blanket	25. screen

D. Around the House

26. B	35. B
27. A	36. A
28. D	37. C
29. C	38. D
30. A	39. A
31. D	40. C
32. C	41. A
33. A	42. B
34. C	43. D

E. Cloze Reading

44. B	48. B
45. A	49. C
46. C	50. B
47. A	

F. Writing Sample
(Answers will vary.)

UNIT 4B TEST: Picture Dictionary Pages 28–35

A. What Is It?

1. rake	7. shovel
2. vacuum cleaner	8. ladder
3. dustpan	9. sponge mop
4. saw	10. hose
5. hammer	11. broom
6. wheelbarrow	12. screwdriver

B. Who Is It?

13. plumber	16. locksmith
14. exterminator	17. carpenter
15. appliance	18. electrician

C. What's the Word?

19. trim	23. wash
20. mow	24. vacuum
21. rake	25. wax
22. polish	

D. Around the House

26. C	35. A
27. D	36. B
28. B	37. C
29. A	38. A
30. C	39. D
31. B	40. B
32. C	41. C
33. D	42. D
34. B	

E. Cloze Reading

43. B	47. A
44. A	48. B
45. B	49. C
46. C	50. A

F. Writing Sample
(Answers will vary.)

UNIT 5 TEST: Picture Dictionary Pages 36–41

A. In the City

1. fire hydrant	7. pedestrian
2. parking garage	8. manhole
3. mailbox	9. bus stop
4. curb	10. traffic light
5. crosswalk	11. street vendor
6. intersection	12. parking meter

B. Where Are They?

13. supermarket
14. park
15. hardware store
16. restaurant
17. jewelry store
18. furniture store
19. library
20. cleaners
21. barber shop
22. video store
23. electronics store
24. drug store
25. pet shop

C. What's the Word?

26. B	34. B
27. C	35. D
28. A	36. A
29. D	37. B
30. C	38. D
31. B	39. C
32. A	40. A
33. C	41. D

D. Cloze Reading

42. B	47. C
43. A	48. B
44. C	49. A
45. A	50. B
46. B	

E. Writing Sample
(Answers will vary.)

UNIT 6 TEST: Picture Dictionary Pages 42–47

A. How Do You Feel?

1. sad	7. tired
2. happy	8. hungry
3. bored	9. hot
4. sick	10. thirsty
5. cold	11. frustrated
6. furious	12. nervous

B. What's the Opposite?

13. old	18. expensive
14. slow	19. smooth
15. messy	20. poor
16. hard	21. loose
17. narrow	22. plain

C. What Do You Look Like?

23–25. (Answers will vary.)

D. What's the Word?

26. B	34. D
27. C	35. B
28. A	36. A
29. D	37. D
30. A	38. C
31. C	39. D
32. B	40. B
33. C	41. A

E. Cloze Reading

42. B	47. A
43. A	48. B
44. B	49. A
45. A	50. C
46. C	

F. Writing Sample
(Answers will vary.)

UNIT 7A TEST: Picture Dictionary Pages 48–56

A. What Is It?

1. tomato
2. lettuce
3. banana
4. apple
5. eggs
6. steak
7. milk
8. fish
9. pear
10. nuts
11. chicken
12. cantaloupe
13. grapes
14. strawberries
15. green pepper
16. onion
17. cherries
18. ham
19. green bean
20. corn

B. What's the Word?

21. loaf
22. carton
23. jar
24. head
25. six-pack

C. What's the Word?

26. B
27. C
28. D
29. A
30. C
31. B
32. A
33. B
34. A
35. C
36. D
37. B
38. A
39. D
40. C
41. B

D. Cloze Reading

42. C
43. B
44. A
45. B
46. A
47. C
48. B
49. A
50. B

E. Writing Sample

(Answers will vary.)

UNIT 7B TEST: Picture Dictionary Pages 57–64

A. What Is It?

1. hot dog
2. spaghetti
3. muffin
4. tossed salad
5. burrito
6. sandwich
7. apple pie
8. waffles
9. pizza
10. bagel
11. ice cream sundae
12. french fries
13. bacon
14. fruit cup
15. hamburger
16. baked potato
17. mixed vegetables
18. shrimp cocktail
19. pita bread
20. sausages

B. What's the Word?

21. Boil
22. Peel
23. Bake
24. Pour
25. Grate

C. What's the Word?

26. B
27. C
28. A
29. D
30. C
31. B
32. A
33. B
34. D
35. B
36. A
37. C
38. C
39. B
40. D
41. A

D. Cloze Reading

42. B
43. C
44. A
45. B
46. C

E. Writing Sample

(Answers will vary.)

UNIT 8 TEST: Picture Dictionary Pages 65–73

A. What Are They Wearing?

1. turtleneck
2. cardigan sweater
3. belt
4. jeans
5. loafers
6. necklace
7. blouse
8. vest
9. skirt
10. high heels

B. Which Group?

11–15. running shorts, sleeveless shirt, swimsuit, T-shirt, tank top
16–20. boots, down jacket, parka, scarf, sweater

C. What Are They Doing?

21. sorting
22. loading
23. hanging
24. unloading
25. putting

D. What's the Word?

26. B
27. C
28. D
29. A
30. C
31. B
32. A
33. D
34. B
35. C
36. D
37. A
38. C
39. B

E. Cloze Reading

40. B
41. A
42. C
43. B
44. A
45. B
46. C
47. A
48. B
49. A
50. C

F. Writing Sample

(Answers will vary.)

UNIT 9 TEST: Picture Dictionary Pages 74–79

A. What Is It?

1. printer
2. DVD player
3. speakers
4. notebook computer
5. clock radio
6. keyboard
7. video camera
8. cordless phone
9. digital camera
10. mouse
11. remote control
12. cell phone
13. battery charger
14. price tag
15. receipt
16. camera case
17. portable CD player
18. surge protector

B. At the Department Store

19. Men's Clothing
20. Home Furnishings
21. Children's Clothing
22. Household Appliances
23. Housewares
24. Customer Service
25. Electronics

C. What's the Word?

26. C
27. A
28. D
29. B
30. C
31. B
32. A
33. D
34. B
35. A
36. D
37. A
38. C
39. B
40. D
41. A
42. C
43. B

D. Cloze Reading

44. B
45. A
46. C
47. A
48. B
49. C
50. B

E. Writing Sample

(Answers will vary.)

UNIT 10 TEST: Picture Dictionary Pages 80–85

A. Banking Actions

1. write a check
2. use the ATM machine
3. open an account
4. balance the checkbook
5. cash a check
6. bank online

B. Who Are They?

7. emergency operator
8. mayor
9. activities director
10. paramedic
11. sanitation worker

C. Using the ATM

12. Insert
13. Enter
14. Select
15. Withdraw
16. Transfer
17. Remove

D. What Happened?

18. fire
19. vandalism
20. explosion
21. burglary
22. drunk driver
23. bank robbery
24. accident
25. downed power line

E. What's the Word?

26. C	34. A
27. B	35. B
28. A	36. C
29. B	37. B
30. D	38. A
31. B	39. C
32. C	40. D
33. D	41. B

F. Cloze Reading

42. A	47. A
43. B	48. C
44. B	49. A
45. A	50. B
46. C	

G. Writing Sample

(Answers will vary.)

UNIT 11A TEST: Picture Dictionary Pages 86–91

A. Parts of the Body

1. head	8. wrist
2. eye	9. waist
3. ear	10. hip
4. nose	11. leg
5. neck	12. knee
6. chest	13. ankle
7. arm	14. foot

B. What's the Word?

15. stomachache	18. fever
16. sunburn	19. blisters
17. cavity	20. laryngitis

C. What First Aid Do These People Need?

21. rescue breathing
22. a splint
23. the Heimlich maneuver
24. a tourniquet
25. CPR

D. What's the Word?

26. A	34. A
27. C	35. B
28. B	36. D
29. C	37. C
30. A	38. A
31. B	39. B
32. C	40. C
33. D	41. A

E. Cloze Reading

42. B	47. C
43. A	48. B
44. C	49. A
45. B	50. C
46. A	

F. Writing Sample

(Answers will vary.)

UNIT 11B TEST: Picture Dictionary Pages 92–100

A. Staying Healthy

1. rest in bed
2. examine your eyes
3. talk with a counselor
4. measure your weight
5. give a shot
6. check your blood pressure
7. take a chest X-ray
8. draw blood
9. take vitamins

B. What's the Word?

10. injection
11. cough syrup
12. wheelchair
13. walker
14. cast
15. cold tablets
16. crutches
17. nasal spray

C. Who Are They?

18. lab technician
19. dentist
20. therapist
21. orthopedist
22. pediatrician
23. cardiologist
24. surgeon
25. X-ray technician

D. What's the Word?

26. D	34. C
27. B	35. D
28. C	36. A
29. A	37. C
30. B	38. D
31. C	39. C
32. B	40. A
33. A	41. B

E. Cloze Reading

42. B	47. B
43. A	48. A
44. C	49. C
45. A	50. B
46. C	

F. Writing Sample

(Answers will vary.)

UNIT 12A TEST: Picture Dictionary Pages 101–104

A. Schools and Places

1. hallway
2. principal's office
3. cafeteria
4. music class
5. classroom
6. gymnasium
7. track
8. main office
9. science lab
10. medical school
11. adult school
12. vocational school

B. What's the Order?

13. nursery school
14. elementary school
15. middle school
16. high school
17. college
18. graduate school

C. What's the Subject?

19. geography
20. art
21. English
22. government
23. computer science
24. history
25. driver's education

D. What's the Word?

26. D	34. C
27. B	35. B
28. A	36. A
29. B	37. C
30. C	38. D
31. A	39. A
32. D	40. B
33. B	41. C

E. Cloze Reading

42. C	47. A
43. A	48. B
44. B	49. A
45. A	50. C
46. C	

F. Writing Sample

(Answers will vary.)

UNIT 12B TEST: Picture Dictionary Pages 105–111

A. What Is It?

1. square	5. magnet
2. circle	6. dropped
3. rectangle	7. microscope
4. pyramid	8. scale

B. Math Symbols

9. plus	12. percentage
10. equals	13. times
11. minus	14. divided by

C. Language Arts

15. subject
16. verb
17. article
18. noun
19. preposition

D. Punctuation

20. quotation marks
21. apostrophe
22. question mark
23. comma
24. exclamation mark
25. period

E. What's the Word?

26. B	34. A
27. C	35. B
28. D	36. C
29. A	37. D
30. C	38. B
31. B	39. A
32. D	40. C
33. C	41. D

F. Cloze Reading

42. B	47. C
43. A	48. B
44. C	49. A
45. B	50. B
46. A	

G. Writing Sample

(Answers will vary.)

UNIT 13A TEST: Picture Dictionary Pages 112–117

A. What's Your Occupation?

1. instructor	7. truck driver
2. cashier	8. store owner
3. pharmacist	9. travel agent
4. mechanic	10. lawyer
5. housekeeper	11. accountant
6. postal worker	12. supervisor

B. What Do They Do?

13. fly	17. translate
14. build	18. operate
15. grow	19. assist
16. prepare	

C. Who Are They?

20. butcherr
21. barber
22. receptionistr
23. reporter
24. tailor
25. factory worker

D. On the Job

26. B	35. C
27. C	36. B
28. A	37. D
29. D	38. C
30. B	39. D
31. A	40. C
32. B	41. B
33. C	42. A
34. A	43. B

E. Cloze Reading

44. B	48. A
45. C	49. B
46. A	50. C
47. C	

F. Writing Sample

(Answers will vary.)

UNIT 13B TEST: Picture Dictionary Pages 118–123

A. In the Office

1. stapler
2. paper clip
3. rubber band
4. job notice
5. coat rack
6. message board
7. adding machine
8. file folder
9. swivel chair
10. vending machine
11. photocopier
12. water cooler

B. At the Factory

13. time card
14. conveyor
15. forklift
16. loading dock
17. dolly

C. Which Group?

18–21. earplugs, mask, respirator, goggles
22–25. shovel, pickax, sledgehammer, trowel

D. What's the Word?

26. C	34. D
27. B	35. A
28. A	36. B
29. D	37. C
30. A	38. D
31. C	39. B
32. A	40. C
33. B	41. A

E. Cloze Reading

42. B	47. A
43. C	48. B
44. B	49. C
45. A	50. A
46. B	

F. Writing Sample

(Answers will vary.)

UNIT 14 TEST: Picture Dictionary Pages 124–133

A. Vehicles and Transportation

1. sedan	7. van
2. hatchback	8. subway
3. motorcycle	9. S.U.V.
4. station wagon	10. taxi
5. moving van	11. tow truck
6. train	12. tractor trailer

B. What's the Sign?

13. handicapped parking only
14. no right turn
15. school crossing
16. pedestrian crossing
17. railroad crossing
18. right turn only

C. In the Car

19. seat belt
20. trunk
21. windshield wipers
22. turn signal
23. oil
24. tires
25. nozzle

D. What's the Word?

26. B	34. B
27. A	35. A
28. C	36. B
29. D	37. C
30. C	38. D
31. A	39. A
32. B	40. C
33. D	41. B

E. Cloze Reading

42. C	47. B
43. B	48. C
44. A	49. B
45. B	50. A
46. A	

F. Writing Sample

(Answers will vary.)

UNIT 15A TEST: Picture Dictionary Pages 134–141

A. Where Do You Like to Go?

1. beach	7. concert
2. zoo	8. yard sale
3. movies	9. historic site
4. museum	10. aquarium
5. playground	11. play
6. fair	12. national park

B. At the Beach

13. sunscreen	16. sand castle
14. shells	17. surfer
15. lifeguard	

C. Which Group?

18–21. backpack, canteen, compass, trail map
22–25. camping stove, lantern, sleeping bag, tent

D. What's the Word?

26. C	34. A
27. B	35. C
28. D	36. A
29. C	37. B
30. D	38. C
31. A	39. A
32. B	40. D
33. D	41. B

E. Cloze Reading

42. C	47. C
43. A	48. B
44. B	49. A
45. A	50. C
46. B	

F. Writing Sample

(Answers will vary.)

UNIT 15B TEST: Picture Dictionary Pages 142–150

A. Sports Equipment

1. skis	5. face guard
2. basketball	6. football helmet
3. baseball glove	7. hockey stick
4. soccer ball	8. baseball bat

B. Musical Instruments

9. piano	13. trumpet
10. drums	14. violin
11. guitar	15. bass
12. clarinet	16. flute

C. Movies

17. western	20. musical
18. comedy	21. horror
19. documentary	

D. TV Programs

22. game show	24. nature
23. sports	25. cartoon

E. What's the Word?

26. C	34. B
27. A	35. D
28. D	36. C
29. B	37. B
30. C	38. D
31. D	39. B
32. A	40. A
33. C	41. C

F. Cloze Reading

42. A	47. C
43. C	48. B
44. A	49. A
45. B	50. C
46. A	

G. Writing Sample

(Answers will vary.)

UNIT 16 TEST: Picture Dictionary Pages 151–159

A. Animals

1. rabbit	7. bat
2. monkey	8. eagle
3. polar bear	9. fox
4. deer	10. parrot
5. kangaroo	11. seagull
6. dolphin	12. hippopotamus

B. Which Group?

13–16. elephant, giraffe, gorilla, jaguar
17–21. crab, octopus, sea lion, shark, whale
22–25. cow, goat, horse, pig

C. What's the Word?

26. D	34. C
27. C	35. A
28. B	36. B
29. A	37. C
30. B	38. A
31. D	39. B
32. B	40. D
33. A	41. B

D. Cloze Reading

42. B	47. C
43. A	48. A
44. B	49. B
45. C	50. C
46. A	

E. Writing Sample

(Answers will vary.)

UNIT 17 TEST (U.S. EDITION): Picture Dictionary Pages 160–166

A. The Legal System and Citizenship

1. pay taxes
2. vote
3. obey laws
4. be arrested
5. appear in court
6. serve on a jury

B. What's the Holiday?

7. New Year's Day
8. Martin Luther King, Jr. Day
9. Valentine's Day
10. Memorial Day
11. Independence Day
12. Halloween
13. Veterans Day
14. Thanksgiving

C. U.S. Government

15–16. representatives, senators
17–18. president, vice-president
19–20. chief justice, Supreme Court justices

D. U.S. History

21. Revolutionary War
22. Civil War
23. World Wars I and II
24. Korean War
25. Vietnam War

E. What's the Word?

26. B	34. B
27. C	35. C
28. D	36. D
29. A	37. B
30. C	38. A
31. D	39. C
32. B	40. A
33. A	41. B

F. Cloze Reading

42. B	47. C
43. C	48. A
44. B	49. C
45. A	50. B
46. B	

G. Writing Sample

(Answers will vary.)

UNIT 17 TEST (INTERNATIONAL EDITION): Picture Dictionary Pages 160–165

A. What Will They Do?

1. go to a museum
2. take a walking tour
3. exchange money
4. rent a car
5. get the baggage
6. mail some postcards
7. take a shuttle bus
8. visit an historic site
9. go to an Internet cafe

B. Travel

10. cruise
11. travel agency
12. study tour
13. expedition
14. business trip

C. What's the Word?

15. declaration form
16. customs
17. traveler's checks
18. souvenirs
19. car rental counter

D. What Are They Saying?

20. May I see your passport?
21. Can I pay with a credit card?
22. I'd like to book a ski trip.
23. Please write that down for me.
24. Please don't bother me!
25. Can I take photographs here?

E. What's the Word?

26. C	34. B
27. D	35. D
28. A	36. C
29. B	37. B
30. C	38. A
31. A	39. D
32. D	40. B
33. A	41. C

F. Cloze Reading

42. B	47. C
43. A	48. B
44. C	49. A
45. B	50. C
46. A	

G. Writing Sample

(Answers will vary.)

WORD BY WORD INTERMEDIATE-LEVEL TESTS ANSWER KEY

UNIT 1 TEST: Picture Dictionary Pages 1–3

A. What's the Word?
1. B
2. C
3. D
4. A
5. B
6. C
7. A
8. C
9. D
10. C
11. A
12. B
13. C
14. D
15. B
16. A

B. Cloze Reading
17. A
18. C
19. A
20. B
21. A
22. C
23. A
24. C
25. B

C. What's the Word?
26. area code
27. phone number
28. e-mail address
29. social security number
30. date of birth
31. apartment number
32. zip code
33. address

D. What's the Word?
34. father-in-law
35. grandfather
36. sister-in-law
37. nephews
38. sister
39. uncle
40. parents
41. father
42. brother
43. grandchildren
44. cousin

E. What's the Answer?
45–50. (Answers will vary.)

F. Writing Sample
(Answers will vary.)

UNIT 2A TEST: Picture Dictionary Pages 4–8

A. What's the Word?
1. C
2. B
3. D
4. B
5. D
6. B
7. A
8. D
9. C
10. B
11. C
12. A
13. B
14. C
15. A
16. C
17. B
18. D
19. A
20. C
21. D
22. B
23. C
24. D
25. A

B. What's the Word?
26. Turn off
27. Open
28. Help
29. Fill in
30. Break up
31. Put

C. What's the Answer?
32. Read page 27.
33. Look in the dictionary.
34. Share a book.
35. No. Work as a class.
36. Write on a separate piece of paper.
37. Print your name.

D. Cloze Reading
38. out
39. over
40. write
41. board
42. unscramble
43. partner
44. turned on
45. overhead projector

E. What's the Word?
46. on
47. above
48. in
49. of
50. to

F. Writing Sample
(Answers will vary.)

UNIT 2B TEST: Picture Dictionary Pages 9–14

A. What's the Word?
1. D
2. A
3. C
4. B
5. D
6. B
7. C
8. A
9. B
10. A
11. D
12. B
13. C
14. D
15. A
16. B
17. D
18. C
19. B
20. C
21. D
22. A
23. C
24. B
25. D

B. What's the Word?
26. thunderstorm
27. hot
28. snowstorm
29. smoggy

C. What's the Answer?
30. Not much.
31. Hold on a minute, please.
32. It's sleeting.
33. See you later.
34. Nice to meet you.
35. Fine, thanks.
36. Of course. I'll speak more slowly.

D. Cloze Reading
37. weather
38. clear
39. used
40. left
41. drove
42. swim
43. cold
44. read
45. played
46. walked
47. cloudy
48. listened
49. lightning
50. got

E. Writing Sample
(Answers will vary.)

UNIT 3 TEST: Picture Dictionary Pages 15–19

A. What's the Word?
1. A
2. B
3. D
4. A
5. C
6. B
7. D
8. C
9. B
10. A
11. C
12. B
13. D
14. B
15. D
16. C

B. Cloze Reading
17. C
18. B
19. C
20. B
21. A
22. C
23. A
24. B
25. A

C. What Time Is It?
26. six thirty
27. a quarter after seven
28. midnight
29. six fifteen
30. half past seven
31. a quarter to seven

D. What's the Word?
32. Tuesday
33. Thursday
34. Saturday
35. Sunday
36. June
37. July
38. March
39. May

E. What the Word?
40. twenty-five
41. dime
42. penny
43. half
44. nickel
45. fifty
46. quarter
47. twenty

F. What's the Answer?
48–50. (Answers will vary.)

G. Writing Sample
(Answers will vary.)

UNIT 4A TEST: Picture Dictionary Pages 20–27

A. What's the Word?
1. B
2. A
3. C
4. D
5. C
6. A
7. D
8. B

9. A   13. A
10. D   14. D
11. B   15. C
12. C   16. B

B. Cloze Reading

17. B   22. B
18. A   23. C
19. B   24. B
20. C   25. A
21. A

C. What is It?

26. soap
27. hamper
28. scale
29. plunger
30. medicine cabinet
31. wastebasket
32. rubber mat

D. What's the Word?

33. chandelier   39. platter
34. vase   40. saucer
35. alarm clock   41. comforter
36. tablecloth   42. serving bowl
37. pitcher   43. napkin
38. nightstand   44. mattress

E. Cloze Reading

45. crib
46. chest
47. changing table
48. playpen
49. stuffed animals
50. baby monitor

F. Writing Sample

(Answers will vary.)

UNIT 4B TEST: Picture Dictionary Pages 28–35

A. What's the Word?

1. B   14. C
2. C   15. B
3. A   16. C
4. C   17. A
5. B   18. B
6. D   19. D
7. A   20. C
8. B   21. B
9. D   22. C
10. B   23. D
11. D   24. B
12. C   25. D
13. A

B. What's the Word?

26. can   29. tape
27. electric   30. cord
28. blower   31. step

C. What's the Word?

32. sprinkler   37. shovel
33. saw   38. flashlight
34. broom   39. wheelbarrow
35. hammer   40. trowel
36. plunger

D. Cloze Reading

41. repairs   46. dead-bolt lock
42. peeling   47. appliance
43. broken   48. clogged
44. cracked   49. toilet
45. handyman   50. plumber

E. Writing Sample

(Answers will vary.)

UNIT 5 TEST: Picture Dictionary Pages 36–41

A. What's the Word?

1. A   9. C
2. C   10. B
3. D   11. D
4. B   12. A
5. A   13. B
6. C   14. C
7. B   15. B
8. D   16. D

B. Cloze Reading

17. B   22. A
18. C   23. B
19. A   24. A
20. B   25. C
21. C

C. What's the Word?

26. health club   29. discount store
27. clinic   30. laundromat
28. hotel   31. coffee shop

D. What's the Word?

32. sidewalk
33. public telephone
34. stop
35. fire alarm box
36. jail
37. subway
38. intersection
39. manhole
40. trash container
41. crosswalk

E. Matching: *Where Are They?*

42. pet store
43. restaurant
44. electronics store
45. park
46. hardware store
47. video store
48. convenience store
49. clothing store
50. day-care center

F. Writing Sample

(Answers will vary.)

UNIT 6 TEST: Picture Dictionary Pages 42–47

A. What's the Word?

1. B   6. C
2. A   7. A
3. D   8. B
4. C   9. C
5. D   10. D
11. B   19. B
12. A   20. C
13. C   21. D
14. A   22. A
15. D   23. D
16. B   24. C
17. A   25. B
18. C

B. What's the Opposite?

26. young   29. rich
27. tall   30. hard
28. thin   31. tight

C. What's the Word?

32. homesick   37. dishonest
33. angry   38. uncomfortable
34. noisy   39. single
35. proud   40. confused
36. jealous   41. narrow

D. Cloze Reading

42. wet   47. surprised
43. embarrassed   48. sick
44. difficult   49. hungry
45. worried   50. exhausted
46. closed

E. Writing Sample

(Answers will vary.)

UNIT 7A TEST: Picture Dictionary Pages 48–56

A. What's the Word?

1. D   10. A
2. C   11. C
3. B   12. D
4. A   13. B
5. C   14. D
6. B   15. B
7. A   16. C
8. B   17. D
9. C   18. A

B. Cloze Reading

19. B   23. C
20. A   24. B
21. C   25. A
22. B

C. What's the Word?

26. loaf   31. head
27. carton   32. six-pack
28. jar   33. container
29. can   34. bag
30. bunch   35. roll

D. What's the Word?

36. scale
37. margarine
38. watermelon
39. shellfish
40. fish
41. soap
42. mix
43. wrap
44. sauce
45. salad
46. butter
47. cheese
48. beef
49. wings
50. chops

E. Writing Sample
(Answers will vary.)

UNIT 7B TEST: Picture Dictionary Pages 57–64

A. What the Word?

1. C	14. D
2. A	15. C
3. C	16. A
4. B	17. B
5. D	18. D
6. A	19. B
7. B	20. D
8. D	21. A
9. C	22. D
10. A	23. B
11. D	24. C
12. B	25. B
13. C	

B. What's the Opposite?

26. a tablespoon	29. a pint
27. a pound	30. a quart
28. a cup	31. a gallon

C. What's the Word?

32. add	37. simmer
33. mix	38. roast
34. bake	39. grate
35. microwave	40. stir-fry
36. slice	

D. Cloze Reading

41. hostess	46. cleared
42. seat	47. set
43. patrons	48. chef
44. poured	49. salad bar
45. booster seats	50. dining room

E. Writing Sample
(Answers will vary.)

UNIT 8 TEST: Picture Dictionary Pages 65–73

A. What's the Word?

1. C	10. A
2. A	11. D
3. D	12. B
4. B	13. D
5. C	14. B
6. A	15. A
7. B	16. C
8. D	17. D
9. C	18. B

B. Cloze Reading

19. C	23. B
20. A	24. A
21. C	25. C
22. A	

C. What's the Word?

26. hiking	30. crew
27. sport	31. three-piece
28. wedding	32. cap
29. bag	33. wrist

D. What's the Word?

34. repair	36. let out
35. unload	37. sort
38. hang up	45. handbag
39. iron	46. earring
40. lengthen	47. jewelry
41. take in	48. suspenders
42. windbreaker	49. pattern
43. size	50. string
44. color	

E. Writing Sample
(Answers will vary.)

UNIT 9 TEST: Picture Dictionary Pages 74–79

A. What's the Word?

1. D	14. A
2. A	15. B
3. B	16. C
4. D	17. B
5. C	18. A
6. B	19. D
7. A	20. C
8. C	21. A
9. A	22. D
10. B	23. B
11. D	24. D
12. C	25. C
13. B	

B. What's the Word?

26. exchanged	29. bought
27. tried	30. return
28. paid	

C. Cloze Reading

31. phone	36. camera
32. charger	37. radio
33. notebook	38. TV
34. fax	39. game
35. printer	

D. What's the Word?

40. Home Furnishings
41. Household Appliances
42. Housewares
43. Customer Service
44. Electronics
45. Gift Wrap
46. Jewelry
47. Children's Clothing
48. Perfume
49. Men's Clothing
50. Women's Clothing

E. Writing Sample
(Answers will vary.)

UNIT 10 TEST: Picture Dictionary Pages 80–85

A. What's the Word?

1. A	9. A
2. D	10. D
3. C	11. A
4. A	12. C
5. B	13. B
6. D	14. C
7. B	15. D
8. C	16. C

B. Cloze Reading

17. A	22. B
18. B	23. A
19. C	24. C
20. B	25. B
21. A	

C. What's the Word?

26. senior center
27. activities director
28. nursery
29. mugging
30. ambulance
31. hall
32. derailment
33. dump
34. outage

D. Cloze Reading

35. library card	39. reference
36. checkout	40. encyclopedias
37. online catalog	41. media
38. periodical	42. on tape

E. What's the Word?

43. fire
44. gym
45. gas leak
46. recycling center
47. drunk driving
48. vandalism
49. playroom
50. spill

F. Writing Sample
(Answers will vary.)

UNIT 11A TEST: Picture Dictionary Pages 86–91

A. What's the Word?

1. C
2. A
3. D
4. C
5. A
6. B
7. D
8. B
9. A
10. C
11. B
12. D
13. A
14. D
15. B
16. C
17. B
18. A
19. C
20. D
21. A
22. B
23. A
24. C
25. D

B. What's the Word?

26. aspirin
27. kit
28. antiseptic
29. bandage
30. gauze

C. What's the Word?

31. shock
32. poison
33. reaction
34. rescue
35. infection
36. unconscious
37. maneuver
38. tuberculosis
39. pulse
40. pains
41. measles

D. Cloze Reading

42. bloody
43. fell
44. bandage
45. ointment
46. dizzy
47. temperature
48. throw
49. heatstroke
50. tooth

E. Writing Sample
(Answers will vary.)

UNIT 11B TEST: Picture Dictionary Pages 92–100

A. What's the Word?

1. D
2. B
3. A
4. C
5. B
6. C
7. D
8. A
9. B
10. A
11. C
12. D
13. A
14. B
15. D
16. C

B. Cloze Reading

17. B
18. A
19. C
20. A
21. C
22. B
23. A
24. C
25. A

C. What's the Word?

26. orthopedist
27. counselor
28. pediatrician
29. ENT specialist
30. obstetrician
31. gerontologist
32. ophthalmologist

D. What's the Word?

33. measured
34. examined
35. took
36. rested
37. went
38. drew
39. dressed
40. pill
41. sunscreen
42. antacid
43. mascara
44. vitamin
45. conditioner
46. clipper
47. wipes
48. lozenges
49. formula
50. lotion

E. Writing Sample
(Answers will vary.)

UNIT 12A TEST: Picture Dictionary Pages 101–104

A. What's the Word?

1. C
2. A
3. D
4. A
5. B
6. D
7. A
8. C
9. B
10. A
11. D
12. B
13. C
14. A
15. D
16. C
17. D
18. B
19. A
20. D
21. B
22. A
23. C
24. B
25. C

B. What's the Order?

26. nursery school
27. elementary school
28. middle school
29. high school
30. college
31. graduate school

C. What's the Word?

32. yearbook
33. health
34. literary
35. international
36. vocational
37. law
38. government
39. math
40. medical
41. adult

D. Cloze Reading

42. high
43. subjects
44. education
45. extracurricular
46. club
47. service
48. guidance
49. community
50. university

E. Writing Sample
(Answers will vary.)

UNIT 12B TEST: Picture Dictionary Pages 105–111

A. What's the Word?

1. A
2. C
3. D
4. C
5. B
6. A
7. B
8. C
9. D
10. B
11. C
12. D
13. A
14. B
15. C
16. D

B. Cloze Reading

17. C
18. A
19. B
20. A
21. C
22. B
23. A
24. C
25. B

C. What's the Word?

26. noun
27. verb
28. preposition
29. article
30. pronoun
31. adjective
32. adverb

D. Punctuation

33. question mark
34. colon
35. semi-colon
36. period
37. quotation marks
38. exclamation point

E. What's the Word?

39. minus
40. divided
41. plus
42. times
43. percent
44. funnel
45. magnet
46. hypothesis
47. Satellites
48. test tube
49. telescope
50. microscope

F. Writing Sample
(Answers will vary.)

UNIT 13A TEST: Picture Dictionary Pages 112–117

A. What's the Word?

1. D
2. B
3. C
4. A
5. C
6. D
7. A
8. B
9. A
10. C
11. D
12. B
13. A
14. C
15. B
16. A
17. C
18. D
19. B
20. A
21. D
22. C
23. B
24. A
25. C

B. What's the Word?

26. landscaper
27. painter
28. barber
29. hairdresser
30. pharmacist
31. cashier

C. What's the Word?
32. built
33. flew
34. grow
35. assisted
36. prepared
37. operate
38. take
39. file
40. sold

D. Cloze Reading
41. aides
42. receptionists
43. cashier
44. Food-service
45. Housekeepers
46. custodians
47. secretaries
48. data entry
49. accountants
50. translators

E. Writing Sample
(Answers will vary.)

UNIT 13B TEST: Picture Dictionary Pages 118–123

A. What's the Word?
1. D
2. A
3. C
4. D
5. B
6. C
7. B
8. A
9. C
10. D
11. A
12. B
13. C
14. D
15. C
16. A

B. Cloze Reading
17. A
18. B
19. C
20. B
21. A
22. C
23. A
24. B
25. A

C. What's the Word?
26. hairnets
27. earplugs
28. respirators
29. goggles
30. helmets
31. safety vests

D. What's the Word?
32. skills
33. previous
34. resume
35. salary
36. interview
37. benefits
38. search
39. dock
40. conveyor
41. hand
42. biohazard
43. forklift
44. clock
45. payroll
46. corrosive
47. defibrillator
48. dump
49. shingles
50. pickax

E. Writing Sample
(Answers will vary.)

UNIT 14 TEST: Picture Dictionary Pages 124–133

A. What's the Word?
1. B
2. A
3. C
4. B
5. D
6. A
7. D
8. C
9. B
10. C
11. A
12. D
13. A
14. B
15. C
16. D
17. B
18. D
19. A
20. C
21. B
22. A
23. C
24. D
25. A

B. What's the Word?
26. wipers
27. pipe
28. tank
29. wheel
30. compartment
31. brake

C. What's the Word?
32. past
33. through
34. down
35. onto
36. off
37. bellhop
38. concierge
39. housekeeper
40. guests

D. Cloze Reading
41. counter
42. security
43. carry-on
44. X-ray
45. metal
46. gate
47. boarding
48. agent
49. compartment
50. seat belt

E. Writing Sample
(Answers will vary.)

UNIT 15A TEST: Picture Dictionary Pages 134–141

A. What's the Word?
1. C
2. A
3. D
4. B
5. D
6. A
7. B
8. C
9. B
10. C
11. D
12. A
13. B
14. A
15. C
16. D

B. Cloze Reading
17. B
18. A
19. C
20. A
21. C
22. B
23. A
24. B
25. C

C. What's the Word?
26. yard sales
27. beach
28. park
29. historic
30. concert
31. aquarium
32. mountains

D. What's the Word?
33. planetarium
34. botanical
35. play
36. national
37. gallery
38. carnival
39. binoculars
40. arrows
41. rowing
42. beam
43. helmet
44. telescope
45. weights
46. racquetball
47. pool
48. knee pads
49. clubs
50. martial

E. Writing Sample
(Answers will vary.)

UNIT 15B TEST: Picture Dictionary Pages 142–150

A. What's the Word?
1. A
2. C
3. D
4. B
5. A
6. D
7. B
8. C
9. D
10. C
11. A
12. B
13. D
14. A
15. C
16. B
17. A
18. B
19. D
20. C
21. B
22. A
23. D
24. B
25. C

B. What's the Equipment?
26. rod
27. paddles
28. glove
29. net
30. shoulder pads
31. towrope

C. What's the Word?
32. served
33. dive
34. kicked
35. bounce
36. shot
37. bend
38. hop
39. pitched
40. lift

D. Cloze Reading
41. entertainment
42. classical
43. conductor
44. orchestra
45. musical
46. film
47. concert
48. band
49. soccer
50. field

E. Writing Sample
(Answers will vary.)

UNIT 16 TEST: Picture Dictionary Pages 151–159

A. What's the Word?
1. B
2. C
3. B
4. A
5. D
6. C
7. A
8. D
9. B
10. C
11. A
12. C
13. D
14. B
15. A
16. D

B. Cloze Reading

17. B
18. A
19. C
20. A
21. C

22. A
23. B
24. C
25. A

C. What's the Word?

26. solar
27. air
28. hurricanes
29. warming

30. geothermal
31. natural
32. earthquake
33. hydroelectric

D. What's the Word?

34. bats
35. squirrel
36. porcupine
37. puppy
38. jaguar
39. worms
40. spider
41. bees
42. bear

43. ticks
44. octopus
45. frogs
46. gills
47. crabs
48. cobra
49. flounder
50. shark

E. Writing Sample

(Answers will vary.)

UNIT 17 U.S. EDITION TEST: Picture Dictionary Pages 160–166

A. What's the Word?

1. B
2. D
3. A
4. B
5. C
6. A
7. B
8. D
9. A
10. C
11. D
12. B
13. A

14. C
15. A
16. B
17. D
18. A
19. C
20. D
21. B
22. C
23. A
24. D
25. B

B. U.S. History

26. Civil War
27. Korean War
28. World War II
29. Revolutionary War
30. Vietnam War

C. What's the Holiday?

31. New Year's Day
32. Martin Luther King, Jr. Day
33. Valentine's Day
34. Memorial Day
35. Independence Day
36. Halloween
37. Veterans Day
38. Thanksgiving

D. Cloze Reading

39. passport
40. I.D.
41. student
42. permit
43. citizen
44. citizenship
45. government
46. test
47. naturalization
48. ceremony
49. Allegiance
50. jury

E. Writing Sample

(Answers will vary.)

UNIT 17 INTERNATIONAL EDITION TEST: Picture Dictionary Pages 160–165

A. What's the Word?

1. C
2. D
3. A
4. C
5. B
6. D
7. B
8. A
9. C
10. B
11. C
12. A
13. D

14. B
15. C
16. A
17. B
18. A
19. D
20. B
21. C
22. A
23. D
24. A
25. C

B. What's the Word?

26. room
27. cafe
28. club
29. tour
30. business
31. exchange

C. What's the Word?

32. declaration
33. visa
34. customs
35. traveler's checks
36. car rental
37. souvenirs
38. use
39. pay
40. exchange
41. book

D. Cloze Reading

42. trip
43. hotel
44. suite
45. double
46. view
47. tour
48. sightseeing
49. reservations
50. show

E. Writing Sample

(Answers will vary.)